Master Ultima®

Ralph Roberts

SAMS
A Division of Macmillan Computer Publishing
11711 North College, Carmel, Indiana 46032 USA

FIRST EDITION
FIRST PRINTING—1991

The material in this book represents the observations, opinions, and speculations of the author, and has not been authorized or licensed by ORIGIN Systems, Inc..

International Standard Book Number: 0-672-22828-9
Library of Congress Catalog Card Number: 91-61192

Publishing Manager: *Marie Butler-Knight*
Acquisitions Editor: *Mary-Terese Cozzola Cagnina*
Manuscript Editor: *Amy M. Perry*
Cover Illustrator: *Ned Shaw*
Production Assistance: *Martin Coleman, Sandy Grieshop, Tami Hughes, Tracy Kaufman, Betty Kish, Michele Laseau, Sarah Leatherman, Howard Peirce, Joe Ramon*
Indexer: *Jill Bomaster*
Technical Editor: *John T. Baumgarten*

Printed in the United States of America

Contents

A Message from the Scribe

Greetings, O Mighty One, O Slayer of Dragons, O Winner of Quests. You hold in your hands a Book of Great Power. It contains great Secrets learned during my many years of journeying throughout the realms of Lord British. Wield this Book with confidence. *They* (the ones who must not be named) labor under the illusion that this is merely another computer game book. I assure you, they will remain in the dark, like the blackness of the evil places from whence they came.

The nameless ones are those who oppose the success of your quests into the realms of Britannia, the ones who attack you in dungeons and attempt to flay the flesh from your bones—the ones who are the evil spawn of enemies to all that is good. If they were to learn that a hero or heroine (that is *you,* O Adventurer) is about to enter the land, they would make preparations for conflict, rendering your battle even more difficult.

We shall fool them, you and I, and thereby retain the advantage of surprise. We shall also pretend that this is just another computer game book. Consider the six Ultima games as merely computer games, Wise One, and not six gateways to the far-off times and faraway places that Lord British surveys. Pretend that you and I are only ordinary humans and not Destroyers of Evil with Powers that far transcend those of mere mortals.

So think of me as only a lowly writer hunched before his word processor and not as a Scribe/Mage, a traveler of far lands who has mastered the vast power of ancient crystals and is now inscribing these words in the endless, soundless library of Lord British. Think of me not as surrounded by towering shelves of scrolls stretching far into the torchlit distance, a magic lamp at my shoulder moving in concert with my hand as the Ink of Power flows smoothly through my white eagle's feather onto the vellum. No, imagine me instead in a cube-like room in the "real world," where only the telephone's jangle interrupts the rapid clacking of the keyboard, a forgotten cup of coffee grows cold on the desk, and clangorous traffic whooshes by outside.

Think of me like that, and *they* need not know the truth. *They* will never suspect that important Secrets are about to be yours.

The Power of this book for you, Adventurer, is not only in the potent strategies it reveals to you. My words are also a glorying in the unique mystique of the Ultima realms—unique in that dragons, knights, and other wonders of medieval life exist simultaneously with such futurities as interstellar travel at faster-than-light speeds.

So gird yourself for adventure, Courageous One. Heed well the Secrets in these pages, and no Evil will withstand you. Master these hints, and *they* will melt as rancid butter before your red-hot blade. This I promise you, if you but walk the Way of Power with me.

Acknowledgments

This scribe would like to acknowledge here, with grateful thanks, the many people who helped in the preparation of this scroll. While not all are named, my heartfelt gratitude goes to everyone.

To Richard Garriott, Lord British, and ORIGIN Systems, Inc. for making it all possible.

For research assistance and most helpful background material—either directly or indirectly through their published materials: Scorpia, who runs the Games Special Interest Groups on the DELPHI and GEnie computer networks (thanks, Scorpie!); Patricia Fitzgibbons; Jason Levine; Lord Thomill, Kevin, and the Phoenix; Greg Ellsworth; Randy Snow; Scott Ward; Targhan; Dave Konkel; and CompuServe's Uncle Andy.

To John Baumgarten of Record Survival in Asheville, for his expertise in reviewing this scroll to ensure completeness and technical accuracy.

To all those at SAMS who do so much to help us scribes look good: Marie Butler Knight, a very resourceful and creative lady; Mary-Terese Cozzola Cagnina, her of the wondrously lilting name who sees all and knows all, but is very, very nice about it and is absolutely fantastic to work for; Amy Perry, who works miracles, turning runes and mystic symbols into English that all can read; Dan Derrick, whose BBS receives manuscripts called in electronically from anywhere, even Sosaria and Britannia; Linda Sanning, who got it all started; Herb Feltner, who oversaw the technical editing; and to all the other valiant workers at SAMS.

Also thanks to Jack Nimersheim, writer of many books, for his encouragement; and to Sprint, the amazing word processor that refuses to die because so many of us scribes will use nothing else.

Trademarks

All terms mentioned in this book that are known to be trademarks or service marks are listed below. In addition, terms suspected of being trademarks or service marks have been appropriately capitalized. SAMS cannot attest to the accuracy of this information. Use of a term in this book should not be regarded as affecting the validity of any trademark or service mark.

Amiga is a registered trademark of Commodore-Amiga, Inc.

Apple II is a registered trademark of Apple Computer, Inc.

Apple is a registered trademark of Apple Computer, Inc.

Commodore 64 is a registered trademark of Commodore Electronics Limited.

CompuServe is a registered trademark of H&R Block, Inc.

DELPHI is a trademark of General Videotex Corp.

Dungeons and Dragons game is a trademark of T.S.R., Inc.

Game Boy is a trademark of Nintendo of America, Inc.

GEnie is a trademark of General Electric Co.

IBM is a registered trademark of International Business Machines Corporation.

Intel is a registered trademark of Intel Corporation.

Lord British is a registered trademark of Richard Garriott.

Mac is a registered trademark of Apple Computer, Inc.

Nintendo is a registered trademark of Nintendo of America, Inc.

Origin is a registered trademark of ORIGIN Systems, Inc.

PART 1

Introduction

1 From Dragons to Starships

You can have it all—castles, pirates, sea monsters, sorcerers, starships, dragons to fight, dungeons to explore, princesses to rescue, journeys to far away star systems—even voyages through the very fabric of Time. The Ultima series gives you all this and worlds upon worlds of imagination more. These are the worlds of Lord British, author of the longest-running and most successful series of computer games in history.

The concept of combining science fiction and fantasy elements in the same story is not a new one. To mention only a few of the many examples, not only were well-known writers such as Jack Vance doing it years before Lord British was born, but even before World War I, Edgar Rice Burroughs' Martian series ("under the hurtling moons of Barsoom!") contained fantasy elements .

However, Lord British gets the credit for the awesome innovation of mixing fantasy and science fiction in computer gaming.

It started in very early times, in the morning mists of the Dawning of the Information Age, in the ancient, almost forgotten year of 1978. In those days the personal computer had been around only a couple of years. A little start-up (also upstart) company in California by the unlikely name of Apple was manufacturing a small computer by the same name. It put brackets after the name and called it the "Apple II." IBM and the other biggies still scoffed at any computer you could actually carry around. Just as the big radio companies ignored radio hams of an earlier generation ("they'll never get out of their back yards with those dinky little sets"), the large computer firms ignored Apple and Radio Shack (now Tandy) computers. They were just toys, right?

Wrong! For, just as the creative experimentation of radio amateurs made radio and television practical today, the creative experimentation of computer hackers (back in the days when the word "hacker" was a term of respect) made the desktop computer practical. The graphical user interfaces and other user-friendly aspects of word processing, spreadsheets, database management, and other software we take for granted today, all had their roots in programming gems and other techniques first developed for computer games.

Many of us saw and felt and *tasted* the potential in the personal computer. We haunted the few and far-between computer stores that were springing up around the country. We scrimped and saved and bought our very own personal computers, and they changed our lives—just as they changed the life of a fifteen-year-old high school kid who was to became legendary under the name "Lord British."

A New Age Dawns

Down in Texas, during those almost prehistoric days of the late seventies, young Richard Garriott had a dream after-school job—he was working in a computer store! He had only to reach out his hand to be able to touch computers. Keyboards were now always at his fingertips. It was riches beyond imagination. It was power, and it was creativity. It was . . . well, wonderful.

This was not Richard's first exposure to computers. His high school had a single programming class, which he took three times. He wrote programs on a Teletype machine that ran at the turtle pace of ten characters a second. Since there were few personal computers at the time, the Teletype was tied into a large computer via the phone lines.

"I had a class without a teacher," he said in a 1986 interview in the DELPHI computer network's Game SIG (Software Interest Group), "and if I had a project I was working on I would get a grade, so I wrote FRPs on the Teletype."

"FRPs" are, of course, fantasy role playing games. They existed on the big computer systems in universities and the like—in a pretty primitive state, but they did exist. J.R.R. Tolkien's classic *Lord of the Rings* series in the 1970s had gotten everyone, Richard included, to thinking about orcs and goblins and hobbits. At the time Richard did not have an inkling of the antipathy that some science fiction and fantasy authors have since expressed toward mixing fantasy and technological elements in the same work. All he knew was that this tiny desktop computer found in the store, the Apple II, was fantastic. His excitement (and that of many others) centered mainly around the fact that it had graphics! Not only could you actually own this small computer (if you scraped together a large enough sum), you could do something with it that the clunky, clanky Teletype terminals hooked up to big computers could *not* do—draw on the screen. Games were no longer limited to displays having a mere twenty-six letters, the digits zero through nine, and a handful of special symbols—you could actually illustrate games.

In his spare time Richard quickly converted his last fantasy role playing game project at high school into a game that could be played on the Apples sold in the store. He also enhanced the game, and named it Akalabeth. Those who saw and played the game were amazed at its depth and precision. Still, it might all have ended there. After all, Richard was a high school kid working part-time in a small computer store in the middle of Texas. That's a pretty strong formula for obscurity—except that Richard's boss, the store manager, saw the game's potential. Without Richard's knowledge, he sent it off to a major software publisher in California.

The company loved the game and immediately made arrangements to publish it. Within a few weeks, this relatively unsophisticated fantasy dungeon game for the Apple II was in computer stores all over the country and had sold over 25,000 copies. Considering that the world-wide ownership of Apple computers was just barely more than 100,000 at that time, these sales figures were nothing short of amazing.

So, while still a teenager, Richard Garriott had found two very important things—financial security and a satisfying career. Yet, not willing to rest on his laurels, he set out to use the interactive potential of the personal computer as fully as possible in new games that he wanted to write. He began creating the absorbing worlds of fantasy and technology that we know as the Ultima games. He became one of the brightest stars in the universe of computer games. He became Lord British.

New Concepts and New Techniques

Ultima I: The First Age of Darkness was published in 1980 by the California Pacific Computer Company. It was originally programmed in AppleSoft BASIC and was a sequel to Akalabeth. From the very beginning, *Ultima I* had a lot going for it. First of all, its scope gave the player medieval fantasy roles mixed with the science fictional elements of blasters, phazors, and starships. You could rescue a princess from a castle prison and become a space ace, all in an evening's time.

Figure 1.1 *The new opening screen of* Ultima I, *recently rereleased. As you might guess from the high level of detail, this game takes advantage of the improved graphics of EGA- and VGA-level screens.*

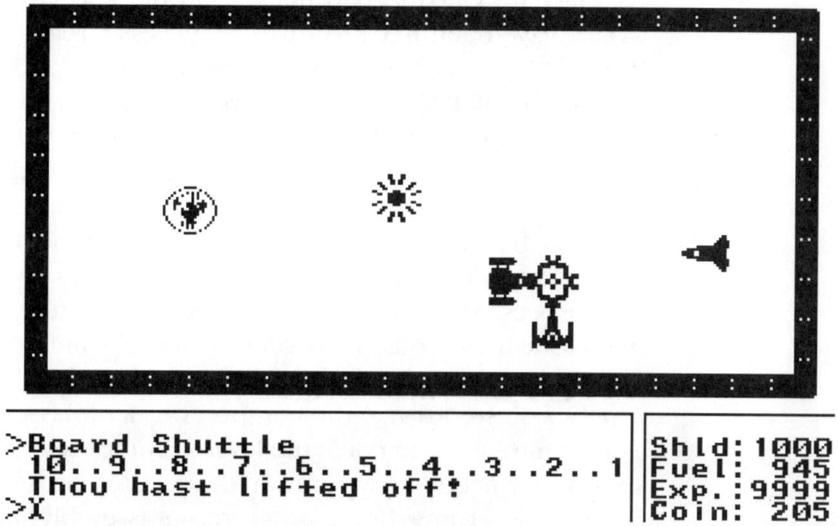

Figure 1.2 Ultima I *takes you from medieval life to the far future. Here you're approaching a space station in your shuttle. Dock carefully! If you're even a little bit off to either side, the station will crunch your shield and you'll die.*

And the graphics were unique for those pioneering days. Akalabeth had featured three-dimensional perspectives (the dungeon had walls and floors and doorways), but Richard made a major improvement over that. *Ultima I* showcased his now-classic tile graphic concept. Tile graphics allow people and monsters—indeed anything that moves—to be built up of little squares that are superimposed on the background scenery. Thus the program can accomplish animation effects easily, because it can rearrange only the pertinent squares and does not have to go through the time-consuming process of rewriting (redrawing) the entire screen.

Richard also first used the name of Lord British in *Ultima I.* Yes, Lord British is both the pseudonym that Richard writes and programs the games under and the name of a benevolent monarch in all six games. (By the way, although Richard has lived in Texas for many years now, he took this name because he was born in Cambridge, England.)

Richard Garriott had his second hit, and Lord British his first. It would have been hard to top the success already achieved, but Lord British, like every true artist, was always striving to better his craft.

AppleSoft BASIC is an interpreted language, meaning it serves as an interface between the human and the computer. As such it provides very, very limited access to the actual power and speed of the machine. In contrast, assembly (or machine language) programs work on a level closer to the microprocessor chip and are real speed demons compared to an interpreted language. In those early days, even the Apple II had little processor speed and little memory to waste. (Almost any standard IBM-clone in use today has over ten times the memory and several times the speed and graphics capacity of the old Apple.) A complicated BASIC program slowed down the computer to a molasses-like crawl. If computer games were to reach the level of complexity that Lord British was seeking, he needed a way to run them faster. So he set himself the task not only of learning the arcane secrets of assembly language, but of using it as a vehicle for his own unique and creative concepts.

He succeeded in "pushing the envelope" on the Apple II, achieving effects that other programmers swore were impossible on such a small and limited machine. (Incidentally, by this time Richard was attending the University of Texas, and the time taken up by this effort cost him a semester's grades. However, he was fortunate: the resulting arcade-quality graphics and exceptional playability brought him royalties that no doubt easily paid for several semesters of schooling.)

The Origin of ORIGIN

In 1982, the new game, *Ultima II: Revenge of the Enchantress* was released by Sierra On-Line, the California company that has since become famous for the games King's Quest and Leisure Suit Larry. *Ultima II,* like its predecessor, was an immediate success, selling over 100,000 copies in its first year.

Figure 1.3 *Although confined to CGA-level graphics,* Ultima II *is still a very complex and enjoyable game to play.*

Quite naturally, this success led Lord British to thoughts of *Ultima III: Exodus,* which he wrote in 1983. With the growing popularity of the whole Ultima concept and series, Richard decided to maintain closer creative control of this game. Thus, together with Robert Garriott, Charles Bueche, and ex-NASA astronaut Owen Garriott, he founded ORIGIN Systems, Inc. to act as publisher. Today all six of the Ultima games are under ORIGIN's control. Robert Garriott is the president, and over fifty computer gaming professionals work at their world headquarters in Austin, Texas.

The world of *Ultima III: Exodus* is filled with power and complexity exceeding that of the first two Ultimas. It introduced multiadventurer parties and colorful dungeon graphics. The combat sequences also were completely overhauled to make the game much more exciting. In the first two games, the combatants remained in the same location on-screen as they fought with each other. Beginning with the third game, as combat starts, the scene changes to a close-up of the player's group and the monsters. Also, all the characters in the player's party appear individually across the bottom of the screen, all the monsters appear individually across the top, and subsequently members of both groups move closer together and engage in combat.

Figure 1.4 Ultima III *was the first of the series (and one of the first computer games overall) to allow the player more than one character.*

Ultima III also made another innovation: a complete musical soundtrack, which Richard Garriott paid for out of his own pocket. (In 1983, music with computer games was not considered commercially viable.) Today, music is an important element in computer games in general, due in great part to Lord British's pioneering efforts.

By *Ultima IV: Quest of the Avatar,* Lord British was taking full advantage of all the advances in color displays and faster computers. This game is more colorful and more detailed than previous games. It also has several nice little animation effects.

Figure 1.5 *In* Ultima IV, *which is more abstract and spiritual than the previous games, you seek the attainment of eight specific virtues. When achieved, they confer upon you the status of Avatar, or example of virtue.*

Ultima V: Warriors of Destiny released in 1988, used EGA-level graphics, thus bringing the level of detail shown on-screen up a notch from that of the previously released games. In it the player was compelled less to fight than in prior games; it increased in subtlety and offered the player many more places to visit and search. Yet, despite this enormity and complexity, in some ways it was actually easier to play.

Ultima VI: The False Prophet sports even more improvements. In addition to letting you use a mouse, which makes it easier to choose commands, the game now has complete 256-color VGA support. On a VGA monitor (which of course makes it possible to show even more detail than an EGA monitor), Britannia seems to come alive—the full color graphics and vivid animations are as dazzling as the original scores are captivating. The world is fully interactive—bells ring, clocks tell time, cannons fire—and everything has a purpose. If an item on-screen is not just a decoration, you can grab it and can use it!

Figure 1.6 Ultima V *was about twice the size of* Ultima IV *and continued Lord British's tradition of showcasing new features. Combat became less necessary and there were more places to visit.*

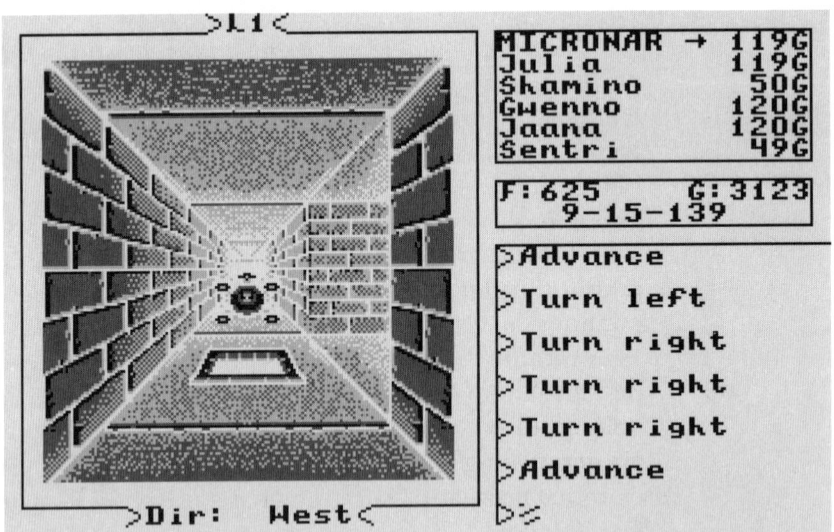

Figure 1.7 *The dungeons in* Ultima V *really look like dungeons when you're using an EGA-level adapter.*

Figure 1.8 *In the opening scene of* Ultima VI: The False Prophet, *you are sitting boredly in your own world when a summoning to Brittania takes you again into the fight.*

It is obvious that just as Lord British's software persona has grown from minor king of an insignificant city-state to ruler of the mighty Empire of Britannia, so too has Lord British the game designer grown in strength and ability from the early days a decade ago. Now he no longer has to essentially do it all alone, as in the early games. He can now call on the best artists and animators, he can commission musical scores, and he can spare no expense in implementing the latest programming techniques to make his games jump out of the screen and become, at least for a few hours, your world.

The Longevity of Ultima

It is nearly impossible to say too much about just exactly how unusual it is to find a computer game still being sold a full ten years after it was introduced! In the course of computer history, that's several ice ages.

Since then, whole species of dinosaurs have come and gone, rain has worn towering granite mountains to mere pebbles, and huge seas have dried and left no trace.

Yet, through all the epochian changes in computer technology, with programs lasting a very short time, only the early Ultima games have survived. True, such word processing packages as WordStar and WordPerfect existed in 1980, but their current versions have gone through many generations of evolution and change. The original programs are nothing like what you can buy today. Not so with *Ultima I* and *Ultima II*—they are substantially the same now as in the early eighties.

Yes, their appearance is different. *Ultima I* especially got a complete facelift for its rerelease (with EGA graphics for the IBM version), while *Ultima II* remains closer to the Sierra 1982 edition (having only CGA-level graphics). Not much effort was required to bring both games up to the performance and play value of the 1990s, since those changes were only cosmetic. "Why?" you ask. "Why have these Ultima games lasted so well when all the rest of the games have sunk without a trace into the mire and muck of ancient computer history?"

It's a combination of factors, really. First, Lord British's unique mixture of science fiction and fantasy lends a huge amount of scope and sheer complexity to the games. Second, Lord British's games never subordinated intrinsic story value to special effects, as did many of the early computer games. Their creators were more interested in the nifty graphics they were trying to achieve on the screen than in plot. These games reflected this lack of understanding of game playing and quickly faded into well-deserved obscurity. But in a manner of speaking, Lord British transcended the medium of computer graphics by giving even his first games intrinsic story value along with state-of-the-art special effects. That is why *Ultima I* is still robust and complex and enjoyable to play.

In fact, the game is more complicated and harder to solve than many of today's slick games, despite their mind-blowing VGA graphics and complete musical scores. There's a logical reason for this. The very strengths of modern games—powerful graphics—can also be their downfall. Here's why: today's simple EGA screen of 320 x 200 pixels has 64,000 places that the computer has to keep updated with the right color information, etc. Even for a fast machine such as one with an Intel 80386 chip, or a color Mac, or an Amiga, that's still a lot of work for the processor to do. As a result, some game designers take short cuts and write simple games overlaid with a few awesome screens. In other words, like with some movies, you get some special effects and very little real story value.

On the other hand, those early computer games, being mostly character-based, could be fast and have considerably more choices in a much smaller amount of memory. A text screen (even one using graphic characters), might be 80 characters per line with a total of 25 lines. That's only 2,000 places the computer has to keep up with, not 64,000. And the early Apple computers only had 40 columns, so they only had 32,000 places to keep updated. (To get 80 columns, you had to buy an extra card and plug it into your machine.) So, a computer (even one of the earliest personal computers) can do a lot more and do it faster on a text screen. True, it's not nearly as pretty, but the game writer can work in more plot and offer more options. Thus this very real limitation actually turned out to be a strength. It resulted in games more powerful than many of today's offerings.

Another reason for Ultima's popularity is the fact that it is a continuing series. People entering into the Ultima universe—at say, *Ultima IV* or *Ultima V*, see references to the earlier games. If you like the games (and well over a million of us now do), you'll probably not only want to play the next game in the series, but the previous ones as well.

The collecting instinct also helps make the Ultima series successful. Because of their profound influence on the course of computer gaming in general, they have become part of the cultural "literature" of personal computing. Ultima games are historically significant because they usually showcased new techniques in game playing, computer hardware, and programming methods. The early games, especially, are very much collector's items now because they pioneered effects that have helped to improve computing in general.

Ultima is very popular worldwide. For example, Japan has Ultima comic books, Ultima Saturday morning cartoon shows, Ultima records, and even Ultima product endorsements in television commercials. There is a Nintendo version of *Ultima III: Exodus*, which is a bestseller in the United States also.

No doubt, in years to come, some college student will do a doctoral or master's thesis on the seminal impact of Ultima—if someone hasn't already.

To sum up, the Ultima games have enjoyed incredible longevity because Lord British had a talent for giving them real story value, power, and complexity that still exert a strong attraction upon players today;

because they are part of a series; because they used graphics and new programming methods so effectively; and because their significant impact on computing in general, even on an international level, makes them legitimately collectible.

The Ultima universe is here to stay. Let's now take a look at this universe and a little of its history.

The History of Britannia

By the time of the most recent game, *Ultima VI,* Lord British (the character in the game) rules the land of Britannia. By happy coincidence, the history of Britannia falls neatly into six parts that coincide with capsule reviews of the six Ultima games.

The First Age of Darkness

In *Ultima I: The First Age of Darkness,* Lord British was a relatively minor king in a land known as Sosaria. The land was divided into small, often warring kingdoms—widely scattered and generally ineffective in maintaining order outside the walls of their castles. The level of technology roughly paralleled that of Earth during medieval times, although advanced weapons such as blasters and phazors existed, as well as aircars and space shuttles. (Actually, Sosaria is Earth—or at least a parallel or alternate Earth. By the second game, North America and other places familiar in outline, if not in inhabitants and localities, appear.)

Power abhors a vacuum, and into this arena of a widely divided, and thus very weak, land stepped the evil wizard, Mondain. With his many minions, the foul Mondain began his horrible reign. Vile and wicked creatures preyed upon the people and ravaged the land. Kine and fowl, fields of grain and fruit, all were no more.

During this time of travail, there came a hero. He (or she) strode forth to fight turtle dragons, evil sorcerers, and all the other despicable subjects of Mondain. The kings, notably Lord British, supplied some help, but it was limited because of their great lack of resources.

The hero rescued princesses, fought many a foe, learned the way into space, became a Space ace, collected all the gems of power, and eventually traveled back into the very beginning of Time. There he (or she) met Mondain in his lair at the only time when there was even a faint possibility of defeating this evil warlock. A frightful battle ensued in which, after much effort and loss of blood, the hero was victorious.

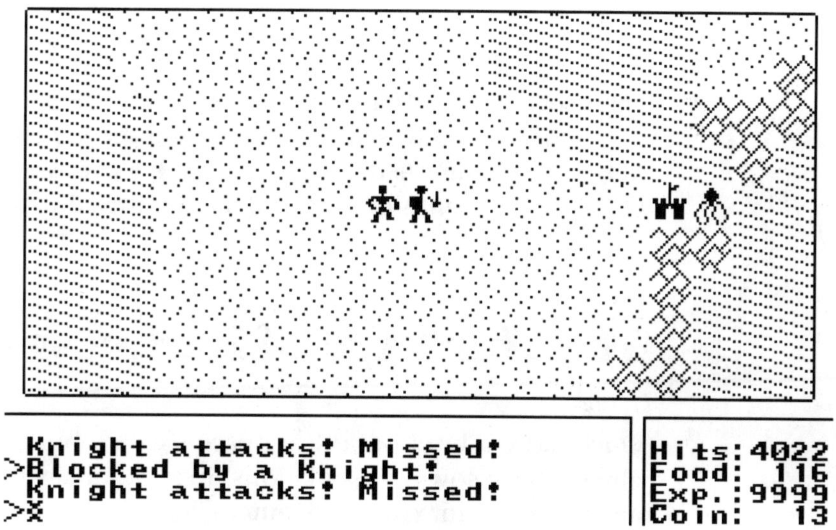

Mondain was slain. A fitful peace came to Sosaria.

Figure 1.9 *In* Ultima I *you (right center) are attacked by an evil knight (left center). On the far right is the castle of a king, next to a giant squid. It's all in a day's work for heroes.*

The Second Age of Darkness

The time of peace after the First Age of Darkness was, alas, short-lived. Minax—enchantress of evil and one-time apprentice to Mondain—

waxed in power. Storms of destruction collapsed society, and horrors of all sorts prevailed. Survivors were forced to rethink the concept of time itself. The only way life itself might once more gain a foothold on Earth was for someone to pass through the mysterious doors of time and influence past events. Many tried and many died. Minax was twice as powerful as Mondain, four times as nasty, and very elusive.

In *Ultima II: Revenge of the Enchantress*, Lord British called for a hero or heroine to save the land. At this time, he had a larger dwelling—an island castle—and many more retainers and greater wealth than in the previous game. He furnished much help while the hero built up his own power. As in *Ultima I*, the adventurer journeyed into outer space. This time, the goal was not enemy ships, but a person whose blessing would mean the difference between finding and destroying the enchantress, or not. That person was on a planet somewhere.

Finding him was quite difficult, but the hero solved the mystery of Minax and triumphed by destroying this ever-so-evil enchantress. He received the thanks of Lord British and the adulation of the people.

The Third Age of Darkness

Once more a brief period of peace existed, but the seeds of evil had already been sown. The relationship of Mondain and the young female apprentice, Minax, turned out to have been more than just that of teacher and student. From that unholy union a child had been born and had grown strong in his own right. In *Ultima III: Exodus*, troubles of the vilest kind once more descended upon the realms of Lord British. No longer was it safe to tend crops in the open, so peasants sought refuge in the walled towns, forsaking crops and livestock to the marauding monsters. Pirates ruled the seas; more evil dungeons appeared, producing even more monsters to plague a suffering Sosaria.

Finding the enemy of Lord British—indeed of the entire world—was not to be an easy task, for nobody knew anything about him. But a single clue was found in the form of a bloody word scrawled across the deck of an abandoned merchant ship: EXODUS.

Again Lord British sent out the call for someone to save the land. This time not one, but four strangers appeared because finding and destroying this new evil called for more than a single hero. And, sure enough, the mix of fighting, spell-casting, and thieving abilities in the party enabled these courageous ones eventually to put an end to the evil Exodus.

The Age of the Avatar Begins

The final destruction of the evil spawn of evil parents, Exodus, rocked the entire known world. Mountains rose and land masses sank. Most of the surface area of the world fused into one large continent. Lord British rose from the rubble of Sosaria and formed a mighty empire, Britannia. He was able, after many years, to unite all of the mainland and a few of the islands under his single rule.

The new Empire of Britannia brought general peace and prosperity. Many of the ancient pockets of evil were wiped out. Travelers had little to fear except an occasional marauding band of orcs or hill giants. Few areas of the Realm remained unexplored, and many were actually mapped. With the Triad of Evil destroyed, Lord British could devote his time to building public works and otherwise bettering the lives of his faithful and loving subjects.

At the time of *Ultima IV: Quest of the Avatar* Britannia had eight major towns. Each town was dedicated to fostering the study and spread of its own particular virtue. There were also numerous small villages scattered about.

Lord British was living in a magnificent castle at the very center of the continent, overlooking Britanny Bay. This tall, stately palace was the greatest architectural achievement of the new age. Loyal subjects paid homage to his majesty and renewed fealty whenever they visited the castle. Nearby was the town of Britain, the cultural center of Britannia, where bards wove tales of legendary deeds and serenaded passersby. Yet a great lack marred the kingdom—the people needed moral leadership; they needed to be shown virtue and enlightenment.

So again Lord British sent out the call, this time for a single individual to become an example of virtue, or avatar, for his people and thus guide them from the Age of Darkness into the Age of Light. The champion who responded was devoted and dedicated. He received the charge to discover the Codex of Ultimate Wisdom.

First the Hero and his party had to visit each of the eight towns to prove themselves worthy in each of the eight virtues of an avatar (Compassion, Honesty, Honor, Humility, Justice, Sacrifice, Spirituality, and Valor), as well as complete many quests. Then they journeyed to the Great Stygian Abyss (a very, very un-nice place), where the Codex was secreted, successfully completing their light-bringing mission.

The Subversion of the Shadowlords

Even after the Age of the Avatar, not all the evil entities in the world had been destroyed. Notably there still existed eight terrible dungeons, all of which Lord British, on the advice of his Council, determined to close up forever.

As the monarch himself recounts in the scrolls preparing adventurers for *Ultima V: Warriors of Destiny*:

> The acquisition of the Codex of Ultimate Wisdom from the deep recesses of the underworld created a karmic imbalance in the universe, resulting in the emergence of the sinister Shadowlords from the shards of the black jewel of Mondain. These grim agents of darkness were the very antitheses of virtue. Their trickery and deceit allowed them to imprison me in their underworld dungeon and, in a perversion of justice, compelled the leaders of Britannia to oppress the people. The once noble Lord Blackthorn became the human agent who fulfilled their evil intent.

When the Adventurer answered Lord British's summons he was already an Avatar. This was fortunate, considering the severity of the problem he was faced with—the entire land ruled by evil and arrayed against him, and Lord British in durance vile in some unknown place. The hero carefully chose a party. Demonstrating patience and perseverance, the adventurers vanquished the Shadowlords, rescued Lord British, and restored him to his consecrated throne. Peace and right ruled once again.

The Threat of the Gargoyles

The Gargoyles were long believed to be mythical creatures. Today, however, as the hero boredly watches television in his everyday humdrum world, a new evil assaults the land. An expedition in the geologically unstable underworld discovered these creatures, and now they apparently are bent on doing vast harm. The creatures pour forth, seeming to search for something of vast import to them and seizing the land's holy shrines, one after the other. Once again Lord British calls on the Avatar of great bravery and virtue to save Britannia. Inexplicably, they turn out to be bent on his destruction also.

Nonetheless, in *Ultima VI: The False Prophet,* the Avatar's mission has a different cast from his previous quests. He spends much less time in combat. (The monsters he meets are usually much easier to defeat; also he finds he needs fewer magic spells.) Instead of spending time fighting, he discovers many colorful places and characters, enjoys intriguing conversations, and encounters fascinating puzzles.

He does rid the land of the horrible plague, but accomplishing this is the most difficult challenge he has ever faced. This hero must possess immeasureable strength, vision, and compassion. In the course of ending the struggle between the Darkness and the Light, the Avatar needs his creativity and intellectual abilities more than he ever has before.

The Benefits of Fantasy Role Playing

This brings us to a good point for digressing from Ultima and Lord British for just a moment and taking a look at the larger picture. As I'm sure you know, although fantasy role playing should not loom extremely large in one's life, it has numerous beneficial effects that make it worthwhile to engage in wholeheartedly.

Most importantly, fantasy games help to keep the imagination flexible and powerful. There is something extraordinary possessed by every young person on this planet: a sense of wonder, a marvelous ability to let creativity soar. A child's imaginary playmates, a teenager's ironic sense of humor and immersion in science fiction and fantasy role playing—these show a power of mind that, if nurtured, is extremely helpful in adult life. The contribution made by a sense of wonder to one's creative powers can be . . . shall we say, valuable financially as well as personally.

Secondly, playing computer games increases one's sense of ease with computers in general and helps develop a readiness to explore and exploit their powerful features. This feeling of being "at home" contributes to computer literacy, and I doubt there is anyone here who thinks the high-paying jobs in the next few years *won't* go to the computer-literate.

Thirdly, the intense concentration required improves the ability to solve problems logically. Computer games require you to logically analyze the game elements and devise a workable strategy to deal with them. This works like a champ in the real world as well.

And fourth, computer gaming is an excellent method of stress management. Entertainment just for entertainment's sake helps relieve the many onerous tensions of everyday life.

Last, but certainly not least, it's fun—isn't it?

This Book

This book's explanation of the philosophy behind the games, as well as the specific strategies, hints, and tips provided, should help you solve the games more easily and add to your enjoyment of them.

After the questions and answers about Lord British and the world he created in Chapter 2, Chapter 3 gives general playing strategies for all six games and on-line sources of help.

Then comes the "good" stuff, an in-depth (very appropriate for dungeons, eh?) look at all six of the Ultima games. Each game gets two chapters. The first chapter lays out the game for you straightforwardly (just like a military briefing based on intelligence reports and the like) and offers a strategy specific to that game. It also tells you what to look for and what to look *out* for, and contains screens representative of those you will see as you play the game. The second chapter for each game follows the adventures of a different character created for our journey through a particular Ultima game. These chapters are intended to stretch your mind rather than simply inform it. Don't be surprised when descriptions of Ultima characters our hero encounters depart from actual game action and dialogue. The goal here is not so much to explain the games—that's what strategy chapters are for—as to inspire your own imaginative approach to playing them. After all, your imagination isn't just another resource here; it's essential to game mastery.

Read carefully these strategy sessions and stories, for they reveal things you will need to know not only for successful completion of the adventure, but just for simple survival!

Which brings us to the general philosophy of this book. I will tell you a lot of explicit facts about the worlds of Ultima, but not *everything* will be completely spelled out. Let's face it, a step-by-step, nuts-and-bolts walk-through would take away all your fun and sense of accomplishment in solving the six Ultima games.

Read the two chapters for each game as you play that game, and try not to get too far ahead. That way, you'll still be in suspense about what will happen next and surprised by it when it does. Also, if you came into the Ultima series late, say at *Ultima V* or *Ultima VI*, it's a good idea to go back and play the earlier games. Not only will this give you a lot of enjoyment, but the more you learn about the universe of Lord British, the more likely you are to survive these later games and new games as they come out.

2 Questions and Answers

Following are some of the most commonly asked questions about Lord British and the world of Ultima with, of course, their answers. This information was mostly gathered from conferences throughout 1985 to 1990 on DELPHI, GEnie, and CompuServe.

Who is Lord British? I see that name given as the author of all the games, but isn't he a character in the games also?

There are two manifestations of Lord British. One is the benign emperor of Sosaria/Britannia, where he has lived for several ages, growing ever stronger, and working toward the common good between periods of total warfare instigated by various champions of evil. Mortals meet this Lord British while adventuring in his realm (where his help is of incalculable worth).

Lord British also is a person who has been living on Earth for a shorter period—just over thirty years, local time. He travels incognito here. Some people, however, have reported meeting him on Earth as "Richard C. Garriott" at various computer trade conventions.

Regardless of where you run across him, he is always gracious, as befits such a powerful monarch.

What does the "C"stand for in "Richard C. Garriott"?

Hmmm. This would make a great question if Trivial Pursuit ever puts out a card set about computer game authors. The "C" stands for "Cantabridgian." This unusually long middle name means "from Cambridge," and refers to the fact that the Lord British who lives on Earth was born in Cambridge, England.

What does Lord British look like when in his earthly guise of Richard C. Garriott?

Look at the portrait of Shamino in *Ultima VI*.

Where did Lord British the game author get his schooling here on Earth? In what did he major?

He attended the University of Texas, which, he told an audience on CompuServe, is "a great school in a great state!" He majored in electrical engineering with a minor in computer science. He left college to work fulltime writing computer games because he realized that his schooling was not helping in his already successful career of computer game design. Well, he does qualify that slightly—it did help him learn to spell better. It's not hard to figure out that he earns more doing this than most electrical engineers, so his decision was personally sound.

Where does Lord British get his creative concepts? From fantasy and science fiction?

His ideas come from various places. As late as 1984, Lord British claimed to have read only twenty-five books, and he had been writing highly successful computer games for over five years by that time. However, as he went on to state, the increasing complexity of the games has caused him to do extensive research and read many more fantasy and science fiction books since then.

A few years ago Lord British was a big Dungeons and Dragons player. (D&D, of course, is the seminal fantasy role-playing game from TSR Hobbies that allows several people to play together and has been very popular for over a decade now.) He has also participated in the Society for Creative Anachronism (a very interesting and fun national group of medievalists).

He reports that he is an avid movie goer; the movie *Time Bandits,* for example, inspired the time doors in *Ultima II.* Everyday events, even dreams, inspire him too.

Of course, for the truly creative person, everything is a potential trigger for something new and exciting.

Where does Lord British get the names of his characters? Some of them seem like common, everyday Earth names, and others sound more make-believe and fanciful.

You're right. Lord British often uses the names of friends and acquaintances. Starting with *Ultima IV*, he held various contests and used the names of the winners in the games. Plus, people send him many suggestions for names and characters, several hundred of which actually appear.

What procedure does Lord British use to create the games?

Lord British says that first he decides upon his main objectives for graphics and plot. Then, he programs the way they tell you not to in school—that is, he doesn't use a top down approach. He gets the outdoor graphics working. Then he makes the adventurer walk around, enter towns, walk some more, and so on.

Next he constructs and activates essential shops, such as the food shops. Monsters start appearing about this time; he implements the routines that allow the adventurer or party of adventurers to attack them and that lets the monsters fight back. In other words, it is a gradual process of adding on. The last items to go in are the main plot phases.

Does Lord British work alone?

Not any more. The first four games in the series were written almost one hundred percent by him, but as the games grew in complexity, it became obvious that there was no way for one man to be able to do all the work in a reasonable amount of time. So, rather than having new Ultima games coming out only every two or three years, which was felt to be too long a waiting period, Lord British assembled a team of creative and technical people to help him.

As he put it himself, in a recent CompuServe conference, "Beginning with number V, I did about half of the programming and none of the art, as I began to utilize professional artists. By the time *Ultima VI* came around, I was basically involved in the design and world creation aspects, having specialists working with me on all areas: four programmers, five artists, three writers and an assortment of testers, musicians, and other helpers." So Lord British has become more like a movie director than anything else. He may not run every camera, so to speak, but he tells them all where to point.

Actually, we can't say too much about the advantage that having a supporting team gives Lord British. He now has the liberty to devise new styles and techniques of gaming without having to do the time-consuming task of making it work in a computer. Thus he is able to come up with *more* innovations.

Does Lord British ever play his own games?

Because it takes two years or so of very intensive work to write and develop an Ultima game, Lord British says, he usually prefers to start working on the next creation instead of playing one already done. By that time, he knows the completed one pretty well. Nor is he much on playing competitors' games, unless it's just to keep an eye on what they're doing out of professional curiosity.

He has long (and rather obviously) enjoyed fantasy computer games very much but, with his considerable success today, has little time for play. Or, as he put it to the CompuServe audience, "these days Ultima seems like my life."

How do the stories of the six games fit together?

The first three games, written between 1979 and 1983, were created, as Lord British admits, somewhat haphazardly and with little internal consistency. However, the sheer raw force of the author's creativity carries them, despite their story flaws. Also they do tie together loosely into a trilogy, a fact reinforced by the documentation that comes with the recent rerelease of all three games in one box as the *Ultima Trilogy*. More recently, due to the game author's increased experience, the games display a lot more polish and craftsmanship. The games in the second set of three are much more interrelated in both plot and character. So, for example, learning how the virtues of an Avatar work in *Ultima IV* helps you in the next two games, and vice versa.

Why does the world's geography change so much from Ultima to Ultima?

Glad you asked that. Lord British the game author has revealed that he changes the layout of the world in each game for two reasons: the necessities of the story and personal whim. The first factor, of course, is the more compelling. During the process of creating the game, he decides to rearrange geography to improve playability, make a better story, and so forth.

How does Lord British react to people who read deep meanings into his games?

Lord British has expressed some amazement at the number of people, even fans, who read things into his games that he never put there. (They remind one of literary reviewers who use thousands of words to detail "the hidden meaning" of a book when all the poor author was trying to do was tell an entertaining story.)

But the Ultima games do have a message, don't they?

Not really, but the earthly Lord British does want them to have a constructive and beneficial impact. He says he realizes that what he creates has affected, even if just in a small way, the lives of hundreds of thousands of people. He often expresses his sense of responsibility to make sure that the net effect of his work is positive, not negative, on these lives.

While not professing any particular religious morality, he does believe that certain ethical principles are based on logic. The example he gives is the old one that goes "Do unto others as you would have them do unto you." In other words, don't beat anybody up, unless you want them to beat you up in return.

We can see the growing concern of Lord British with moral and philosophical realities becoming more evident from the fourth Ultima on, when the virtuous attributes of the Avatar play a big role. Lord British is pleased that this new direction has been well received as the Ultima series continues to grow in popularity.

Does Lord British think computer games will replace board games?

Yes, he thinks computer games will eventually prevail over board and other manual games. The popularity of Nintendo's Game Boy and other similar electronic games is one indicator as, of course, is the extraordinary sales of the Ultima series and other popular computer games. As this age becomes more and more the Information Age, Lord British foresees games of increasing complexity, as well as awesome graphics and sound capabilities. For avid computer game players, this is a wonderful time to be alive.

Does Lord British have any plans for adapting the gaming system used in Ultima to other game genres, such as mystery or science fiction?

Yes, Lord British has expressed an interest in writing other types of games. However, as he says, he's been kept busy by the demand for new games in the Ultima series, and if he does branch out he probably will just oversee those projects and turn the programming over to others.

What can I expect to see in future Ultima games?

You can expect the games to become even more complicated. The reason is that Lord British has a stated goal of developing a wide game "universe" in which an infinite number of scenarios are possible. He avows that he has always tried to use each new advance in computer technology whenever he possibly can, to enhance the Ultima series.

We can see this goal of his in the last three games, which incorporate moral dilemmas that the player must answer questions about. The player's character is determined by the beliefs expressed in the answers. There is wide latitude in where and how characters start off, making each adventurer's journey unique at least in part.

Still, in these games the end goal is the same for all. But Lord British acknowledges an even more ambitious goal—that of a variety of *solutions*.

How much money does Lord British make writing games?

The short answer is "a lot," just as is true of many other computer game writers, and of movie stars, members of popular rock groups, and best-selling authors. (We reward those who entertain us well.) Lord British prefers not to give actual figures, but did reveal several years ago that he received eight dollars in royalties for each copy of *Ultima III* sold, and that monthly sales for the first six months of its release were running between 2,000 to 6,000. Things have improved since then.

It's obviously a good way to make a living, and Lord British expresses his gratitude to the many fans who continue to buy his games.

Does Lord British ever read his own fan mail?

Oh yes, and he gets tons of it. He reports receiving thousands of letters since the first game came out in 1979, running the gamut from complaints (from religious fanatics who oppose the portraying of demons and magic) to compliments (from an army of true fans). You may write to him here on Earth in care of ORIGIN Systems, P.O. Box 161750, Austin TX 78716.

3 A Toast to Fallen Heroes

O Hero, take heed of this chapter lest it be you that we toast in sad remembrance these long, cold winter nights in the Great Hall of Lord British.

Britannia's extensive repository of learning, knowledge, and wisdom is the Lycaeum, which is located on the northwest slopes of Verity Isle. Here are libraries, laboratories, and various academies of learning. Together they constitute a haven for scholars and all others who would seek truth. A regular occurrence at the Lycaeum is the meeting of the Inner Circle of Mages in certain labyrinthine chambers within the walls. This happens four times during the year, and many esoteric secrets are reputed to be exchanged.

Yet, amidst the striving for truth and the other lofty goals of academic pursuits, there exist areas devoted to more mundane endeavors. One such is the Hall of Inactive Personnel Records—an entity of Lord British's civil service. In this huge, rambling, out-of-the-way stone pile are kept records of service. One entire wing several levels high is devoted to the scrolls of those Heroes who failed in their mission and fell in agony on the field of battle, or expired horribly in the darkness of a dank dungeon to the echo of some monster's fiendish laugh. Millions of these scrolls lie quiet and pale as the light of a visitor's torch goes down endless aisle after endless aisle—a terrible and sad waste.

How may the addition of your own scroll to these dusty shelves best be avoided?

This chapter presents you with certain precautions and general rules of strategy that will help you have a much greater chance of survival when you undertake any of the six grand adventures.

Persistence

There is one great secret to success in life, and it exists not in gems of power, nor is it written in flaming runes on some far altar. It is a thing so simple that many overlook it and fail in their endeavors. Whether one is seeking the lair of the evil Mondain or is striving to write a computer program, find a job, or obtain the love of fair maid or lad, there is this one secret that ensures success—persistence.

As some anonymous person once wrote:

> Nothing in the world can take the place of persistence. Talent will not; nothing is more common than unsuccessful men and women with talent. Genius will not; unrewarded genius is almost a proverb. Education alone will not; the world is full of educated derelicts. Persistence and determination alone are omnipotent.

When you reach a sticking point, and there are many in a game as complex as an Ultima game always is, do not stop. Keep experimenting until you surmount the obstacle. Luck won't do it—the games are just too complicated. Guessing won't cut it—there are just too many possibilities. Instead, you need to keep on trying to acquire the knowledge and items required to solve each phase of the game and to reach the goal.

I repeat: Do *not* give up. There are many people who—unknown to them—come within inches of achieving a treasured goal, only to give up when a mere smidgen of extra effort would have secured the goal.

In football this means that the halfback with three tackles from the opposing team viciously hanging on and trying to wrestle him down, takes those two additional agonizing steps that drag him, the tackles, and the ball into the end zone for a touchdown. In a computer game, it means you restore from the saved state once more, and *this* time manage to defeat the monster that seemed invincible the forty previous times. You may not immediately win the game, but you will feel wonderfully triumphant as you quickly save the game after that victory, then proceed determinedly onward.

By continuously trying, you will learn your way through the game. With determination, you'll overcome all odds and master Ultima!

But, there are just a few other things to learn.

Save Early, Save Often, and Save a Lot!

To be persistent, one must have a point from which to spring forward again.

If you've made a thousand moves, built up hundreds of hit points, and accumulated several important gems or tools or other important objects, being drop-kicked back to the beginning of the game is *not* a viable option. It might take you hours or even days to get back to the point where your character was so foully done in. And, in reaching that point again, you might not find or capture all the items you originally had. Therefore, saving is all-important.

The Ultima games all offer a command for saving the game. In the first five games, this is the letter `Q`.

Using this save game feature does have restrictions. In general, you must be in the open, and you must first dismount from any vehicle you might be in or on—whether it's a horse, frigate, skiff, aircar, raft, or space shuttle. This general requirement presents the further restriction that you must be on open land to dismount.

In other words, if you get killed while in a dungeon, a town, a king's castle, a tower, or space, you lose everything gained since the last time you were on the ground in open terrain and pressed `Q` to save the game. So save frequently.

A wise hero knows when to save. For example, the dungeons in *Ultima I* go ten levels deep, and there are some very, very nasty creatures that dwell in those dark depths. So it is wise to explore and map them in stages, returning frequently to the surface to save the game.

Figure 3.1 *A party in* Ultima V *is about to enter a moon gate near the town of Skara Brae. While you can save at more places in this game than prior ones, it's still always a great idea to save before going somewhere new—just in case you don't like where you wind up and can't get back.*

A disadvantage (or at least a minor annoyance) of the first five Ultima games is that to restore the game, you must reset the computer and restart the game, which then gives you an option to proceed from your last saved point. This happens because Lord British wrote these five games in machine language so that he could pack more power and faster action into them. In other words, the game takes over the computer totally, and you have to reboot before you can do anything else at all.

Ultima VI, utilizing newer programming techniques, offers much more convenience in saving and restoring games, especially in the MS-DOS version. There you use Control-S to save the game. (You will be asked if you really want to save the game; type N for "no" if you've changed your mind.) Control-R immediately restores the last saved game state. Control-Q exits the game and returns you to DOS, where you can then run other programs. This, too, is a big timesaver over the first five Ultima games.

Regardless of the difficulty of saving, however, you should do it very often, especially when you are first starting out and your character or characters have few experience points and few hit points. Then, almost any monster that feels like it (and they all do!) can wipe out your Hero or party of Heroes with ease and the greatest of beastly glee. If that happens, and you have not saved recently, you have to go back and retrace many steps.

One caution, however. You might want to think a little before saving if your hero is in a position where he cannot retreat. For example, if you are far from any source of food and your food supply is very low, so low that starvation is a certainty long before you can reach any food source, don't save the game here. This is one time when it is wise to start over at an earlier point and stock up on plenty of food so that the situation won't happen again.

True, in some games you can be resurrected, but resurrection has its disadvantages. In *Ultima I* you usually are resurrected with reduced hit points. Also, you retain your armor, vehicles, and spells, but lose your weapons. If you formerly had 2,000 hit points and a blaster, you will find it quite an inconvenience to come back to life with only 99 hit points and your bare hands as a weapon. So ignore resurrection, reset your computer, and restart the game from your last saved point (which should be relatively close if you've been saving regularly as you should have).

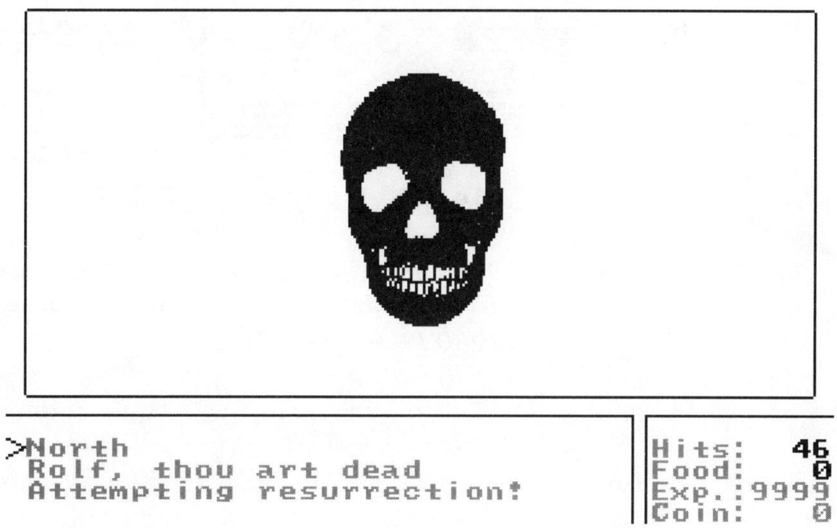

Figure 3.2 *Death in all of the Ultima games (except* Ultima II*) is not final, but you lose things when you are resurrected, as here in* Ultima I. *Better to reset your computer and restart the game from the last saved point than to be resurrected.*

In *Ultima II*, if you get killed, you are dead. Save early, save often, and save a lot!

Adventurers who die in *Ultima III* are not automatically restored. You have to get them resurrected manually. A high-level cleric of your own can do this, or you can buy a resurrection (assuming you've got the necessary gold) at one of the healing shops in various towns.

In later games, such as *Ultima V*, a dead adventurer returns through a resurrecting void to Lord British's castle. Which is fine, except you now have to take a long and often arduous journey back to where your party expired. Far better to have saved the game just before that and to proceed from there.

Save early, save often, and save a lot!

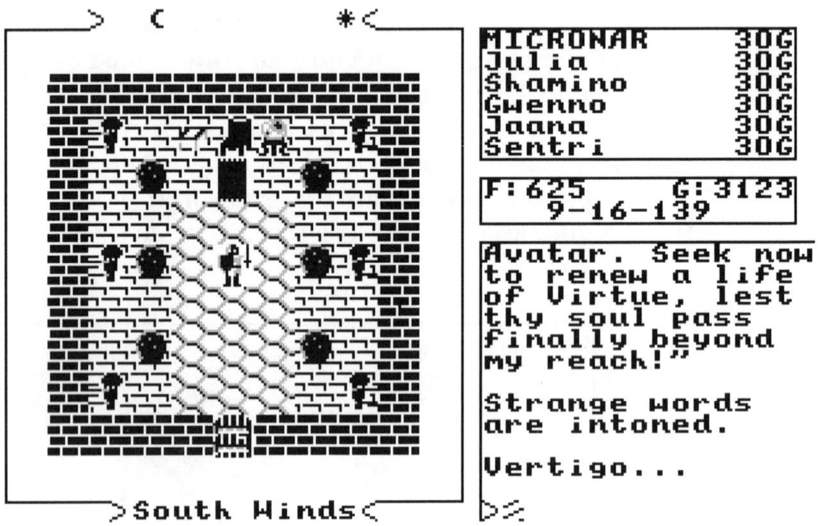

Figure 3.3 *In* Ultima V, *your party has been totally wiped out, is resurrected, and finds itself back in the castle of Lord British, ready for another try.*

Food

Ah, food. Succulent, juicy dragon steaks flame-broiled over an open fire. Tender leeks in a broth of barley. Great hunks of fresh-baked bread. Tubs of butter and delicious jellies. Great wheels of golden, flaky cheese. Pheasant and mutton, roasted and basted with their own flavorful drippings.

Yes, one eats well in the realms of Lord British. This must be so, for the many exertions of a Hero quickly sap your energy and, if you don't keep a wary eye on your food supply, you could starve quickly. (By the way, riding on a horse or in a vehicle helps you conserve energy, as well as enabling you to travel farther and faster.)

At the very outset of the games, especially of *Ultima I* and *Ultima II*, finding food is of utmost importance. Even in *Ultima II*, your initial provision of 400 hit points, 400 units of food, and 400 gold pieces isn't all that much help. You had better see to getting some food, not to mention armor and weapons, right away. Throughout the game check your food supply often, and replenish it before the level becomes so low that it's death not to do so immediately.

Develop the habit of shopping for food whenever you are near a food source. Shops selling food may be found in most towns in all games except *Ultima II*. There, you need to go to a village to get food. (Sometimes you may wonder whether a place is a town or a castle. One way to find out is to go inside and look around. To do this, place your character on the symbol for the town or castle and type E for Enter. By the way, this is the way you enter everything from towns to dungeons in all six games.)

Naturally, these groceries and Ye Olde Food Shoppes and Convenience Stores are not in the business for the fun of it. They require hard cash in the form of good, solid coin of the realm. (None of these shops take VISA, MasterCard or American Express.) So, while you may occasionally have to risk stealing food (don't get caught!), you should be sure you have a good supply of gold before entering an establishment selling food. You get gold by killing monsters, or finding it in chests or coffins in dungeons.

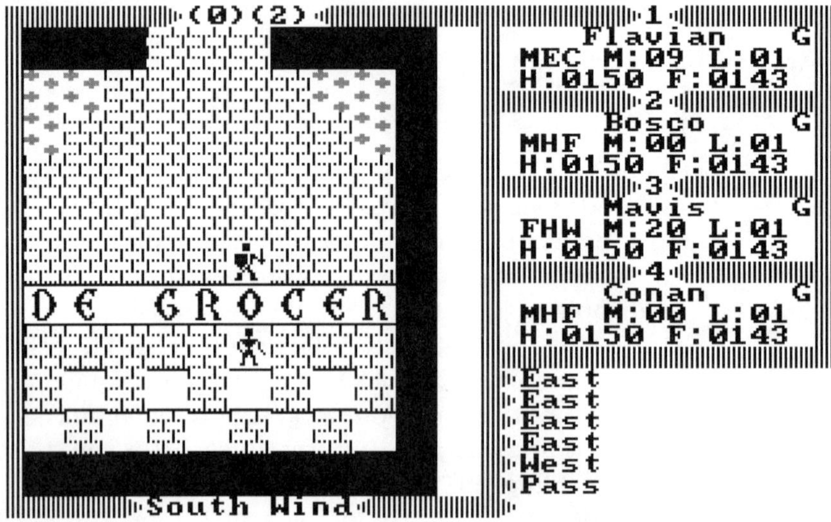

Figure 3.4 *Food is usually found in towns, such as here at De Grocer in* Ultima III. *You need lots of food to survive.*

There's another way to get gold in *Ultima I*. If you steal two blasters or two reflective suits, you can use one and immediately sell the other back to the shopowner (who doesn't recognize his or her own merchandise). Although stealing weapons or armor is very dangerous, when you are broke and desperate for food, it's a quick way to raise enough gold to buy a considerable amount of food (more than you can safely steal directly).

In the first three games, stealing anything—food, weapons, armor, or *any*thing—is always very risky. Guards, who don't like stealing, are omnipresent. They're also extremely strong and seem to take forever to kill. Most of the time, you don't have forever. In the last three games, stealing is not virtuous and delays completion of your quest.

Luckily, since it is very much a recurring expense, food is not all that dear. In *Ultima III*, you need to purchase food for each member of the party, but in *Ultima IV* and *Ultima V*, one food purchase is divided automatically among the group. In *Ultima VI*, food plays a much less important role.

Keep your food supply very high. Don't worry about getting fat; the realms of Lord British are definitely one place where you will stay lean, mean, and in fighting trim. No matter how much food you have, there's going to be plenty of exertion to burn up those calories.

Food, you can't live without it.

Arms and Armor

If you want to live long enough to risk starvation, you had better be well armed and well armored. So, in addition to obtaining food, make sure you have as much protection and fighting power as possible, as soon as possible. In *Ultima II*, for example, you start with only your hands as weapons and your bare skin as armor. Definitely not a winning combination! So you need to find a town immediately and equip yourself for survival, avoiding combat in the meantime. In other words, though it goes against the grain of being a Hero, run like a rabbit.

Figure 3.5 *A weapons shop in* Ultima II. *Outfit your character or characters with the best equipment you can afford (or steal).*

Building up your supplies can be a long, slow, painful process. In the first two games, for example, the level of gold you start with is insufficient to buy the higher classes of armor and weapons. One solution to this problem is to amass enough cash to buy them later. This takes time, because it involves getting hit points by defeating monsters in the countryside, then descending into the dungeons with your added strength and killing monsters for even more hit points and gold.

Fortunately, a wily thief can speed up the process somewhat in *Ultima I*. There, in an armor shop, you see strictly medieval items such as leather, chain mail, and plate armor displayed, but behind the counter are vacuum and reflective suits. You'll definitely need a vacuum suit when you go into space; otherwise you will find space travel a very breathtaking (and brief) episode. To get these suits at this stage means stealing (just press the S key). Later, when you've accumulated experience, you'll actually be offered the high tech weapons and armor, but they are very expensive.

(Save early, save often, and save a lot!)

In the later four Ultima games when you can (indeed must) have a party of adventurers, make sure that they are all equipped and provisioned to the very utmost you can afford. Parties usually encounter groups of monsters, and parties with weak members are soon minus those members.

Magic

Magic exists and works on Sosaria and in Britannia, in the form of various kinds of spells, including healing. Spells are very useful in dungeons in *Ultima I;* they aren't really necessary in *Ultima II;* and beginning in *Ultima III* they are an important part of general fighting strategy.

In the latter three Ultima games, there are two ways to cast magic spells. First, a character who is a magic user, such as a mage, can cast a spell if he or she has advanced to a high enough level and has prepared the spell beforehand by mixing various reagents in the proper way for that particular spell. Second, anyone in your party, magic user or not, can cast any spell, even one of a level higher than that attained by the character, by using a special type of scroll or potion. Naturally, finding these precious items is a bonus, and you should constantly search for them.

Transportation

You travel in the games by various low-tech and high-tech means, ranging from foot, horse, skiff, and wind-powered craft, to space vehicles, time doors, and moon gates. These last transport you instantly to another location. In the last four games, learning when moon gates appear and how to use them is a major key to success on your quests.

Expertise

In the Empire of Britannia there is a word for those who are not smart and do not learn from their experiences, and that word is 'dead.'

In all of the Ultima games it is supremely important to take notes and make maps. It also pays to talk to all who are willing to hold a conversation with you, from bartender to princess, and listen to the hints they divulge.

Princesses are especially important sources of information in *Ultima I.* Luckily, there, princesses are never hard to come by. Every castle, even Lord British's, has them in its prison. Also, after you manage to rescue one, you can immediately reenter the castle, rescue another, and receive another helpful hint. (In later games, with the emergence of equal rights for princesses in Britannia, princess captivity came to be frowned on as very insensitive and backward.)

In *Ultima II,* the only way you can win the game is to obtain expertise on how to use various items (gems, skull keys, brass buttons, various tools, and the like) that you pick up during combat with monsters. After every fight with a monster, check your statistics to learn what you've garnered (by pressing the letter Z—for Z-stats), and be sure to listen to everybody you meet for helpful info on how to use your finds.

Keep records of what happens. The last three games are almost impossible to complete unless you take extensive notes. You will talk to scores of people in each, many of whom can be induced to give you a helpful, even critically important, clue. Keep a list of people's names and locations, just in case you asked the wrong question in your first meeting and later get referred back to them.

When *Ultima IV* starts, it suggests very emphatically that you read the booklet that comes with the game. As Lord British said once, most people ignore this but eventually find themselves forced to read the material in the box and then start again. In fact, some of the traps are based on the assumption that the player has not read this information and will ignorantly blunder into the jaws of death. So, to succeed in solving *Ultima IV*, read the booklets that come with the game—*The History of Britannia*, *The Book of Magic*, and the Player Reference Card—thoroughly before beginning play (as well as Chapters 10 and 11 in this book).

Figure 3.6 *As* Ultima IV *opens, you'll pass through this timegate, or moongate. You need to have read the booklet that comes in the game package to know what to do next.*

You can never know too much in any of the Ultima games! Search, listen, make notes, map. Expertise can be a more powerful weapon than blasters, phazors, or the strongest of magic spells.

General Strategy

The plots of the Ultima games, as they progress from *Ultima I* through *Ultima VI*, become more and more tightly woven. However, none are so rigid (as are some games) as to require one particular strategy or order of play to win. There are a lot of different ways to achieve the goal—some of them easier than others, but none very easy.

Overall, think of your campaign as having three phases (of course always saving early, often, and a lot). The very first stage is sheer survival. That means getting your character or characters properly equipped, and making sure that they have plenty of food. In other words, logistics is the primary order of business. This phase may take some time, as you cautiously venture out from towns and castles, looking for easy battles as a source of experience points and of gold to buy food, better weapons, and better armor.

Speaking of equipping your characters, a general word about the last three Ultima games: the virtues that an Avatar must show play a large part in your success or failure. Being humble, for example, is more effective than being arrogant. (It's OK to be aggressive, however.) Also, the games watch your every move and make you pay for bad deeds. After a dishonest act it takes a lengthy period of honesty and good deeds to recover and work your way back to the top.

Figure 3.7 *From* Ultima IV *on, your answers to a series of questions establish the virtues of a new character. It's very important to answer honestly and to the best of your ability.*

As your experience builds, you enter a second phase, that of exploration. (The later the game, the more this phase overlaps with the first.) Now, reasonably confident of surviving most battles, you can venture further afield, searching for the items and information you need to eventually solve the game. This should be by far the longest stage. Use it to build your character or characters up to their maximum potential, and to acquire the very best weapons and armor as well as magic spells and anything else that's not nailed down. You will need every edge possible for the final stage.

Last, fully informed and fully armed, you can confront the evil with a chance of actually succeeding. The final stage should be relatively short. Evil wizards and monsters guarding the Codex or Lord British are no pushovers, but you'll have all the tools at hand to defeat them if you did the second stage properly and thoroughly.

Boiled down to its essence like this, this three-part general strategy sounds absurdly simple, but it is not simple to accomplish. Each stage involves scores of battles (and sometimes other challenges), and much travail and effort on your part. (If it was easy, Lord British would not have called for you, the greatest of all Heroes, would he have? Of course not. He'd have gotten cheap labor instead, like the idiot fighters in *Ultima II* who stand around saying, "Me tough.")

In the chapters specific to each of the six Ultima games, we will go into the strategy you should employ to win each particular game, but remember always the three basic tenets above (which work for most fantasy role-playing games): prepare for survival by arming and provisioning; prepare for the final conflict by exploring, learning, and building experience; and (when fully ready) enter the final conflict with all the tools you need to quickly and decisively win it.

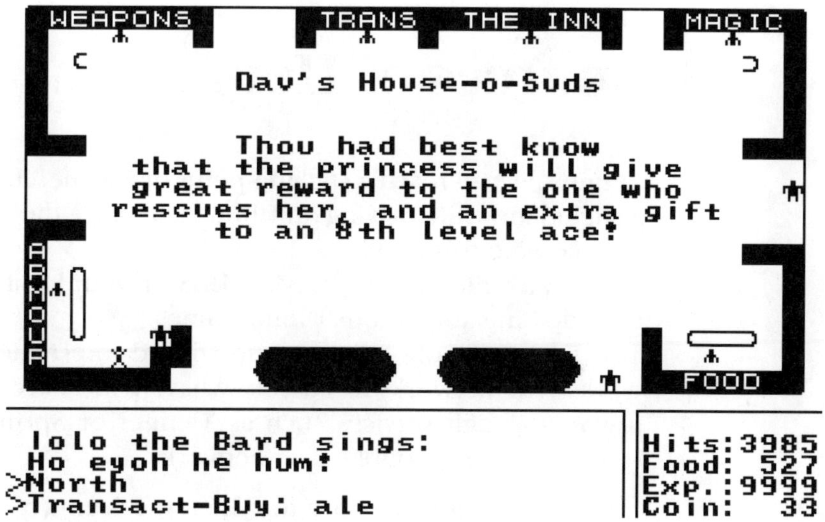

Figure 3.8 *In* Ultima I, *as in all Ultima games, it pays to talk to everyone you can and listen to what they say, such as this bartender who is giving you a very valuable tip.*

Installation

Installation is the process of setting up the game to run on your computer. This is usually a one-time process involving copying your disks, either to backup floppies or (if you have it) a hard disk.

As a general caution, you should always make copies of your game disks in case one becomes corrupted. The earlier Ultimas require a key disk (that is, you must insert one of the original disks before the game will work). You must treat those disks very carefully. Beginning with *Ultima VI,* you no longer have this aggravating worry.

In the games that require a play disk even if you have a hard disk, be sure to make a backup copy of the play disk periodically. There is nothing so frustrating as building a character or characters almost up to the strength needed for the final conflict and then losing your play disk. Always, always have a backup.

Sources of Help

At times, we all reach a sticking point in a game. If you find yourself in a slight jam while playing an Ultima game, try the following ideas:

Look in this book.

Try a bulletin board service (BBS) in your local area; many of these provide hints for various Ultima games.

Log on to one of the national and international computer networks. The networks listed below have a local access number in most towns, through services such as Tymnet or SprintNet data network (formerly Telenet public data network).

- CompuServe: Go into the Gamers Forum (type `GO GAMERS`). Search the library and the messages for the keyword 'Ultima.'
- DELPHI (the world's friendliest computer network): From the MAIN prompt type `groups games`. This takes you to Scorpia's GAMESIG. You might mention to Scorpia that you read about her games group in this book, since she very kindly provided helpful input.
- While on DELPHI, you can also pop over to the WRITERS GROUP and say "hi" to AUTHOR, Ralph Roberts. Incidentally, please feel free to E-mail me with comments about this book or any of the Ultima games.

- GEnie: From the main menu select (Games), then select 1 (Games Round Table). The Games Round Table is also run by Scorpia.
- Prodigy: Go to the PC Club and enter the adventure games forum (Jumpword: `PC CLUB`).

For more information on the computer network services mentioned above, and how to join them, call these toll-free numbers:

DELPHI	(800) 544-4005
GEnie	(800) 638-9636
CompuServe	(800) 848-8199
Prodigy	(800) 822-6922

You can do more than just "walk through" files when you're on-line. These services are also a meeting place for many people with interests the same as yours. Just as the Ultima games open worlds of fantasy, on-line services can open worlds of friendship.

PART

2

Ultima I—The First Age of Darkness

4 The Adventure Begins

Hail, Noble One! The land is in need of a stalwart hero, one who will brave perils too horrific to consider. A plague has befallen the Realm, a scourge is upon the land! 'Tis the doing of one so evil that the earth trembles at the mention of his name. The situation is desperate and resources so scarce that only a solitary adventurer can be sent back to effect the rescue of an entire civilization. The outcome of this mission of salvation lies on your strong shoulders. Give careful attention to this briefing, so that you may succeed.

Background

First, the background. Sosaria, an ancient land, is divided into minuscule kingdoms, small city-states spread widely over four continents. Historically the level of technology was completely medieval; people relied on wind, muscle, and animal power. Peasant farmers eked out a living on tiny plots of farmland, selling their surplus foodstuffs to the towns and castles, which were all heavily fortified against attack. Strife was rare, limited to forays by mountain orcs and only an occasional brief burst of warfare between one fiefdom and another.

From the tiny bobbit to the tall human, the folk of town and country lived usually in harmony, working together in a spirit of comradeship. Each of the four races recognized its own strengths and weaknesses and assisted the other races in areas were they were lacking.

It was an idyllic period, where gaining the necessities of survival did not take an overabundance of effort, and people could devote much time to contemplation and various leisurely pursuits. Even the kings, Lord British included, tended to accept their domains as they were and to spend their time in revelry and otherwise enjoying life, rather than engaging in arduous campaigns of conquest that would necessitate tramping about the countryside in the summer heat and being forced to drink one's wine not properly chilled.

Civilization overall was placid, static, almost smug. No one wished to make changes. But now that the scourge of Mondain has begun, wicked and detestable creatures prey upon the people and despoil the land. Villages lie sacked—they are mere ruinous mounds of ashes. The fields are bare where peasants stout of heart and sound of mind once flourished, where grain and fruit once blossomed, where kine and fowl grew fat upon the bounties of fair Sosaria. Formerly honorable citizens have been seduced to evil and are wreaking destruction upon their fellows.

The troubles are in full swing at the time you arrive in Sosaria, with only a bare minimum of arms and armor. You need to act immediately to secure the means of your own survival, and to begin the quest to rescue this land from the evil that has horridly befallen it.

Your Character

There is one set of decisions, however, that you must make before being injected into this situation, and that can greatly help or harm you—your character. While your provisions are limited, you do have some flexibility in that you can modify your characteristics slightly. You may choose your race, sex, and profession, and adjust your personal character traits.

Upon arrival you have ten points each in the categories of intelligence, strength, wisdom, agility, charisma, and stamina. You can distribute an additional thirty points among these attributes. For initial survival, select strength and agility, one reason being that there are several weapons that require agility to wield, as does the sometimes necessary art of theft. In the long run, of course, you'll need as much as possible of the other four attributes too. For now, give an edge to strength and agility and plan to enhance your other attributes during your mission.

Figure 4.1 *Distribute your points carefully. As this character you have an abundance of intelligence, which you'll need to build up your other attributes.*

The following sections will assist you in making workable choices regarding your race, sex, and profession (as well as in assessing people you meet).

Race and Sex

The people of Sosaria fall into four general categories—human, elf, dwarf, and bobbit.

Of the four racial groups of Sosaria, humans have the advantage of a higher average intellect. Humans are the ruling class in Sosarian society, and found in every walk of life. They are usually strong in both body and spirit.

Elves are shorter than humans—on the order of about the width of three hands. They are slight of build, very agile, and fast on their feet. Their natural abilities make them excellent musicians and thieves. Whether among the trees of some deep forest, or in the alleyways of a town, the Sosarian elf can be a stalwart companion or a relentless foe.

Shorter than elves, but usually outweighing them because of their stocky build, are the dwarves. Dwarves are mountain folk. None surpasses them in mining ability—they wrestle riches from the ground with a strength greater than humans. They are extremely courageous.

The bobbits are small and gentle. No one knows their origin, although many say that they came to Sosaria from some distant place and are not native. They favor mountainside meadows and—being shorter than dwarves and not nearly as strong—avoid all tasks that involve hard labor. They prefer instead to study and contemplate. In fact their strong points are their serenity and profound wisdom.

Now which race should you choose?

Elves have a huge advantage in their agility. This is helpful early on because it is a good idea to avoid combat until you're properly weaponed and armed. Because fighting earns you cash, avoiding combat means no source of gold; as a result, the only course left is to steal the food and equipment needed to get started—and, as you might expect, elves steal very well. However, their lack of strength can often turn into a real impediment later in your campaign.

Dwarves are very strong, always a blessing in a fight to the death. They also are undeniably courageous. Alas, however, they generally are dumber than moatwater, which can become a disadvantage later.

Bobbits are weak but wise. Being wise, they seldom go on quests.

The compromise between these pros and cons is the human. Humans are of moderate strength (only dwarves are stronger). They have the highest intelligence, although not necessarily the wisdom to go with it. Human agility is usually at least barely adequate to the task at hand in the early going. In sum, blessed with good intelligence, humans are able to acquire the agility and strength needed to survive and progress.

As for which sex to choose, males are stronger at the beginning. On the other hand, females are more agile. During the early going, strength has a slight edge, but as you build up your points in these categories, the sexes become equal.

Profession

Although there are many varied professions in Sosaria, you are limited to one of these four professions, each of which has advantages and disadvantages: fighter, cleric, wizard (mage), and thief.

A fighter is strong, agile, and proficient with every weapon likely to be found in Sosaria. If you choose to be a fighter you can have these attributes without having to actually spend the time sweating under a hot sun in the practice yard of some castle doing endless calisthenics or hacking eternally at a post with a heavy great sword until your arms feel like lead and you wish they *would* fall off. Instead, you may just conveniently declare yourself a fighter and proceed from there with all the benefits accruing thereto.

A cleric enjoys a gentler calling than that of a fighter, although in the present emergency men and women of the collar and robe must battle just as hard to survive as any fighter. The cleric spends many years in patient and diligent study and thereby gains great wisdom. The calmness and concentration won by his holy lifestyle give a cleric a decided advantage in spell casting. At no time does the proper spell cast by a cleric fail; it always achieves the desired result. Should you choose to be injected into the First Age of Darkness, this benefit is yours without the many years of prayer, study, and fasting that it would otherwise require.

Magic has always been important in Sosaria, although it has not always been popularly used. Becoming proficient in the arcane arts is not an easy task—as in the case of the cleric, the years pass slowly in study. He or she who would be a wizard and use magic must master secrets written in barely decipherable runes on ancient dusty scrolls. You will find it a great advantage to be a graduate wizard, however, because magic supply shops cater only to a recognized wizard.

Thieves are not well thought of in any society, but there are advantages to being a thief in Sosaria. The nimble fingers and dexterous hands of a master thief are often of great advantage in disarming the many traps in dungeons and securing the goodies inside. Locks are no barrier for a thief. Shoplifting while in stores is also much easier for a thief than for other mortals, and the likelihood of being caught is less. Should you choose this profession, your fingers become instantly nimble as you awake in Sosaria.

Which profession offers the greatest advantage is a matter hotly debated among adventurers whenever they meet. Many a barrel of wine has been broached and emptied without the argument being resolved. As with the races, there are various stages in the quest when one or the other has the edge. During the initial stage of this venture, for example, an elfin thief (the fastest and most nimble of thieves) could steal weapons, armor, and food easily, moving like a shadow among the merchants of the towns. (You can also steal in castles, but the chances of being caught are greater.) And in dungeons, no coffin or chest foils an elfin thief.

Alas, obtaining the finest food, weapons, and armor is not necessarily a guarantee to survival. Having lots of gold does not buy your way out of combat. At some point, all who enter Sosaria must fight, and no thief is long a match for a knight, a dragon turtle, or one of the dungeon monsters who live only for battle and have had years of experience finishing off adventurers.

If thief is not the best profession for long-term survival, what of cleric or wizard? These are definitely more viable. The powerful spells available to each at times can definitely make the difference between life and death. But those years of arduous study do little to build muscles, or skill with weapons. It is not possible to use magic to stand off and avoid all physical combat. You will often be in battles where you must stand toe to claw with an evil monster and batter it into the ground, or become a permanent part of the landscape or a blotch on the dungeon floor yourself.

Select the profession of fighter as the most appropriate for long-term survival. Fighters are agile enough to open most traps and to steal when absolutely necessary. They can use all the weapons found in shops and are strong enough to deliver killing blows with these weapons. They can also cast some spells (true, not always reliably, but usually well enough).

The best choice of race and profession is to become a human fighter. In fact, the next chapter relates how a human fighter named Rolf became one of the greatest heroes in the history of Britannia.

Of course, there is nothing to stop you from experimenting with different combinations such as dwarf/fighter, bobbit/cleric, elf/wizard, human/thief, etc. There are sixteen possible combinations. Think carefully before you choose. For example, you might not get far as a bobbit fighter. Poor little guy would be awfully weak and, to him, a dagger would be heavier than a great sword to a human.

The Lay of the Land

Naturally, no matter what your profession, you need to understand the layout of the planet, both its geography and the types of terrain you'll be crossing.

Geography

The world of Sosaria consists of four continents and a number of islands. It also is continuous and twisted. This means that the continents are laid out in a row of four when you are going east or west, but in two columns of two each when you are going north or south.

Specifically, when you arrive on the planet you are on the continent appearing at the top right of the map in your adventurer's kit (Continent One). If you go east, you'll hit the continent on the bottom right (Continent Two). Further east is the continent on the top left (Continent Three), and still further east is the one on the bottom left (Continent Four). If you go east from that one, you'll hit Continent One again. So, going east or west, the map looks like this:

1 2 3 4 1 2 3 4. . . .

This setup is pretty simple, no? However, the twist is, literally, as follows: If you start from Continent One and go *either north or south*, you'll hit Continent Three; and, not surprisingly, if you start at from Continent Three and go *either north or south*, you'll hit Continent One. By now you might have guessed that if you start at Continent Two and go either north or south, you'll reach Continent Four, and if you start at Continent Four and go either north or south, you'll reach Continent Two. So, going north or south, the map looks like this:

1
3
1
3
.
.
.

and

2
4
2
4
.
.
.

These continents contain many towns, castles, dungeons, and landmarks that you must explore. The only way to leave the continent on which you are first injected is to purchase a seagoing craft or an aircar. The map that you will find in your adventurer's kit should prove to be of considerable use in getting to various spots on each continent.

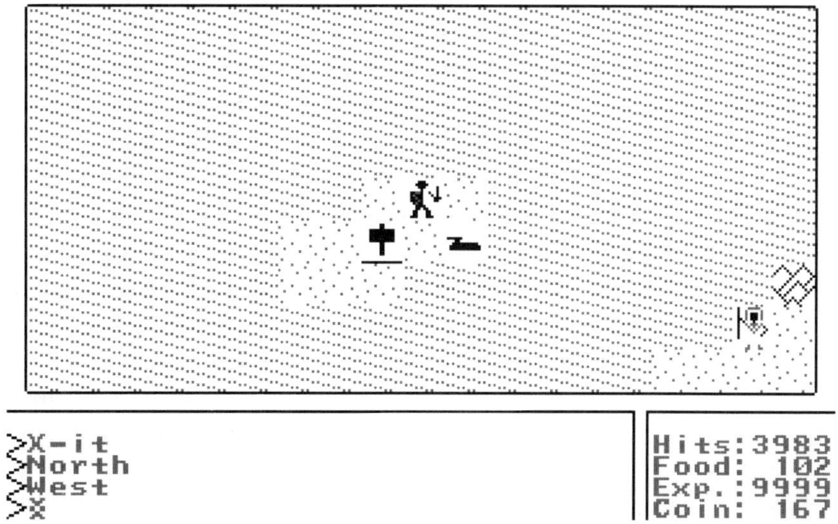

Figure 4.2 *Small islands sometimes have landmarks that you are wise to find and enter.*

Know where you are at all times. Keep track of your movements and the location of places that you might need to find again. Here is a description of the four continents:

Continent One (top right)	This is where you find yourself first. It has two small kingdoms, that of the Lost King and of Lord British. There are also eight towns. These are Britain (next to the castle of Lord British), Yew, Fawn, Moon, Tune, Grey, Montor, and Paws. There also are nine dungeons—Death's Awakening, Lost Caverns, Mondain's Gate to Hell, Perinia, Unholy Hole, Mines of Mt. Drash (1 and 2), Montor (not to be confused with the town of the same name), and Doubt.

	Continent One has two notable landmarks—one on an island just off the northern coast and one on a small southern coastal island. These are the Pillars of Protection and the Tower of Knowledge. Enter these landmarks if at all possible.
Continent Two (bottom right)	This lies to the east of Continent One. There are also two kingdoms on this continent, Barataria and Rondorlin. Eight towns are spaced around the continent—Gerry, Arnold, Snake, Linda, Helen, John, Owen, and Wolf. Eight dungeons blot the landscape and lie in wait for the traveler. They are named Scorpion Hole, Dead Warrior's Fight, The Labyrinth, Where Hercules Died, Advari's Hole, The Savage Place, Horror of the Harpies, and Gorgon's Hole. As with Continent One, there are also two landmarks—The Pillars of the Argonauts and the Pillar of Ozymandias. Go to the first for some useful items and to the latter for wisdom. The former is on an island just west of the continent, and the latter on an island off the southwest coast.
Continent Three (top left)	This lies even further east. The two kingdoms here are Black Dragon and Olympus. There are eight towns: Ponder, Clear Lagoon, Poor, Nassau, Gauntlet, Wealth, Stout, and Imagination. Nine dungeons full of death and torture await. They are The Long

	Death, The Metal Twister, The End, Viper's Pit (1 and 2), Guild of Death, Troll's Hole, Tramp of Doom, and Slow Death.
	To the northwest and southwest of Continent Three respectively are two landmarks. One is called 'Sign Post,' which you will find if you have the stamina to reach it, and the other is 'Southern Sign Post.' Visiting the latter raises your charisma points.
Continent Four (bottom left)	This is even further to the east. Two kingdoms are to be found here as well—that of Shamino and that of White Dragon. Here, too, are eight towns, namely Gorlab, Brother, Magic, Wheeler, Bulldozer, Turtle, Dextron, and Lost Friends. Nine dungeons lurk in the underground strata: Dead Cat's Life (1 and 2), Skull Smasher, Doom, Dead Man's Walk, Spine Breaker, Hole to Hades, the Morbid Adventure, and Free Death Hole.
	There are also two landmarks, which you will find to the northwest and southwest of the continent. You gain strength by visiting the Grave of the Lost Soul, while the Eastern Sign Post is merely a sign reading, "Go east to go east."

I repeat, keep in mind where you are at all times. You never know when a king is going to send you on a quest to some specific place. You'll need the ability to navigate there quickly and surely, and to plot a safe return course.

Terrain

The ground over which you operate is not very complex. The wide open areas are grassy plains, which don't impede travel in the least (nor that of any monster who might be chasing you). There are many wooded areas. These you can move through easily on foot or on horseback, but they stop a vehicle such as an aircar.

Those you meet outside of town invariably are enemies—don't waste time on talk, strike hard and fast. Out in the open you find nothing hidden. Everything is as it appears which is both good and bad. You cannot be surprised by an enemy but, on the other hand, there is nowhere to hide either.

The mountains of Sosaria (each continent has several ranges) tower high. No vehicle can take you over them, and the sides are too steep for climbing. The only way to deal with mountains is to go around them.

In the oceans on Sosaria are the additional flavorings of pirate ships and sea monsters, none of which are very friendly. You cannot walk on water or swim, so you'll need a seagoing vessel, or a high-tech craft like an aircar, to cross the oceans.

Your Resources

Regardless of your identity and of the depth of your knowledge of the planet, it's a sure bet you'll need to seize upon every bit of help possible to build up your attributes (which are measured in points), experience (measured in experience points), and cash (which you need to buy the transportation, food, magic spells, weapons, and armor that you need). You'll find both help and traps in almost every part of Sosaria; next you'll be briefed on how to stay alive, find out information, and gain the essential points and cash that you'll need.

As your experience points increase, you rise in level. The highest level is eight. Keep in mind, however, that the maximum number of experience points you can have is 9,999; the same goes for hit points. In fact, your hit points roll back to zero if you attempt to push them beyond this limit. Your attributes of strength, agility, intelligence, wisdom, charisma, and stamina also have a top limit of 99. Once past 99, they roll back to zero too. When you are as close as possible to these limits (and have become a Space Ace and found out from a princess where to find Mondain), you are ready to go fight this wily, scaly, slimy, bad-breathed wizard.

Castles and Towns

Castles and towns are of great value. For one thing, they provide shelter from attack, as long as you do not transgress their simple laws. If a monster is getting the best of you, and your hit points are dropping like a stone, run to the nearest town or castle and enter. The monster cannot follow and you can safely recoup some strength before returning to the fight.

castles and towns are havens, the average individual you meet in castle and town may or may not help you during your mission. Some may be thieves and likely to take what you have—keep a wary vigilance. Watch also wenches and bards.

Both castles and towns are policed by huge, ill-tempered guards of immense strength and the dispositions of junkyard dogs. If you are law-abiding, you have nothing to fear from these brutes. Unfortunately, a spot of thievery is sometimes in order just to insure simple survival. So if you must steal, do it carefully! Should you be caught, every guard in the place converges on you, and it's extremely hard to defeat one, much less several. If you let them hem you in, it's all over, even for the staunchest of fighters.

A word about finding towns. The towns in *Ultima I* have blue flags, and the castles of kings have red flags. Also you can tell the difference between towns and castles by their size and shape—the castles are narrower and have more pronounced battlements. Or you can find out which is which by entering one.

Castles are built of massive blocks of stone and are all homes of kings—each being ruler of the region that you are currently visiting. Never try to kill a king—it takes a lot of hit points, and his guards will get you sooner or later. And if you do manage to kill one, he'll be right back there the next time you enter the castle. Instead of wasting your time like this, transact with kings. They are excellent sources of information and provide additional hit points for money. For this reason, when fleeing from a fight in the countryside, if you have only a few hit points but a decent amount of cash, run to a castle rather than a town.

Transacting with these minor kings (even Lord British himself falls into this category during this period) is easy. They want only two things from you—gold, which they reward with hit points, or some sort of service. The latter they reward with hit points, information, and sometimes essential jewels. Of course, you may never return from some of these quests, for they are not always safe by any means. Yet, they are something that must be done sooner or later.

In addition to the king and his numerous burly guards, several other types of individuals live in castles. There are courtiers, fools or jesters, princesses, and a few merchants.

Lovely Princesses in Durance Vile

While kings are mostly nice, helpful guys, they all—even Lord British—have a dark quirk in their personalities that causes them to hold princesses captive in prisons. There is an incredible surplus of princesses; in every castle you can find them pacing their cells, presumably dreaming of a Hero or Heroine to rescue them. If you rescue a princess and immediately reenter the castle, you'll find that the king already has yet another princess in captivity. (Rescuing them could become a full-time profession if you don't watch it.)

Rescuing a princess at any time is beneficial (if you are strong enough to do so). A grateful princess always awards her rescuer 500 hit points, 500 experience points, and 500 pieces of gold. Princesses are generous to a fault, and if you are a Space Ace as well, you'll get an even greater award, information on where to find the time machine that will transport you to Mondain's lair.

To free a princess, you need the key to her cell. The jester claims to have this key; sometimes he doesn't, and sometimes he does. The only way to find out for sure is to kill the jester, take the key, and try it. Of course, the minute you waste the jester, all the guards in the castle are out for your blood. Like their brutish cousins in the towns, castle guards are close to invincible.

Therefore if you're wise, when engaging in princess rescue, you'll pick carefully where to kill the jester. The closer you are to the prison, the better. Then, run like the wind to the prisoner. If you move fast enough, you can get there and unlock the door before the guards are upon you.

Two possibilities exist. You have either the right key or the wrong key. The right key unlocks the door and frees the princess. Either way, you'll have to make a run for the exit next. One false move and the guards have you cornered.

If you have the right key and manage to release the princess, she can be of great help in effecting an escape. Keep her between yourself and the guards, because they won't attack a princess. (Princesses, being so numerous, have a very strong union.)

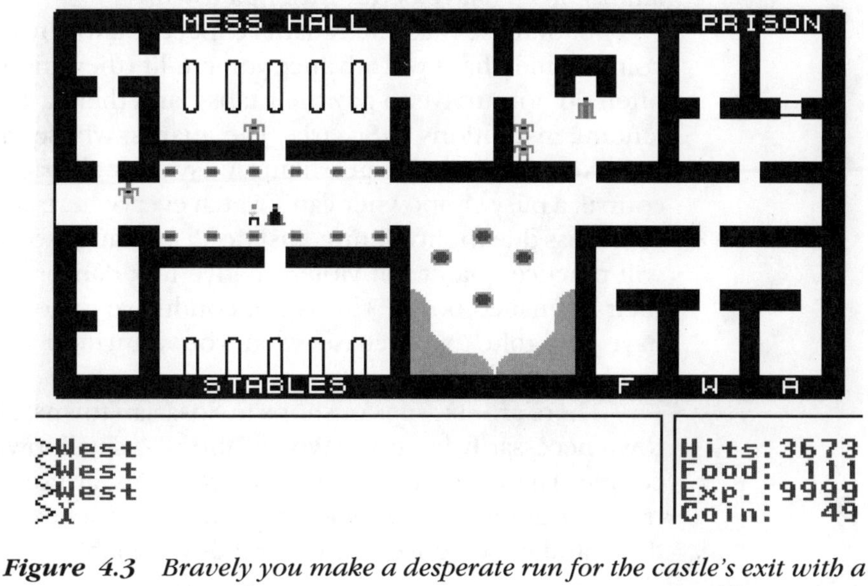

Figure 4.3 *Bravely you make a desperate run for the castle's exit with a rescued princess in tow.*

Quickness is the only solution here. One careless bump into walls, trees, or ponds can trap you. If the guards manage to corner you, you'd better have a *lot* of hit points because it takes considerable effort to defeat even one guard, and all the time you are doing it, two or three may be banging on your hide.

However, if you can just gain the castle's exit, all the rewards described above are yours. If you become really proficient at princess rescue (and this takes much practice in between invoking 'Q' spells), it is a quick way to maximize your hit points, cash, and experience.

Shops

The merchant class of Sosaria is large and energetic. Every town has its share of stores selling such products as foodstuffs, weapons, armor, various means of transportation, magic, and liquid refreshments. Although you can sometimes obtain food and equipment at castles, you almost always have better luck in a town.

All of these these merchants expect you to pay in good, solid gold coin. No merchant will advance you credit (they know that adventurers often do not survive to pay their tabs), and there are no banks or other lending institutions in Sosaria. The guards, whose salaries are paid by the taxes levied on the merchants, unswervingly back up this policy. Of course, a busy shopowner can't watch everywhere at once, and there is some loss due to shoplifting. Just don't get caught or those huge guards will practice quaint but violent native folk dances on your chest with their hobnailed boots. This is not conducive to good health. So either have the gold to purchase what you want and need, or steal very carefully.

There are six types of shops in Sosarian towns, although not every town necessarily has every type of shop—a small town may only have a couple. These six types are food emporiums, armories, weapon shops, transportation sellers, magic stores, and pubs or taverns, wherein strong drink and good conversation is readily available.

Food

As a newly arrived adventurer, equipped only with a dagger and flimsy leather armor, you'll want to visit the first town you find and attempt to purchase a few necessities, such as additional provisions. Being a hero does burn up the old calories fast.

Food shops feature fresh produce and meats for the locals, and carefully treated food that lasts for weeks in your pack with no special care for adveturers. The latter is not tasty but it is cheap. Prices vary only slightly from location to location. Buy plenty and don't worry about saving a pence or two—it is far worse to run out of food while out in the countryside or down in a dungeon. In fact, it is absolutely fatal.

Figure 4.4 *The provisions for adventurers stocked in the food shops are not tasty but they are cheap. Buy plenty.*

Arms

The next place you enter might well be a weapons shop. Step right up and transact with the clerk behind the counter. You'll find that he gives you two choices every time—either to sell to you, or to buy surplus weapons. Weapons available to a newcomer are those you would expect to find in any medieval society—daggers, maces, swords, and the like. They are of the highest quality, however, for the metalsmiths of Sosaria have few equals. From carved hardwood maces reinforced with iron, to the expensive and marvelously crafted tempered steel great swords, you are assured of the finest instruments of killing that your purse can bear. They are true works of art.

After you've survived for awhile, gaining in experience and hit points, the weapons merchants begin bringing the *good* stuff out from the back rooms and under the counters. You will be able, should you have the exorbitant amounts asked, to buy lasers and phazors.

By the by, it should not surprise you to find such high tech, futuristic weapons in the midst of castles and knights—with the astronomically powered evil wizardry of Mondain tearing the land apart, there have been all sorts of ripped areas in space and time. Anomalies are to be expected. Suspect that which appears usual and expect the unusual.

So, after many battles and the gathering of much gold, which may take hundreds of moves, you may expect to finally have enough status to be offered a laser or phazor, and to have the resources to purchase such a powerful weapon. Or, if you are newly arrived and sufficiently nimble-fingered, you might want to see what you can pick up behind the counter. Just because you are not offered a particular weapon doesn't mean it isn't in stock. Just don't get caught.

Armor

Armories are abundant, being found in most towns. The finest craftsmen in the land will quickly tailor and fit a suit of armor to your requirements, just as long as your purse plays their favorite song, the clink of gold coins against many others of the same kind. Leather suits are the cheapest, such as the one you possess on arrival in Sosaria. Chain mail and plate armor are also available, with the latter being incredibly expensive. Still, without life, gold is worthless.

As with weapons, when you have proved yourself worthy and risen in rank you may expect to be offered armor that could only have come from a highly developed society. For very large prices, you can buy reflective suits, which reflect energy beams harmlessly back to their sender (harmless, that is, to you), or armored vacuum suits like those that astronauts wear in the void of deep space. As a newcomer you won't see these high tech garments for some time, although you never know what might be found under the counter.

Transportation

Transportation is always a concern. Not only does riding an animal or traveling in a vehicle burn fewer calories, and thus make your sometimes meager food supply last longer, but traveling across oceans or going into space requires a vehicle of some sort. Even for relatively short journeys over land, using a vehicle or animal is quicker than going by foot.

Horses, as would be expected in this medieval society, are plentiful and cheap. For a somewhat greater outlay in gold, you can purchase a seagoing vessel that enables you to sail, comfortably dry-footed, from continent to continent. It is virtually impossible to steal transport; you'll have to buy it.

Those of higher level find other vehicles available in establishments specializing in transport. There is nothing like cruising in comfort in your own heavily armed aircar. Sometimes even surplus space shuttles are for sale in the transportation shops of Sosaria. That a simple medieval merchant deals in huge spacecraft costing many times the price which he asks you is, indeed, a graphic indication of the gargantuan turmoil going on in space and time. Expect no warranty or flight instruction on these advanced vehicles. No fuel is available either—you have to find a space station for that (just be sure to have the necessary funds with you).

Magic

Magic in Sosaria was important, but the kings long deemed it too corrupting for the general populace. Its use was discouraged or even stamped out to varying degrees of success in each town. The coming of Mondain has changed all of that and magic now flourishes openly. Many believe that, as the only way to fight fire is with fire, the only way to fight the sorcery of Mondain is with sorcery.

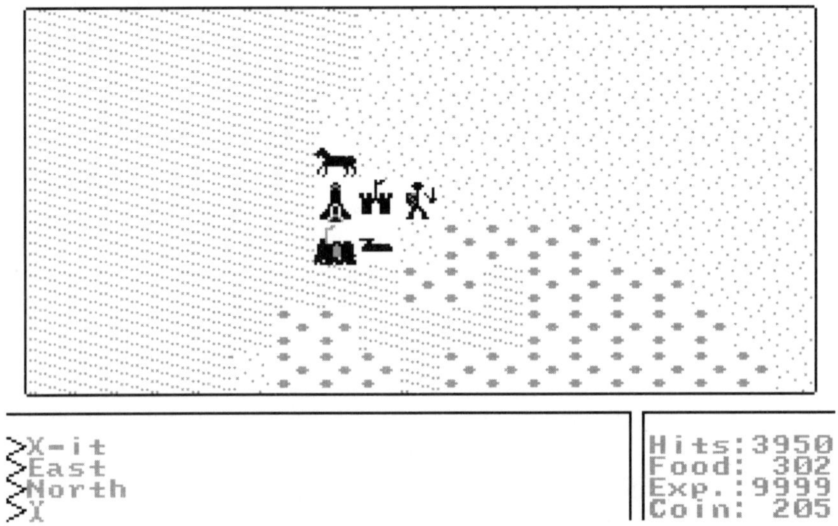

Figure 4.5 *Here you have plenty of vehicles. Just outside the castle of Lord British and the town of Britain, you have a horse, an aircar, and a space shuttle. Parking is free and no one will steal or otherwise bother the vehicles you leave while off on a quest somewhere.*

So magic shops do a steady and profitable business in many towns. There are shops specializing in the types of white magic that you might find of use, for example Ladder Up and Ladder Down spells. You should learn to use magic. However, it is seldom wise to depend on it totally, even if your profession is that of wizard.

If you're a wizard, you need one or more of four artifacts that may be purchased in towns—the staff, wand, amulet, and triangle. The latter is a magical sword that also serves as a weapon. There are also ten spells widely available in the magic shops of Sosaria, albeit far from cheaply. As a wizard, you can use most of them effectively.

Other professions can use a lesser number of spells (a good clerk usually lets you buy only what you can use). Most magic is of use only in dungeons but, unfortunately, you *will* be spending a lot of time in dungeons.

The spell called Blink is very handy in dungeon emergencies. It physically transports you a short distance underground—a great way to escape a monster you are having trouble defeating. Like all spells, it is good for one use only. Thus, if you have four Blink spells, you can escape from four monsters.

The Ladder Down and Ladder Up spells also are reliable and extremely useful. Both may be used by almost anyone, regardless of profession. These spells are relatively inexpensive compared to most magic supplies, and are absolutely necessary in dungeons, the only place they can be used anyway. They create a ladder that allows the spellcaster to go up or down a level. The ladder disappears afterwards, so carry as many of these spells as you can afford.

Often you enter a dungeon to kill a specific creature on a quest for a king. Your best course is to use Ladder Down spells to get rapidly down to the level the creature is on (hopefully you have made notes in earlier explorations of dungeons), do the deed, and use Ladder Up spells to get to safety. Quickness pays, because the longer you are in a dungeon, the more chance there is of a monster you cannot defeat finding you.

A Create spell creates a wall of magical force directly in front of you. This shield is very handy.

Opposite in effect is the Destroy spell, which removes a field of force. Often, in exploring dungeons, you find force fields blocking your path. A Destroy spell dissolves these barriers.

And why hack and hack at a foe if one simple spell will blow him or it away? The Kill spell can do just that. Unfortunately, like all magic, it sometimes does not work. A good sharp sword is the best backup you can have. Or a fully charged blaster will wreak a magic of its own in turning an enemy into molten slag.

The spell of Magic Missile is a nice offensive weapon. It is a searing blast of magical force that, when cast by a skilled and properly equipped wizard, can melt opponents most satisfyingly, or at least cause great damage. Other professions find this spell gives them lesser results and often fail to get the spell off at all.

Coffins are very common in dungeons and often contain valuable coins. Unfortunately, they are also often booby-trapped. The Open spell, if it works, opens a coffin for you, disarming any traps in the process.

The Unlock spell is used to open the many chests that you find littering the floors of dungeons. Like coffins, they are often booby-trapped, and an Unlock spell makes that trap harmless, allowing you free access to the goodies stashed within.

Another type of magic is Prayer. This gives you the ability to call on your personal deity when in dire straits. Because a rescue doesn't always happen, prayer is risky and you should use it only as a last resort.

Magic has its place in your arsenal, but use it sparingly and with caution. Nothing replaces courage and a good, swift sword.

Taverns

Most towns have pubs and taverns. The inhabitants of Sosaria love the strong drink and companionship to be found in such establishments. Ale and mead are plentiful and cheap. Many of the people you meet are friendly and helpful. Bartenders, as is a requirement of their profession, are often veritable fountains of wisdom and gossip. Carefully note what these men and women who serve the foaming tankard, especially Varg, have to say.

Your Challenges

Now that you know how best to mold the attributes you start out with, get around on the planet, and obtain the wherewithal to eventually rid the land of the evil wizard's dastardliness, you're ready to learn more specifics about the challenges facing you.

Dungeons

At the edge of mountain ranges, both on the continents and on a few islands, are the dungeons. Many civilizations rose and fell during the long course of Sosaria's history, some of which created vast underground labyrinths as mines or for other reasons now unknown. Others of these mazes have also been created since the coming of Mondain by various of his unspeakably evil slaves. Mondain and his followers no doubt dance with glee when you explore these dungeons, sure that it will be the last thing you ever do.

Whatever their origin, none of the dungeons of Sosaria are safe! They have all been preempted as living space by the teeming hordes of Mondain's monsters. Their living space can quickly become your *dead* space if you aren't careful.

So why enter these pits of peril at all, you might ask? The problem is that you desperately need money for weapons, armor, food, transportation, and magic. The only good thing about dungeons is that there are tons of gold down there. Every monster you vanquish yields up a few pieces. The deeper you are and the stronger the monster, the more gold you get. Chests and coffins abound, all with coins glinting richly in the little light there is down here. Dungeons are ever a ready source of financing.

There are certain minor disadvantages to dungeons, of course—such as instant death around every corner. First of all, except for Mondain (when you at long last meet him for the final showdown), the most dangerous foes you fight are concentrated in the dungeons. You'll find yourself fighting not just one foe, but monstrous enemy after monstrous enemy as you struggle to escape up a level and get away from them.

Worse, you can spend hours down in a dungeon, amassing considerable wealth and experience points, only to have it all taken away from you in the blink of an eye as some vicious monster triumphs and rends your life from your quivering, defeated body. For you cannot save your game to disk while underground or, for that matter, while in a town or castle, or riding in a vehicle, or traveling in space. You can only save while on foot and in the open. This means that when dungeoning you should make frequent trips back to the surface, keeping a detailed map of each level, and (when in the open) press the letter 'Q' to save the game to disk.

Another reason, other than financial necessity, exists for entering dungeons. That reason is a quest assigned by a king. Various monarchs ask you to travel to the nearest dungeon and to slay a certain type of beast. If you can do so, and report back, the king will reward you handsomely. Before agreeing to such a quest, however, be certain that you are strong enough and properly equipped to undertake it, or the word 'undertaker' may acquire a different and tragic meaning for you.

Dungeons can be deadly—be forewarned.

Monsters

The malevolent magic of the monstrous Mondain has created many monsters that now act as his minions. During your travels in Sosaria you will be forced to combat many of these.

A list of the beasts to be found in Sosaria and its dungeons follows. This material was adapted from official game documents, and it includes additional information of overwhelming interest to you, if you like life and prefer to survive.

archer, hidden	Hidden archers are demented or possessed humans, elves, dwarves, or even bobbits. They hide themselves in trees and rain arrows down on travelers with such unerring aim that the victim often dies without ever seeing them. The best part of valor in fighting archers is to retreat until you have enough experience and hit points to take their fire while searching them out and destroying them.
balron	These are huge, leather-skinned daemon lords. They are perhaps the most dangerous of Mondain's monsters, casting devastating fireballs at their victims and whipping them with long barbed whips. Their habitual dwelling place is on the ninth and tenth levels (the lowest) of dungeons. Venture down there with extreme care.
bat, giant	Giant bats live on a diet of animal blood and are not averse to feasting on unwary adventurers. Luckily they are easily defeated. They most often are found on the upper levels of dungeons.
bear	Bears inhabit the forests of Sosaria, venturing out onto the plains in search of a tasty morsel such as the next adventurer to come along. They are ill-tempered and attack with no provocation.

carrion creeper	The midlevels of any dungeon, especially levels five and six, are filled with the horrid slithers of the carrion creeper. These loathsome worms have numerous legs with small barbs that allow them to creep up walls and across ceilings to drop on you.
cyclops	These one-eyed giants hate humans and, in fact, just about everything. They are vicious fighters who attack on sight. Levels three and four of dungeons abound with them.
daemon	Like their cousins, the balrons, these fierce bat-winged horrors inhabit the lowest levels of dungeons. They drink human souls and seem to love the screams of those they torture above all else.
dark knight	In the gloomy forests you will often be set upon by dark knights. Once the pure chivalry of the land and now corrupted by the foul Mondain, they roam the countryside, living only to kill. Engage in combat with one of these only if you are well-armed and armored.
dragon turtle	The beaches of Sosaria are not safe. Huge fire-breathing aquatic dragons inhabit the seas and make life both miserable and short for all who dare approach the shore or venture out onto the water. Their shell is tougher than enchanted plate mail and they are very difficult to kill. Be sure you have weapons of great power before engaging them.
ettin	These two-headed monstrosities live on the surface in forests (where sometimes they find you first) and on levels five and six of dungeons. They love to attack travelers and require some effort to defeat.

gelatinous cube	Some call these blobs "dungeon sweepers." They ooze along the dark corridors, absorbing any material they find, whether alive or dead at the start of the process, and regardless if it is organic or inorganic. More than one adventurer has fought a cube victoriously, only to find afterwards that his armor has been absorbed right off his body, leaving him unprotected. These creatures are most prevalent on levels three and four of dungeons.
gremlins	Gremlins are dungeon creatures that are always hungry, and thus prone to steal your provisions if you are careless, leaving you to starve to death far underground. They haunt levels seven and eight of dungeons.
hood	Peasants subverted by the evil influence of Mondain have become highwaymen who roam the countryside. They are mostly unarmored and poorly armed. They fight with little skill, yet can be pretty much of a nuisance.
invisible seeker	One of the more dangerous creatures on the lower two levels of dungeons, this creature is, as its name implies, invisible. It is susceptible to most weapons, but you'll have to guess in which direction to strike, and guess fast! They prefer the lowest levels of dungeons in which to ply their deadly trade.
knight	Like the forest-dwelling dark knights, these are warriors who have forsaken the ways of chivalry and walk the paths of Evil. They are fierce opponents.
lich	The lich is an evil spellcaster who, through the perverted practice of his dark arts, has entered into a state of living death in order to better serve his master, Mondain. This undead mage attacks without warning, especially on levels seven and eight of dungeons.

lizard man — The evil filth that is Mondain, when he was first starting out, performed various genetic experiments on the fierce reptiles that inhabit the streams of Sosaria. From these he developed the lizard man to serve him. These creatures are a mixture of reptile and human, and have a disposition as ugly as they are. Expect their vicious attacks on the midlevels of dungeons.

mimic — You probably love treasure chests, but sometimes that innocent-looking chest in a corner of a dungeon may have teeth! Mimics patiently wait for a greedy, careless adventurer, then attack fiercely as he or she unthinkingly opens the "chest." View all chests on the midlevels of dungeons with exceptional suspicion.

mind whipper — The mind whipper has the body of a human, a face that looks like the underside of a squid, and an unquenchable thirst for the mental energies of its victims. They are one of the most terrible creatures on the lowest two levels of dungeons.

minotaur — Mondain was less than fastidious in his experiments of creating beasts. The minotaur was his attempt to create the ultimate soldier, which he bred by mating some of his followers with the famed Baratarian fighting bull. The resulting horror walks on two legs like a man, but has the head and cruel sharp horns of a bull, as well as the bull's strength and disposition. Keep a sharp watch for minotaurs when you are on levels five or six of a dungeon.

necromancer — Necromancers are mages who specialize in the practice of the arcane arts pertaining to the dead. You will encounter many of these as you travel the countryside of Sosaria. They are not overly dangerous to you if you are well armed and armored, but should not be underestimated.

Ness creature	As if dragon turtles were not enough trouble for the seafarer, there are also Ness creatures. These huge reptilian beasts are incredibly strong and can easily sink a ship and all those on it.
orc	Orcs are small humanoids with a face like a pig. They are stupid but fierce and roam the countryside of Sosaria looking for humans. Orcs love humans . . . love to eat them, that is.
pirates	With the coming of Mondain, the seas of Sosaria now abound with pirates. They are demented fighters who, once engaged, never quit. If you can't prevail against them, at least escape inland.
ranger	The rangers, at one time the hardy conservators of the woodlands, have been swayed to evil ways by Mondain. If a ranger attacks you, sooner or later you must kill him; otherwise he will follow you continually and keep attacking. Occasionally Rangers also roam the top levels of dungeons.
rat, giant	The Sosarian giant rat dines on the victims of Mondain's evil minions and is a nasty predator in its own right. Look for it on the top levels of dungeons.
skeleton	Skeletons are the animated corpses of dead warriors from whom the very flesh has withered and fallen away. They fight tirelessly. You will see many of them as you explore the top levels of any dungeon.
spider, giant	On levels three and four of dungeons roam giant spiders. They are very agile and possess a paralyzing sting. They immobilize you so that you can suffer the horrible fate of being a living hatchery for their young.

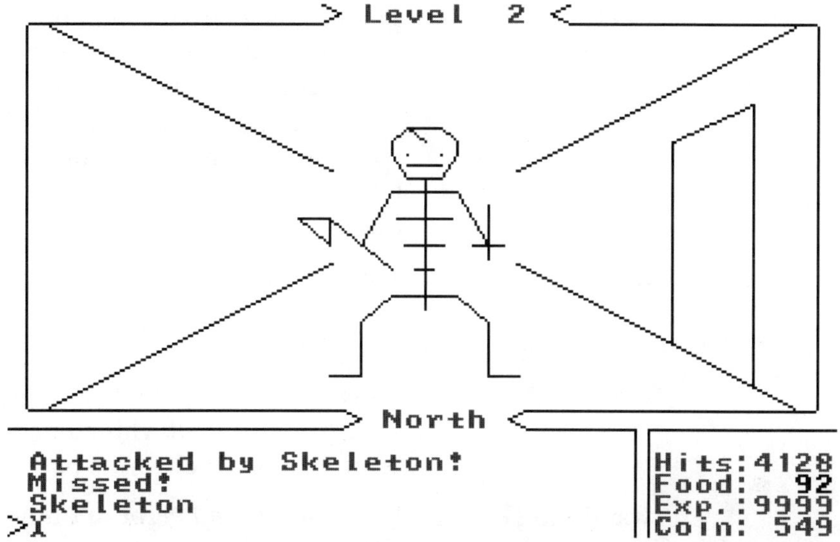

Figure 4.6 *A skeleton is one of the easier dungeon monsters to defeat, but here your food is getting low, and you may soon have a very big problem—starvation.*

squid, giant — Giant squids, along with dragon turtles, Ness creatures, and pirates, make sea travel in Sosaria pretty much uninsurable. You must venture out on the water with only your trusty weapon as protection. Giant squids have been known to entangle entire ships in their tentacles and drag them beneath the waves forever.

tangler — Down in the dank darkness of dungeon levels seven and eight lives the tangler. It looks very much like a vine-covered tree stump, until you get close. Then the tentacles snake out and hold you fast until death comes, after which the monstrosity feasts on your corpse.

thief	Thieves get around. You find them in towns, hiding behind trees, or lurking on the top levels of dungeons. They are always scheming to relieve you of your valuables and your life. Sosarians consider it both polite and a service to your fellow citizens to kill a thief whenever you find one.
trent	The evil trent lurks in the forests, looking like an innocent oak tree until you get near. Then its pliant branches shoot out to ensnare you.
viper	Vipers are snakes, fierce and poisonous. They strike rapidly at all who come within their range. They lurk on levels three and four of dungeons.
wandering eyes	Levels seven and eight of dungeons are home to a peculiar monster that is all eyes and teeth. Beware the wandering eyes, for it weaves a hypnotic spell that could very well be the death of you.
warlock	These are evil practitioners of the arcane arts, serving Mondain by casting bolts of magical energy at travelers. They are difficult to fight unless you, too, can slay at a distance.
wraith	Wraiths are the restless souls of dead clerics suborned by the evil Mondain. They are always in search of converts to their way of wickedness. Since one must die to be "converted," use caution in approaching and fighting wraiths. Levels seven and eight of dungeons are the places in which wraiths proselytize.
zorn	The mysterious zorn seems to defy logic and the laws of nature. It can burrow through anything and is completely omnivorous. When it fights, it seems to generate far more force than you would think possible from a creature of its size. It is found in the lowest and most dangerous levels of dungeons.

Your Strategy

Even if you boast the optimum combination of personal characteristics, know your geography and resources thoroughly, and are up on the horrors you're up against, you'll be a goner if you don't make and follow an effective plan.

The First Stage

The pain of transition from this world to that of Sosaria is minimal. As you return to awareness, you find yourself in the middle of grassy plain. You have with you a dagger and leather armor, a little food, and a small amount of money such as a single gold crown (a common but valuable coin in Sosaria). You should *immediately* ready your weapon for use and don your armor. Just carrying them offers you no protection.

Your entry point, as far as I have been able to calculate, is usually near the castle of Lord British and the town of Britain. You should see those in the distance. Go first to the castle and transact with Lord British. For now, avoid any monster or person you may see in the countryside, because you are probably too weak to stand much chance of victory. Discretion, at this vulnerable moment, is definitely the better part of valor.

In the throne room of the castle, Lord British asks you if you wish to give him service or pence. Since you are not strong enough yet to undertake a quest, give him pence—twenty, for example, causes him to graciously grant you an additional thirty hit points. You could use more hit points of course, but save most of your money for shopping in town.

While in the castle, keep away from the jester for now. Leave the castle and enter the nearest town. Buy some additional food at the shop specializing in provisions for adventurers. Visit the tavern, have a cold one, and talk to the bartender. Don't drink too much, however. More than one drink often results in seduction, which mostly just wastes your time.

Visit the weapons, armor, transportation, and magic shops if you like, but most of their wares at the moment are beyond your means. Should you feel sufficiently lucky and agile, you might see what you can pick up behind the counter. If you successfully shoplift something, you can immediately sell it back to the shopowner, who is so dumb he doesn't recognize his own merchandise. Of course, if you get caught, the guards immediately kill you. Shoplifting in Sosaria is a capital crime, not a misdemeanor.

Once you have built up your hit points by a visit to the castle and purchased extra provisions in town, it's time to explore the countryside. If you managed to steal better weapons and armor, you'll find these a plus in combat with any enemy you might meet (and meeting enemies is something you can count on).

There are several general rules of strategy to keep in mind. Until you have built up many points it is usually best to avoid combat unless you are absolutely sure that your opponent is a pushover. Be advised, however, that there are few pushovers in the First Age of Darkness, when Mondain's slaves ask no questions, neither give nor ask quarter, and fiercely fight tooth and claw for their diabolical master. Run away and live to build your strength.

Improve your financial situation by stealing and selling as much armor as possible. This is a risky and desperate course of action, but one which does work admirably. Even if you are caught sometime in the process and killed by the guards, you can either be resurrected or go back to your last saved position.

Should you accept resurrection, all the armor, vehicles, and spells you have at the time of your demise will be retained after resurrection. You lose all weapons, however. You'll find yourself back outside, with hit points returned to 99, food to 99, and experience points as they were before death. Obviously going for resurrection is logical only if you do not have a lot of hit points. Also, if you have an especially good weapon, such as a light sword or blaster, restore your abilities from the previous saved state instead of accepting resurrection. In that manner, you can proceed from the last point at which the spell was invoked, and perhaps not make the same mistake twice.

The objective you should keep in mind during this initial phase is to build up your resources. Exploring is nice, but worry first about becoming strong enough to survive long journeys.

The Second Stage

There is no escape from the fact that if you wish to build experience, strength, and finances quickly you must journey to a dungeon and perform arduous tasks in the deep darkness. In these underground labyrinths you will find the greatest concentrations of monsters and loose wealth in all of Sosaria.

Dungeons are all built similarly. They all have the same kinds of corridors and rooms. The ladders from level to level are all the same type, and there are always exactly ten levels. Finally, you can *always* count on a high population of monsters, who all take a sudden and violent interest in your presence. You need to kill as many monsters as you can in dungeons and accumulate all the gold you are able to find, which builds you up for the larger, more important battles to come. A few cautious but successful forays into dungeons should give you enough gold to have an ample supply of food, as well as good weapons and armor.

The next consideration is travel. To reach the final goal of your mission, you'll have to visit all four continents and most of their castles and towns. The minimum vehicle needed to cross oceans is a frigate, and an aircar would be even better because you can use it over land also.

In addition to ease of travel, an added advantage of owning a frigate or aircar is that both of these vehicles come heavily armed. There are cannon on the frigates and lasers on the aircar which, if you are the legitimate owner, are yours to do with as you please. Killing sea monsters, for example, is a pleasant and profitable way to while away those long voyages over water, and blasting pirate vessels livens up those dull afternoons.

The object of travel, of course, is to further your mission. Transacting with every king you can find and performing their quests gets you hit points and information, as you know; it also garners the four gems that you need to run the Time Machine that will take you to Mondain's lair.

Space, the Final Frontier

The troubles caused by the immense evil power of Mondain during the First Age of Darkness strained the normal relationships of time and space. Through these cracks in reality have come weapons, armor, and transportation devices from the highly technological societies of the far future. And not only high tech artifacts have come through—the skies themselves are filled with ships of invaders.

As you visit the pubs of Sosaria's walled cities, you may hear talk of the fight against these invaders. Only a few are able to make the transition from turnipseed peasant or hayseed knight to astronaut, much less survive in the very different environment of a space battle. However, with your experience with computers you should do very well and quickly attain the rank of space ace. Besides, all princesses really go for space aces, whether male or female. You will find the friendship of a princess worthwhile.

Unfortunately, even after you raise the money to buy a shuttle in one of the transportation shops and blast off for space, you may not find it as easy as you thought. If you go up into the interstellar reaches smug and overconfident, space indeed could very well be your final frontier as you suck vacuum in those last few agonized moments of airless life. Be sure to don a vacuum suit.

On the other hand, the requirements for belonging to the space forces of Sosaria are very lax. You go and come as you please and fly missions only when you feel like it, and a mere twenty kills relieves you of your service obligation and grants you the rank of Space Ace.

You can't do it in your shuttle, however. That is only your means of getting off the planet and up to the first space base. There, after docking very carefully (even a minor crash in space can damage your shields and be fatal), you'll have your choice of two ships. The larger one has lots of fuel but little shielding. The smaller fighting craft has less fuel, but heavy shielding. The weapons of the enemy ships are very powerful, so opt for short missions and take all the protection you can get.

With the laxity of the Sosarian space service goes a low budget and some downright cheapness. Take plenty of gold with you because you'll have to pay a fee of 500 gold pieces every time you exchange or refuel a ship.

The ships are highly computerized, so that piloting them is relatively simple, although tricky. Use a delicate touch and painstaking care during the docking process. Otherwise, flying and fighting the starfighters of Sosarian Space Command are as straightforward as you might expect in craft designed for those of only medieval educational attainments. There are four buttons marked with 'up,' 'down,' 'left,' and 'right' arrows. The first two control the rocket engines. The up arrow button fires a burst from the rear engine, moving you forward. Hitting that button again increases your speed. The down arrow button activates a retro rocket burst that slows the craft. All these maneuvers, of course, consume fuel.

The left and right buttons rotate the ship to the left or right. When using these, remember that your inertia in space is canceled only by firing a rocket in the opposite direction. There is nothing so embarrassing as sliding sideways into a space station while attempting a docking maneuver. It is often quite fatal, too.

The button on your panel designed with the letter 'I' activates the Inform and Search detector. This device scans all the sectors and informs you which ones have enemy ships in them, and which have space bases where refueling facilities are available. The 'V,' or view, button changes what is shown in your forward viewport. You must be looking out at the stars to properly navigate to another stellar sector, which by the way requires traveling in hyperspace (because otherwise the journey would take thousands of years).

To enter hyperspace and travel faster than light to another sector, just start your craft moving in the direction of that sector and push the big button in the center of your control panel—the one marked 'H.' Be sure you are firmly strapped in, as the ride can get a bit bumpy going through the interfaces between normal and hyperspace and back again.

Once in the sector, you don't have to worry about finding the enemy. They find you with their laser cannon—and of course they'll use the most powerful aperture. When they find you, you'll need to react fast. In the forward view, there's a set of crosshairs on the screen. Maneuver your craft so that an enemy is in the crosshairs and punch the

'F' or Fire button. Of course, the enemy craft is doing rapid and violent evasive maneuvers all the time you are attempting to line up a shot. Just get them as fast as you can—otherwise you'll either run out of fuel or be blasted into tiny globules of molten metal.

Groups of three seem to be the enemy's largest formation. Once in a hostile sector, you can't retreat until you destroy all the ships. If you run out of fuel or food before then, a suitable plaque in your memory will be installed among the many others at Space Forces Headquarters.

Hey, if it was easy, the rank of Space Ace would not mean so much.

After you manage to kill three or four enemy ships, return to the main base, switch to their space shuttle (be sure to have 500 pieces of gold set aside to pay the fee), and return to the surface of Sosaria (just aim the ship at the planet and the landing computers handle the approach for you). Once back on the ground, exit the spacecraft and invoke that old 'Q' spell to make sure that your kills to date are saved.

Then it's back to space. It may take several trips, but eventually you'll get that twentieth kill and become a Space Ace. You need to do this before you can find the time machine.

The Final Stage

At a certain point the climax of your mission is at hand. All the preparation is finished, the building stage is completed, and you are ready to face the final test, and to kill or be killed. It will be the battle of your life.

You get to Mondain's lair in the time machine, which needs all four jewels to run. Getting there is the easy part.

Once in Mondain's place, you can see all of it from any one position. It's small and all it contains is you, the machine you rode in on, Mondain, and the Evil Gem that is the source of much of his power and all of his immortality.

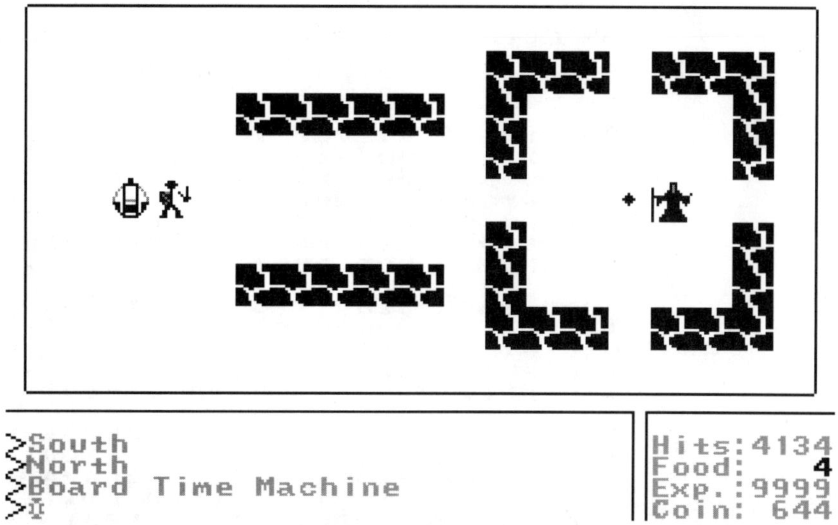

Figure 4.7 *You have arrived in Mondain's lair with only four units of food left and not as many hit points as you should have. You'll have to move quickly and carefully to have any chance at all. To the far right is Mondain with his Evil Gem.*

The elements of your problem are quite simple. You can't kill someone who is immortal, at least not permanently. So you need to take that immortality away. Do this by grabbing the gem. You need close to the maximum number of hit points when you arrive because contact with the gem is excruciating and draining. Once you've taken Mondain's immortality away, it becomes a straight fight to death between you and old dragon-breath.

No matter how good you are with spells or how powerful a wizard you may be, you aren't going to out-wizard the Wiz. You'll only make him stronger and hasten your demise. So forget about Kill spells, he just laughs them off. Also, don't bother with Create spells (they put a shield of force in front of you). No defensive tactic is going to do any good. Your only hope is to attack and keep right on attacking until Mondain falls.

Like most bullies, once you start getting the best of him, Mondain attempts escape, but unsuccessfully, if you are adequately prepared and smart enough. It is surprising that Mondain doesn't have a bolt hole or an escape tunnel of some sort, but perhaps he has made the mistake of vastly underestimating you, his opponent.

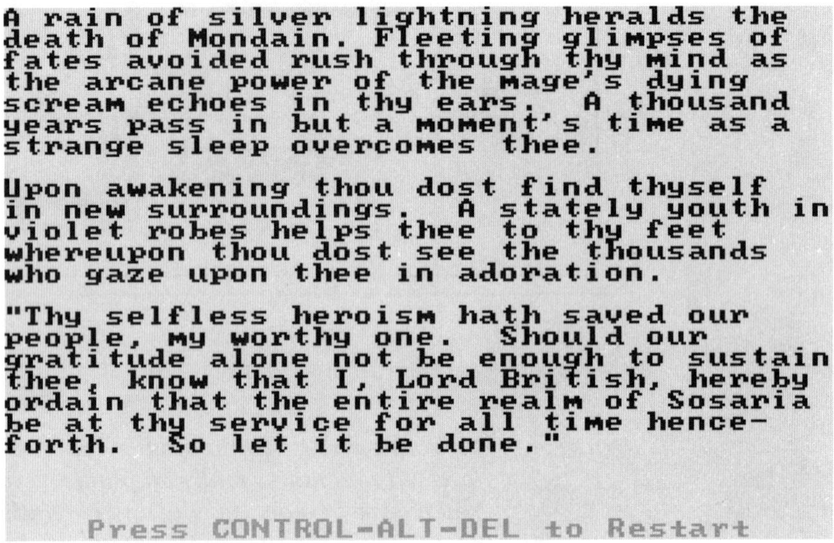

Figure 4.8 *To the victor go the spoils, and you're victorious here!*

On the other hand, if he kills you, he hasn't. Be careful when in Mondain's lair. Very, very careful. And make sure you are fully prepared before you go.

This briefing should have helped you immensely, but read next about Rolf the Warrior. He has gone this way before you, and his story can add many helpful insights. Theory is nice, but the words of one who has actually been there can often mean the difference between success and dismal failure, between life and death.

5

Rolf the Warrior

The tall man with one arm and a black eyepatch on his scarred face stood on the stage in front of the Adventurers Academy's graduating class.

"Look to your right," he commanded. The cadets, used to obeying orders immediately for the past four years, swiveled their heads right.

"Look to your left!"

Again, heads obediently swiveled.

"Those men and women will most likely not return from their first mission," the tall man said harshly. "If you ignore what we've taught you here, if you do not think on your feet, and if you are not resolute in the pursuit of your goal, you will not return either."

There was a nervous silence now in the hall. The thought of the extreme dangers to come spread a heavy blanket of dread that dampened the spirits of the graduates.

The tall man snapped a crisp salute with his one arm.

"Good luck, graduates!"

Sober now, the euphoria of graduation day gone, they filed out.

Agility and a little luck were the only things keeping him alive.

Rolf Karlson dived sideways, just as the Evil Knight's great sword whizzed through the space where his body had been a second before. He hit the grass on his wounded shoulder, but ignored the pain and bounced back to his feet, gripping his pitifully little dagger in a knife fighter's practiced hold—point slightly down, ready to parry, thrust, or slash his opponent. Not that all of his expertise was doing much more than scratching the plate armor of his fanatical enemy.

The Sosarian sun beat down unmercifully, roasting friend and foe alike. Sweat dripped from his skin, mixing with the blood from several minor cuts. His grip on the dagger, his only weapon, was dangerously slippery now. His flimsy leather armor was already ripped in several places.

"Well, cowardly varlet," the Evil Knight said hollowly from behind his closed visor, puffing as he moved menacingly closer, "dost thou quake in thy boots at the thought of approaching death? Thou shalt have it soon enough."

But the minion of Mondain was not rushing in for the kill. He was moving cautiously, obviously with effort. Rolf knew that the Knight must really be suffering in that huge collection of iron and steel now clanking toward him.

Rolf backpedaled a little and risked a quick glance to his rear. The grassy plain was empty of other enemies at the moment, although a dark forest to the left could conceal more danger. Far across the plain were the stone walls of Lord British's castle, and just behind that a walled town.

"Die!" the Evil Knight gasped, charging forward with a din like a kitchen in an earthquake.

Rolf was prepared. He slid aside gracefully and slashed his dagger across the Knight's arm in the hope of penetrating a chink in the armor. The only result was another scratch on the impervious metal. The enemy stumbled to a halt in a cloud of dust, and clumsily whirled to face Rolf again.

That's what they don't tell you, Rolf thought. It all looked so smooth and clean in the simulations, but being on actual terrain in Sosaria was different. There were lots of bare places in the grass; dust boiled up with your every move. Rocks and animal holes in the ground could trip the unwary. Even if he could stand still, the flies and gnats would make him miserable, and the sun would continue to toast him.

The Evil Knight charged again, and once more Rolf sidestepped. This time the Knight was anticipating the move and the great sword's point hit Rolf's upper arm, tearing easily through the leather and into his flesh.

Rolf ignored the pain, moving warily backwards. Now the Evil Knight, puffing from exertion but laughing, was stalking forward, great sword held high in both hands for a killing blow.

"Thou art weakening fast," the Evil Knight gloated. "Thy strength is dwindling. I shall soon send thy soul to my master, Mondain!"

Shaking his head to keep perspiration out of his eyes, Rolf knew that what his enemy said was true. The loss of blood from his several wounds, the heat, and his desperate maneuvers were rapidly taking their toll. Although he knew it had only been two or three minutes at the most since he arrived here in Sosaria to undertake his quest, it seemed like ages.

The Evil Knight was moving faster now, evidently getting a second wind. To survive, Rolf had only one course left, no matter how distasteful and undignified it might be. He turned and sprinted for the castle, running for all he was worth.

"Coward!" the Evil Knight yelled. "Milksop! Deserter! I shall carve thy gizzard into a memento for milord Mondain." Rolf heard his armor clank as he started running too.

Rolf's lungs were laboring, but he managed to fall into a jogger's steady rhythm. The gasps of the armor-laden knight were becoming less audible as he fell further and further behind. Feet pounding, Rolf continued to race for the castle and safety.

Rolf passed two guards as he entered the castle. Hulking brutes dressed in chain mail, both guards had low foreheads and bushy, unkempt beards. Their swords were drawn, and one was reflectively running his thumb over the blade of his—a blade appearing to be well-used and having brown stains that Rolf was sure were something other than rust. Rolf stopped, chest heaving from his long run. The puny dagger in his belt would be even more useless here. He felt two pairs of beady eyes, close-set and suspicious, surveying him.

Rolf knew that he was not a figure to inspire confidence at the moment. True, he was tall and well-muscled (thanks to the extra strength points he had asked for before starting this mission), and he had shiny dark hair and snappy brown eyes (which a former girlfriend once described as piercing). But his armor was torn and bloodstained, and he was dirty and sweaty—not exactly someone to roll out the red carpet for.

Surprisingly, one of the guards waved him by.

Nodding, Rolf walked on down the corridor and out into a courtyard, in the center of which was a sparkling fishpond shaded by small trees. He circled it, glancing down into the depths at the cavorting goldfish. There were other guards around, watching him closely, and other people in various walks of life—merchants, knights, servants, guards and more guards, and other travelers like himself, most of these latter as battered and dirty as Rolf. He supposed that the battleworn look was common in these troubled times.

The corridors of the castle were long and poorly lighted, but deliciously cool. No guard seemed inclined to bar his progress; there seemed to be free access to every spot in this huge pile of stone. He walked along, looking into the rooms as he passed.

Lord British's storerooms were well stocked with plenty of food, weapons, and armor. All the running and fighting had made him ravenously hungry. He was tempted to steal some of the bread and cheese, but the eyes of the guards seemed especially watchful when he was near the storerooms. He sighed and moved on, munching on a packet of the adventurer's rations he carried. He would have to get some more food soon, but it was too dangerous to take any here.

At the end of a corridor he came to the prison. The guard standing there ignored him, so Rolf entered and looked into the cells. There were two. The first was empty, albeit locked. The second was occupied by one of the most beautiful women he had ever seen. She was blond and grand-looking. Noticing him, she rose from her chair and came to the barred door.

"Greetings, Sir Knight," she said grandly, ignoring Rolf's disheveled appearance. "I am the Princess Julia. You may rescue me now and I will reward your valor handsomely."

"Thanks," Rolf said a little shyly in the face of her beauty, "but not just yet. I'll need to get better weapons and armor first."

Princess Julia shrugged and nodded. "Watch the jester," she said. "He's not to be trusted."

Rolf thanked her and promised to return.

He then walked toward the throne room. A man dressed in a clownish costume suddenly capered up to him.

"I've got the key," the jester said, giggling. "I've got the key."

Out of the corner of his eye, Rolf saw the jester's hand moving toward his dagger. He darted away and entered a throne room. He approached the dais respectfully.

Lord British sat on the throne, a large man of dignified face, dressed in the fine purple cloth and gold chains of a king.

"Thou art most welcome, O Hero," Lord British said, his voice deep, resonant, confidence-inspiring. It was the voice of someone obviously destined for a far greater position than that of a minor king in a fragmented land.

"Dost thou wish to give me service or pence?" Lord British continued, while Rolf dropped to one knee in what he hoped was a knightly sign of respect.

"Pence, milord," he said.

"And how many?"

Rolf thought fast. His purse was slim; he had only the equivalent of 99 gold pieces and he desperately needed to purchase provisions for the long campaign ahead.

"Twenty, milord," he said, counting them out into the hand of a court official who had immediately stepped forward. Obviously Lord British did a cash business, a not unwise policy in a land full of suborned knights.

Lord British waved his hand in a regal manner. "I grant thee thirty hit points."

A big chunk of Rolf's hurt and exhaustion from his abortive battle with the Evil Knight melted away. He thanked Lord British and rose.

"When thou dost wish to undertake a quest," Lord British said, "come back and I will assign such to thee. Succeed and great rewards will be thine."

Indicating his intention to return, Rolf left the throne room. Now was not the time, he thought, to ask Lord British why the Princess Julia was locked up.

"I have the key," the jester hissed, making a grab at a packet of Rolf's food.

Rolf slapped the jester's hand away and cautiously wound his way through the corridors to leave the castle . He stopped to peer out the gate to make sure the Evil Knight was not waiting, causing much finger-pointing and mimicry among the guards, which he ignored. Right now, better safe than sorry. He took time to scan the countryside as far and wide as he could see. The path over to the town of Britain looked clear for the moment, so he took it.

The walls of the town enclosed a stereotypical small medieval trading center. Narrow, smelly cobblestoned streets teemed with humans, elves, dwarves, and diminutive bobbits. Inside, life went on pretty much the way it had before the troubles, except that the merchants were extremely happy to be doing such a land office business with the many adventurers who came and went. The town seemed an island of sanity in the midst of the evil knights and bloodthirsty monsters who he knew were prowling and howling in the countryside.

Guards as large and brutish as the castle guards patrolled the streets and shops.

One scowled at Rolf as he passed.

He entered the tavern first, since his mission so far had been very dry work. Males and females of various races sat quaffing the good brown ale of the region. The bartender served him a cold one, and said:

"Best watch out for the wench."

Rolf nodded, seeing a female sneak an object from an adventurer's pack down the bar. He kept his eyes on his own possessions, listening without seeming to as Varg placed a foaming flagon in front of another customer.

"Destroy the evil gem."

Rolf committed that comment to memory also, drained his own flagon, and left. He walked to the food shop. The prices looked okay. Packets of rations were selling for three pence each. He could afford twenty packets—that was all. He made his purchase.

With his purse now flat, Rolf faced a hard choice. He could go out into the countryside and fight some enemies, and maybe get a few more gold pieces that way. Yet his encounter with the Evil Knight had taught him this would not be easy. He needed better weapons and armor, and he needed them now.

His decision made, Rolf went just outside the walls and invoked the 'Q' or 'Quit and Save' spell he had learned at the Adventurers Academy. He then reentered town and went directly to the weapons shop.

The shopowner's grizzled white beard and black eye patch told Rolf he was a veteran of some long ago campaign. He was polishing a sword.

"Buy or sell?" he asked Rolf curtly.

"Just looking," Rolf said, pretending an interest in a display of daggers, all as cheaply made as the one he was carrying.

The shopowner grunted and turned his attention back to his task.

Rolf sidled around behind the counter, careful to stay on the shopowner's blind side. The man appeared not to notice him. He made a quick grab, holding his breath. There were no cries of detection and he looked down to find he now had a mace. He walked around in front of the counter.

"Buy or sell?" the shopowner asked.

"Sell," Rolf replied, holding up the mace cautiously.

The shopowner looked at it. "I have a lot just like that," he said. "I'm not hot for it, but I'll give you three gold pieces."

Rolf smiled and accepted the coins. Not much, but it was a start. As the shopowner turned to put the mace on a shelf he went behind the counter and made another grab. Ah! A blaster!

"You sell blasters?" he asked.

"Sorry, bub," the shopowner said. "Those are high tech weapons. We aren't allowed to sell them. This is a medieval society—didn't you smell the horses outside?"

Rolf nodded, deciding to keep the weapon since it was likely the most powerful weapon he would ever find.

The shopowner looked around to make sure no one could overhear them. Satisfied, he said, "Now if you were to gain some experience and come back here with a pile of gold, there might—just might—be some high tech weapons for sale."

"I'll keep that in mind," Rolf said, deciding not to press his luck with another attempt at theft in this shop. He'd heard that the guards loved to tear the limbs off shoplifters. Time to go outside, invoke that all-saving 'Q' spell, then back inside to do this all over again in the armory.

Well armed with the blaster, and wearing a suit of plate armor taken from under the nose of an unsuspecting clerk in the armory, Rolf ventured forth into the countryside. During the next few weeks in Sosaria, Rolf fought many battles. There were some close scrapes, but he prevailed.

One fight that gave him especially great satisfaction happened one evening as he was approaching the edge of a small woods, his visor open to gain what small breeze there was to relieve the constant mugginess. Suddenly his old acquaintance the Evil Knight ambushed him.

"Ha! We meet again, varlet!" the Knight shouted, readying his sword for a decapitating swing.

Rolf whirled and pressed the firing stud on the blaster. A wave of brilliant red energy washed over the knight, burning off what little paint remained on his shield. The colors were the remmants of a design that was once an honorable heraldic device, but now this heritage was shamed by the Knight's allegiance to the diabolical wizard Mondain.

The Evil Knight staggered and screamed, but recovered and resumed his clumsy charge.

Rolf fired again, and again. The Knight was close now and got in a blow that glanced off Rolf's own armor. Rolf fired once more. The Evil Knight went down for good, a pile of deflated armor clattering to a final stillness in the dust.

"Never call me 'varlet,' " Rolf advised the dead knight as he took the few gold pieces he had and departed whistling.

Now Rolf's strength and level of experience were growing as he confidently ranged the continent, fighting all the monsters he could find and visiting the various towns for food. He also started buying a few magic spells, just for safety's sake.

He begin making cautious trips into dungeons. He carefully mapped his way and stayed on the top two or three levels at first. He could recall similar scenes in the computer simulation back at the Adventurers Academy, but nothing prepared him for the dankness, the darkness, and the eerie sound of distant slitherings mingling with the dripping of moldy water from the ancient stone walls. Above all, he thought, nothing prepared you for the *smell*. Thousands of monsters lived and died down here, and none were housebroken.

Later he bravely ventured deeper as his gold supply increased and he was able to buy plenty of hit points from kings. He also bought a horse, since horses were cheap. Then he was able to travel faster across land and with less expenditure of energy, thus stretching out his food supply.

He was transacting such business one day with the Lost King. The king had just asked him the usual question of whether he offered service or pence. Deciding he was ready for a quest, Rolf replied that he would gladly do the king a service.

"Go thou to a dungeon," commanded the king, "and slay a gelatinous cube."

Rolf left the king's presence and traveled to the nearest dungeon. He readied his blaster and entered the dungeon, fighting his way down to level three.

A dim corridor stretched before him. He stepped forward, only to feel a breeze on his back. Turning, he blasted a giant spider that was swinging from the ceiling. Even as the monstrous spider and its filthy web flared under the blaster's beam, he felt a pang on his right shoulder. The attack this time was from a cyclops. The combat was brief and Rolf won, but the giant cyclops got in several more good blows before succumbing.

Rolf could feel himself weakening. The real danger in dungeons was this cumulative effect of assault by monster after monster as you desperately fought your way back to the surface. In quick succession, but at the loss of more strength, he victoriously battled two orcs and a viper.

He rounded a corner to see a gelatinous cube blocking the corridor. It would not do, Rolf reminded himself, to get too close. Even as he thought this, his finger contracted and the blaster's beam melted its way into the cube's screaming body. Victory!

Just beyond the cube was a chest. Rolf stepped forward and opened it, setting off a trap that it weakened him to escape. After he scooped up a few coins, he decided to get out while the getting was good. He had completed the Lost King's quest—if only he could live to report it!

An orc appeared before him and he crisped it before he could be hit. He grinned but his triumph was short-lived: another cyclops attacked—from behind. He turned and managed to defeat the one-eyed giant, but knew that he could not win many more battles like that. He was too weak and he'd never make it back to the ladder up to the next level.

Down the corridor, he could see a giant spider charging across the ceiling toward him. Quickly he readied a Ladder Up spell and scurried up the ladder that popped into existence. He was now on level two, but there would be plenty of thieves, rangers, skeletons, bats, and giant rats to battle before he could reach the ladder to level one. Rolf cast another Ladder Up spell.

Ah, top level, and the ladder to the surface was relatively near. He begin jogging in that direction, only to encounter a skeleton. He attacked without hesitation, blasting aggressively because he knew it was the only hope he had. To be delayed would only allow more monsters to come up and join the fray, leading to a quick downfall in his weakened state.

With a sigh of relief, he got to the ladder and shot up it. Outside again, he blinked in the bright sunlight and saw a wandering warlock in the distance. He quickly rode his horse in the opposite direction, curving around toward the Lost King's castle. Now was definitely not the time to mess with wandering warlocks.

The Lost King welcomed Rolf back. "Thou hast been successful in fulfilling the quest assigned thee. Here is thy promised reward." He handed a peculiarly cut red gem to Rolf. "Thou wilt need four of these of divers colors to launch the Time Machine."

"The what?" Rolf asked, placing the gem securely in his pouch. (The jester capered closer.)

Ignoring his question, the Lost King asked, "Dost thee now offer me service or pence?"

Rolf reluctantly offered him pence, because he needed to build up his depleted hit points.

"I've got the key," the jester whispered in his ear.

Might as well rescue a princess, Rolf thought, but first he stepped outside the castle to invoke the 'Q' spell. One could not be too careful.

He returned to the castle, entered the throne room, and maneuvered the jester to the door, then attacked the posturing fool. A key was now in his hand, but the floors were reverberating to the pounding of the guards' hobnailed boots as they rushed him.

Moving quickly and surely, Rolf eluded the guards and ran to the prison. Princess Julia jumped to her feet and ran to the door as he approached.

"Hurry," she said urgently. "The guard will be on you at any time."

Rolf unlocked the door with shaking but deft hands. He said, "Follow me, please, your highness," and ran toward the entrance. He heard her scurrying behind; no doubt she was daintily holding up her long skirts.

"Hurry," she said again, "hurry! And watch out for the fishpond!"

Two hulking guards loomed up in front of him, blocking their way. He'd have to blast his way through. The flame roared out and washed over the first guard, who just grinned nastily and swung his huge two-handed sword, dealing Rolf a telling blow. He blasted again, but both guards got in solid hits. Rolf staggered and spun halfway around.

"You better have a lot of hit points," the princess said, her foot tapping a little impatiently.

Wham! Stars before his eyes as a sword clanged on the side of his helmet. He blasted and blasted. How long would this go on?

Suddenly both guards were down—the way was clear. Knowing he'd never survive another guard, he dashed forward. He could hear the princess panting to keep up with him and was glad that shield was still there, because he could also hear the clomping of several guards' boots behind her.

"The fishpond," she prompted breathlessly.

He angled around the fishpond, heading away from an approaching guard. Finally they stumbled out of the castle just inches from the pursuing guards, who all slid to a stop in a clanking of armor and refused to go outside.

The princess stopped and drew a deep breath. "Thanks," she said. "For rescuing me, I reward you with five hundred hit points, five hundred experience points, and please take these five hundred gold pieces also. Now I must go. Why don't you give me a call sometime after you finish your mission? Maybe we could take in a joust or something." And with that, she waved gaily and moved off.

Rolf shook his head in surprise and went back into the castle. It was *déjà vu*. There was already another princess in captivity, another jester was dancing around and whispering about keys, and the king was as gracious as before. Rolf grinned and offered him pence for some more hit points.

Several more weeks passed, although certainly not uneventfully. Rolf had accumulated a good amount of gold now and was anxious to find the other three gems that the Lost King had told him he would need.

He offered service to Lord British, the only king on the continent that he had not served yet. Lord British asked him to visit the Tower of Knowledge. Rolf bought a raft in the town of Britain, because he remembered from his days at the academy that the Tower was on an island just off the southern coast. When he returned from the tower to

Lord British, he felt smarter and stronger, but Lord British did not hand him a gem.

Although disappointed, Rolf shrugged in acceptance and rescued another princess. She gave him the standard princess reward. Returning immediately to the castle, he found she was already in the prison again, and rescued her once more.

By this time, Rolf had recalled enough about the geography of Sosaria to come to the conclusion that he needed to travel abroad. Four gems, four continents—it sounded logical. He went to the town of Britain and spent most of his gold on an aircar.

The aircar enabled Rolf to traverse the entire world. He found the high-tech vehicle's integral laser cannon extremely useful. He discovered other castles, rescued an occasional princess, invoked the 'Q' spell often, and undertook quests for each of the kings he found. Sometimes his reward was simply an increase in one of his attributes such as stamina, charisma, or agility. He took these gratefully, for every little bit helped in his violent world.

Sometimes his reward was one of the four coveted gems. The King of Rondorlin on Continent Two ordered him to kill a carrion creeper. Rolf found and killed this vile creature on one of the middle levels of a dungeon. His compensation was a green gem, which he carefully placed in his pouch with the red one.

A few weeks later, he received a blue gem from the King of Black Dragon's Castle. After long searching and many dangerous fights, his last quest, from the King of Shamino Castle, was to descend to the lowest level of a dungeon to kill the dreaded balron.

Rolf prepared himself for the deep descent by purchasing a dozen each of Ladder Down and Ladder Up spells. After entering the dungeon, he wasted no time, using nine Ladder Down spells to descend immediately to the bottom of the dungeon. There, after desperate combat with a mind whipper and an invisible seeker, he vanquished a balron. The quick casting of nine Ladder Up spells in a row allowed him to escape the dungeon, barely alive but triumphant. His prize was a white gem.

Four gems—red, green, blue, and white—now rested in Rolf's pouch. He knew he needed them *somehow* in order to wipe out the evil that persisted in its horrible rule over the land, for disgusting monsters continued to prey outside of the few safe towns and castles. In fact, he wondered how long it would be before the remaining towns and castles would fall. Not long, he concluded, feeling a chill. If only he knew what to do, where to go next. It all seemed so aimless now.

He decided to concentrate on talking to people. So he began spending more time in the taverns and less out in the field. Battling the monsters had become easy. His purse bulged with gold coin, so there was no reason to further explore the highly dangerous dungeons. He kept the gems secure from the wandering hands of bards, jesters, and the wenches that one was liable to meet in the taverns.

Then one night in a noisy pub, when he ordered his second ale, the bartender said, "The princess will reward you if you save her and will give an additional gift to someone of eighth level or higher."

"Ah ha," Rolf thought, "perhaps here's the path onward." Although he had rescued several princesses in his travels, he was not yet eighth level and had never received an extra gift. The thing to do now was to become eighth level. How was that done? No answer popped into his head, so he resumed his travels, fighting only occasionally and visiting taverns far more than he should.

Then, on an especially oppressive and muggy night that seemed to reflect the menacing evil closing in around the town, another bartender gave him a tip.

"Best you should know that space travel is possible for you, and that you must destroy at least 20 enemy vessels to become an Ace!"

Rolf thanked the man. He journeyed back to the town of Britain, where the same transportation dealer from whom he had bought first a horse, and later a raft and an aircar, had offered him a space shuttle. He was now determined to buy it and try his luck in outer space. He was eager to fight the high tech enemy ships that gossips said had invaded the skies above Sosaria and the adjoining "stellar sectors," he believed the phrase was.

Rolf recognized the air traffic controller as a peasant boy he had met once. He had left his pigsty behind to help Lord British fight the invaders from above. He had a strong and confident voice.

"Five, four, three, two, one. . . . We have ignition. . . . We have liftoff! Good luck, Sir Rolf!"

A polite grunt was about all Rolf could manage as the sudden additional gravity of the shuttle's liftoff pressed him back into the acceleration couch. Six Gs, seven Gs, eight Gs! With each breath he felt as if the weightiest anvil imaginable was on his chest. The rocket engines thundered and the spacecraft vibrated beneath him. It was hot in the vacuum suit he wore, but he was sure that he would need its protection later.

Then, abruptly, there was the absence of gravity, and silence. Into it wafted the voice of another peasant, a warm voice, that of a female pressed into high tech service by the troubles below.

"Shuttle, you are cleared to dock with Sosarian Space Base One. Please exercise caution in your docking maneuvers."

"Thank you, Space Base One," Rolf acknowledged, and proceeded to carefully orient the nose of his ship to fit exactly within the open docking collar on the space base.

As his shuttle coasted toward the station through airless space, Rolf noted two starfighters also docked there, a clumsy-looking craft with large fuel tanks, and a small, lean, mean machine that immediately appealed to him.

He docked smoothly, glad of his care in positioning and orienting the shuttle. A Sosarian Space Forces enlisted person signed him into the station and into the Space Forces.

"Thou mayest undertake a mission immediately," an officer told him. "Thou wilt find plenty of enemy ships to occupy thy time."

Rolf said he understood and handed over the five hundred gold pieces required to rent a starfighter. He chose the small, mean fighter because he intended to make only short, effective missions, protecting whatever gains he achieved by trips back down to Sosaria to invoke his beloved 'Q' spell. Pity that spell did not work up here in space.

He began regular periods of patrol and exploration of nearby stellar sectors, alone in the cockpit. He discovered that combat in space, or almost anywhere for that matter, consists of long periods of boredom interspersed by brief moments of intense action and total horror. Rolf was later to say that anyone who tells you differently, or claims he isn't frightened, is lying through his teeth.

Occasionally as he entered a sector his warning horns would blare as enemy craft approached, their long-range lasers and smart rockets flashing out toward the intruder. The view in front of him would become a whirling kaleidoscope of star fields as Rolf desperately maneuvered to lock his target acquisition crosshairs on an enemy and stab the 'fire' button at just the right moment, all the time conscious of his dwindling fuel supply and of the possibility that another enemy might be coming up in the blind spot on his tail.

Slowly his kills mounted up and at last the day came when Rolf Karlson blasted his twentieth enemy fighter into a blob of red energy that quickly dissipated into the void of interstellar space. He was a Space Ace!

Of course, the universe didn't stop to applaud, and the two remaining enemy ships in the sector were not impressed, only angry at the loss of their sister ship. Space combat continued, and so Rolf returned to Space Base One with twenty-two kills. Getting out of the starfighter, he gracefully accepted the accolades and congratulations of his fellow members of the Sosarian Space Forces.

However, being a space hero did not give him all that many special privileges. He found he still had to pay the five hundred gold piece fee in order to change back to his shuttle for the trip back down to Sosaria. That was when he decided he had flown his last mission for the Space Forces. But he retained his vacuum suit and proudly wore his Space Ace patches.

Back on Sosaria, Rolf bought provisions and got out his aircar. He toured around just for fun, wiping out a few pirates and strafing monsters here and there on the mainland. He even visited the higher levels of several dungeons to replenish his gold supply, which had been depleted by all the docking fees.

During his travels, Rolf could see that, if anything, events had worsened. Mondain's monsters still were wreaking havoc outside the towns and castles. How long could these few islands of good hold out? Would not their food supplies soon be exhausted? A frightening thought. It definitely was time to end all this, and achieve the final triumph.

Rolf landed the aircar near a castle and entered.

A guard scowled and waved him on by.

The king was also unimpressed by Rolf's service patches, ribbons, and medals of valor. "Dost thou offer me service or pence?" the monarch asked.

"Pence," Rolf said, paying out all he had to maximize his hit points.

He then went in search of the jester, who soon capered into view chanting "I've got the key, I've got the key."

"You *better* have it," Rolf said, and immediately attacked.

There was the sudden thunder of the guards' huge feet as they ran to do battle with Rolf, but he had already grabbed the key and was dashing toward the prison.

Seeing him, the princess jumped to her feet and ran anxiously to grip the bars of the door. As he fumbled with the key, she gushed, "Ooooh, I love Space Aces. You're just so darned handsome, big guy."

"So I've heard," Rolf said, swinging open the door. As he led the way out of the prison, a guard chopped at Rolf's head with a massive battle ax. Rolf ducked the whistling swing and beamed his blaster on full power on the broad armor-covered chest.

His foe launched another blow, and another. He seemed invulnerable as three times more the blaster sent a raging stream of red destruction against him. Rolf finally downed him, only to see several of his brutish fellows press forward to take his place. But, taking advantage of a momentary opening between two guards, Rolf led the princess through it and they outran the guards to the entrance.

"Thanks, big guy," the princess said, giving him a chaste peck on the cheek. "Here's five hundred hit points, five hundred experience points, and five hundred gold pieces. Have a nice life."

"Whoa," Rolf said. "I thought Space Aces got a little something extra."

She pecked him on the other cheek.

"Nice, but I meant something to help me on my quest."

She snapped her fingers and smiled. "Oh, yes. You'll find some time machines far to the northwest."

"Thanks," Rolf said. "Will you come with me?"

"Just what kind of girl do you think I am?" the princess snapped, departing in a huff.

Rolf smiled ruefully. So much for the legend that Space Aces had good luck with women. He reentered the castle to buy some more hit points from the king.

Time machines, huh? Well, he thought, no wonder he had not been able to find Mondain in all his travels! The Evil One was hiding back in the mists of time somewhere and directing the dismemberment of Sosaria by remote control. Yes, it was definitely time for Mondain to receive a visitor. He would go outside, invoke the 'Q' spell, and leave right away.

The time machines were easy to find now. He soon saw them gleaming in the distance and swooped the aircar down to land nearby. Inside the machine were four sockets in the control panel. He took from his pouch the four gems he had carried for so long, sparkling red, green, blue, and white. They clicked easily into place.

A powerful humming started, then intensified. Dials started registering. Evidently the process would go on without any aid from him. Rolf gripped a handhold as the machine rocked beneath him and a loud high-pitched warble pressed upon his eardrums. The machine's fall into the space-time continuum was torturing the very fabric of reality. He held on tighter, his mouth wide open in an attempt to lessen the pain.

Just as he thought he could stand it no more, the machine jolted to a halt and the door slid open. Rolf stumbled out. He was in a corner of a relatively small rectangular area with a low ceiling. The only light came from the faintly glowing stone walls, so he figured he was far underground. Not far away was an dark cowled figure so sinister-looking that he could almost see the evil radiating from it in steady streams. At the figure's feet was a small object, pulsing as if with some diabolical life of its own.

"Rolf Karlson, I believe." Mondain's words slithered out arrogantly. "Welcome to thy death. I had intended it to occur much sooner, but my—ahem—assistants all failed me in this matter. It's so hard to get good help these days, eh? Well, methinks thy demise will require little effort."

Rolf gulped and started forward, inadvertently brushing his left shoulder against the wall. A burst of force sent him flying and he landed in a clatter, feeling much weaker.

"Like my walls?" Mondain asked gleefully. "Having them thus charged doth cut down on fingerprints and smudges. By the way, thou wilt not leave this place alive."

With a great exertion of will, Rolf got to his feet and staggered unsteadily toward Mondain.

"Thou comest close. Good. I do so hate chasing victims around and around; it doth strike me as undignified."

Rolf reached the Evil Gem. His hand shot down and grabbed it.

Pain! Horrible pain shot through his body again and again. He could feel his strength dimimishing swiftly. His body vibrated and the very core of his being screamed and screamed in agony.

Then it was gone. There was silence. Mondain's gaze fell briefly on the shards on the floor and then steadily on Rolf, red gleams of anger pulsating from those eyes all but hidden in the shadows of the cowl.

"Thou hast angered me," Mondain spit out. "I must needs fabricate a new Gem of Immortality, which will take some time. I shall have thy soul for this, and have it now!"

Rolf was already holding down the firing stud of his blaster. Its destructive energy flowed over Mondain, who replied with a bolt of his own, knocking Rolf backwards almost to the floor.

They battled for what seemed like an eternity, the air smelling of ionization as both combatants continually unleashed megawatts of force at each other.

Rolf knew he had precious little strength left, and that he was in his final, greatest battle. Yet, yes, there *was* a slim chance he could prevail. A few scorched places had appeared on Mondain's robes, and one small hole had actually been burned into the magical cloth just above his right knee. Rolf was getting some telling blows through. He fired again, and again.

Mondain screamed as red energy flowed through the hole, and backed away. Completely disregarding his own safety, Rolf bore forward, firing steadily, aiming for that widening hole.

Suddenly, Mondain winked out of existence. In the spot he had last occupied, a great, black vile-looking bird was flapping its wings menacingly as it sailed upward.

From then on, Rolf, even as terribly wounded as he was, found the battle almost hilarious. The bird was darting from wall to wall, from corner to corner. It could not seem to find a way out of the dungeon! Nor did it seem to possess any magical bolts of force or other defenses. Relentlessly Rolf chased it, getting in a shot whenever he could.

Finally he cornered the bird and aimed a steady stream of death from the blaster's firing aperture on its foul and detestable feathers.

All at once the bird exploded in a brief burst of oily smoke. Suddenly fatigue and pain stabbed through Rolf and threatened to overcome him. Although he knew that anytime he could slide down into mental darkness, he felt great satisfaction. He had triumphed! Live or die, he had triumphed and destroyed Mondain!

The tall man with a scarred face stood on the stage in front of the Adventurers Academy's graduating class. He looked out over the pasty inexperienced faces of the class. Could these babies survive? He doubted it, but one had to try to give them an edge.

"Look to your right," Rolf commanded, and waited while heads swiveled obediently. "Look to your left!"

PART

3

Ultima II—Revenge of the Enchantress

6 A New Evil Gains Power

O Brave One, you are needed once again. The peaceful and posperous world that Lord British welded together from the small fiefdoms of the First Age of Darkness has all but vanished. Evil stalks the land and seas. Wars again rage, and a holocaust has torn down wise and ancient civilizations and almost destroyed the entire planet. If the beleaguered people of the world could only find a way to use the mysterious doors of time and influence past events, then life itself might once more gain a foothold.

Beware, Adventurer. Armies of evil minions protect the dastardly one responsible for this destruction with single-minded fanaticism. You have your work cut out for you.

Background

In the few years of peace between the First and Second Ages of Darkness, one of the more persistent rumors had to do with a possible successor to the vanquished Mondain. At the time of his death, so the story went, he had been training a young and impressionable protegé—an apprentice in the masterworks of evil that he so despicably crafted.

A few souls, foolhardy and curious, followed in the footsteps of the great Hero who was the slayer of Mondain in the final cataclysmic battle of that age. They entered the shattered chambers of Mondain's fortress soon after the mortal combat had ended, and many searched for loot or souvenirs. Yet they found little but piles of smoking rubble, an occasional clot of dried blood and, where Mondain had expired, a few scorched black feathers. There was no sign, not even the tiniest shard, of Mondain's dread Gem of Immortality. Historians still wonder whether someone had gotten there before them, while the Hero still lay unconscious, and had taken what remained of the Gem.

The debate in the taverns went on for years. General peace prevailed in the land, but great events were also taking place. Lord British, a minor king at the time, had stepped in to pick up the broken traces of government. Peacefully, through his benign and wise leadership, he brought the many small kingdoms together under one flag. Trade and good fellowship prospered equally all over the world.

Yet, obviously, something mysterious was at work. The appearance of the time doors was the first major sign. Traders were the first to make use of these gateways to other times and places. Other disquieting signs were appearing also. A single orc was found, a normally vicious being created by sorcerers, although this one was too sick and hurt to fight.

Then, bit by bit, evil began making itself known once more in the land. People died horribly, outlying farms were burned, and even the livestock tortured and killed. Wanton damage was done to small villages and the rural folk all fled to the walled towns and villages.

Soon the source of evil, now grown strong, was known. Minax was her name. At age eleven she had been apprenticed to Mondain and had shown an amazing aptitude for sorcery from the very first. Mondain had warped her vast power toward evil and now, even from the grave, his training was bearing its horrid fruit of death and destruction.

Societies collapsed. Wars again raged. In the time of 2111, a holocaust, inspired and guided by Minax, devastated the planet.

Lord British realized that only one of great courage, a Hero like the one who had saved Sosaria in the First Age of Darkness, could now save the world again. Once more, that Hero or Heroine would have to travel back and forth in time, brave the unknown, and finally fight a great battle to kill the evil enchantress.

You have already read the Scroll of Calling, but we repeat here the closing words of Lord British:

> If you understand all this and are still willing to venture forth, then go now with our abundant well wishes and the promise that our hopes will be with you ceaselessly until your return.

The need is great. On your shoulders rests the fate of the entire world.

Your Character

As with your previous adventure, before you take any action at all, you determine your race, sex, profession, and personal traits. For these last, you can choose from among strength, agility, charisma, stamina, intelligence, and wisdom. Thanks to advances, there are now a total of ninety points which you may distribute among the six qualities just mentioned.

Enhancing one or two of these attributes over others, obviously can be desirable. For example, strength determines which armor you can wear. Agility or dexterity determines which weapons you can wield, and how skillfully you can steal. Intelligence affects the efficacy of spells cast by wizards and clerics. Other factors are charisma, which determines how much others like you; stamina, which determines your endurance; and wisdom, or the ability to properly use what your intelligence reveals.

Before I say anything else, let me tell you that there is *no,* repeat *no,* resurrection here like there was during the First Age of Darkness. You must take the precaution of invoking the 'Q' spell at regular intervals, or else death is the end.

When you distribute your ninety points, give an edge to strength and agility, as in the last mission. These provide the most favorable configuration for early survival, and you can enhance the other attributes later.

Race and Sex

The races you may choose from are very similar to those prevalent during the First Age of Darkness—human, elf, dwarf, and hobbit. Their strong points vary and should weigh heavily in your choice of identity.

Humans have the advantage of a rather high intellect. They are strong (only dwarves are stronger) and their dexterity, while not matching that of elves, is usually sufficient for the job.

Elves are the most agile and dextrous. Their quickness makes them excellent thieves. This can be very helpful early on, when the key to survival is accumulating weapons, armor, and food.

Dwarves are shorter than elves, but more compact and thus usually heavier. They are stronger even than humans. Dwarves also are brave, but unfortunately they lack intelligence, which is a disadvantage as the mission moves into later and more complex stages.

Hobbits are short and cute and have hairy toes. They are also gentle and seldom go on quests.

The compromise choice is the human. Blessed with good intelligence, humans are able to acquire the agility and strength needed to survive and progress.

It doesn't matter very much which sex you choose to be, because, although males have slightly more strength and females slightly more dexterity at the beginning, the differences even out after a time.

Profession

Also as in the First Age, you can choose among four professions, each profession with its own particular advantages and disadvantages: fighter, cleric, wizard, and thief.

A fighter is strong, agile, and proficient with every weapon likely to be found in Sosaria. If you choose to be a fighter you can have these attributes without having to actually spend years in practice.

A cleric must battle just as hard to survive as any fighter. The cleric spends many years in patient and diligent study and thereby gains great wisdom. Spells cast by a cleric are less likely to fail, but this fact is unimportant in this mission, because magic works only in towers and dungeons, and you really don't need to set foot in these.

Wizards (also known as mages) are users of magic. As with clerics, this is less of an advantage in the Second Age than it was in the First. However, should you choose this profession, all the benefits of years of study are yours without having to open a scroll.

There are advantages to being a thief. Shoplifting while in stores is easier for a thief than others, and the likelihood of being caught less. Should you choose this profession, your fingers will become instantly nimble.

Select the profession of fighter here as the most appropriate for long-term survival. Fighters are agile enough to open most traps and to steal when absolutely necessary. They can use all the weapons you will find in shops, and are strong enough to deliver killing blows with these weapons. While fighters can not do much with magic, this is not really a drawback, as you know.

By extension, becoming a human fighter is the absolute compromise in race and profession.

The Lay of the Land

The planet of Sosaria has changed a lot. Here are the salient facts about it and its present terrain as well.

Geography

There are six areas you need to know about: five time periods (because the geography of the world changes from era to era during this mission) and outer space. A total of twenty time doors interconnect the five time periods. It's pretty much up to you to figure out which one you're in.

When you arrive in Sosaria it will be 1423 B.C. The landmass you find yourself on is Eurasia. Land bridges connect to North America, Africa, and South America. Important locations are Towne Linda in Italy,

Le Jester Village down in Africa, a tower in South America, a dungeon in Greenland, Lord British's castle in (naturally) England, and a signpost in Australia. You will be able to visit the overseas locations only by frigate.

Four time doors are active in this period. They wink in and out of existence rapidly, so be quick to use them. Two are relatively close together in Europe. The left one takes you to England in 1990 A.D. The right one is a connection to the eastern peninsula of the solitary landmass that existed during nine million B.C. A door in North America takes you to Legends—a timeless and very dangerous place that you have to pass through, much in the manner of the Dallas-Fort Worth airport, to get anywhere else. Finally, the door in South America opens to North America in 2112.

Places of note in 1990 A.D. are Lord British's castle and Port Boniface in England, the town of New San Antonio in North America, a tower in Africa, a dungeon in Greenland, and a signpost in Australia. Again, you will need to board a frigate to cross oceans. Or, you can go to the airport in New San Antonio and steal an aircraft.

There are four time doors in this age as well. The door in South America opens to North America in 2112, just like it does in 1423 B.C. The time door by the signpost in Australia goes to nine million B.C. The one near Lord British's castle connects to 1423 B.C., and the one by the dungeon in Greenland also bridges to nine million B.C.

In the very ancient time of nine million B.C., there is only one huge continent and three places of interest—Baradin's Village, a dungeon, and a signpost.

Four time doors are here also. The one by the dungeon in the northeast of the continent connects to Legends. The door on the eastern peninsula opens to Europe in 1423 B.C. The one by the signpost is a portal to England in 1990 A.D., and the one to the north of Baradin's Village goes to North America in 1990 A.D.

The age of 2112 A.D. is the devastated world of the Aftermath, when the wars spurred on by Minax have destroyed most of civilization. Not much remains but a village in Europe called Pirate's Harbour. There is also a dungeon in Greenland and a signpost in Australia. You need to taxi an airplane through the time doors in order to fly to Europe from North America.

As is to be expected, there are four time doors in this age too. The northern time door in North America connects to South America in 1990

A.D. The southern time door on that same continent takes you nonstop to Legends. In Eurasia there are two doors—the southern one takes you to the east of the continent in nine million B.C., and the eastern one is your connection to Europe in 1423 B.C.

Which brings us to Legends—a timeless place heretofore known only in legends (hence its name). It's a huge single continent, but different from the one in nine million B.C. Signs of Minax's presence abound: daemons, balrons, evil wizards, orcs, and devils remind you at all times that her castle is nearby.

Stay in the small area bounded by mountains and containing the four time doors and the signpost; there the creatures leave you mostly alone. Venture out, and you'll have the fight of your life on your hands, maybe the *last* fight of your life. Minax's castle is in the center of this continent.

The four time doors in Legends are in a row just below the signpost. The left-hand door takes you to the northeast of the continent in nine million B.C. The next one to the right connects to Europe in 1423 B.C., the one after that to England in 1990 A.D., and the furthermost door to the right opens up on North America in 2112 A.D.

Terrain

The terrain in all places in the Second Age is much the same as the First Age of Darkness, with one notable exception. In addition to water, grass, and mountains, Minax has thrown in large swampy areas to slow down adventurers. If you're low on hit points, stay out of swamps or you'll lose more points with every squelchy, mud-clogged step through the thorny brambles and tough-edged sawgrass. No self-respecting horse will enter a swamp at all, so you'll have to leave yours to graze if a swamp blocks your way.

As to the oceans, only sea monsters swim there. You'll have to either take a frigate or fly over stretches of water.

Mountains are as impassable as ever. Forests have monsters hiding among the trees, and the grass plains are reasonably smooth and featureless.

Your Resources

No matter who you are and how well you know the times and places of Sosaria, you need to take every opportunity you can to build up your attributes (which are measured in points), experience (measured in experience points), cash (which you need to buy the transportation, food, weapons, and armor that you need), and your supply of crucial items. Every part of Sosaria has both monsters and traps; next you'll be briefed on how to keep yourself alive and obtain the points and objects that you'll need.

Remember, however, that your experience points can go only as high as 9,999; the same is true for hit points. In fact, if you attempt to push them beyond this limit, your hit points roll back to zero. There is also a top limit for the attributes of strength, agility, intelligence, wisdom, charisma, and stamina—99. Once past 99, they roll back to zero too. When your totals are as close as possible to these maximums you can set out to trounce Minax.

Villages, Towns, and Castles

Villages are represented on your map as a collection of small circles. These are filled by simple folk who are glad to sell their wares and share their knowledge with visitors—for a price. Villages are the only places where you'll find food, and you will need lots of food to survive the rigors of adventuring—which has been said to be the most effective diet ever devised.

Towns are larger than villages and are indicated by a cloverleaf symbol. They're more sophisticated than villages, offering taverns and other necessities not found in bumpkinland. Towns also have weapon and armor shops. Both towns and villages have lots of guards, who will do a polka on your chest if you even think about breaking the rules of the municipality.

Castles are seats of government and show on the map as square symbols with a gateway. They have prisons and chapels where you can

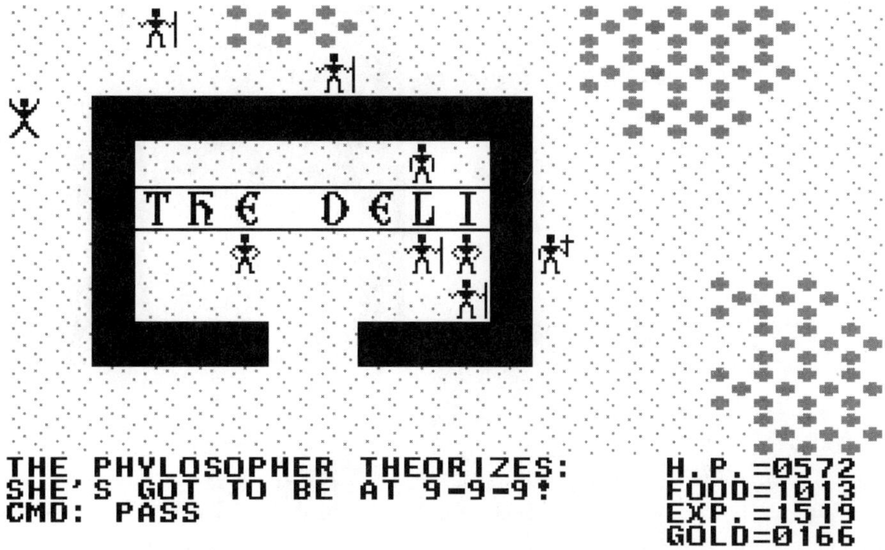

Figure 6.1 *While stocking up on food in a village deli, you have a chance encounter with a philosopher. His tip can save you millions of miles of travel. Literally.*

obtain useful information, as well as private vaults and chambers. Explore them carefully—castle guards are the largest and meanest of their kind.

People

No matter what their race, there are only eight types of people that you meet—fighters, clerics, wizards, thieves, merchants, jesters, kings and queens, and guards. Here is what to watch out for and what to try to gain from each type of inhabitant.

Fighters are of humanoid shape and very strong. Their typical conversation is usually limited to "Ugh, me tough," but you should talk to all fighters. Fighters usually stand with their hands on their hips and are thus easily recognizable from a considerable distance. They carry something you need in your quest so, when you are strong enough, you'll want to pick a fight with a fighter or two.

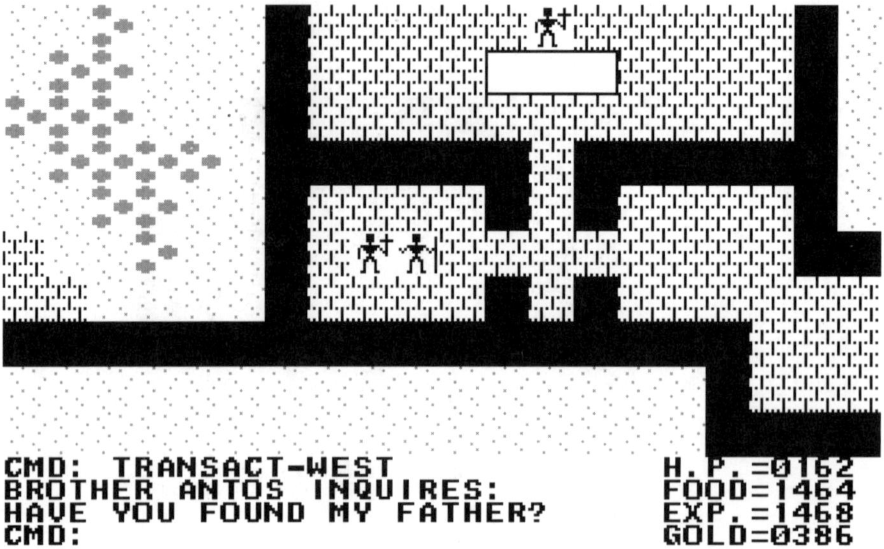

Figure 6.2 *Visiting the chapel in Lord British's castle gives you yet another valuable hint.*

Clerics are humanoid figures who carry a cross in their left hand. They are not always good or wise, and their message is generally restricted to exhortations of "Believe!" However, there are a few clerics whom you will very definitely want to listen to closely, and one kind priest on a far planet whose blessing you must have to complete your mission.

Wizards carry staffs in their left hand. Most wizards in towns are haughty people whose comments are limited to something inane such as "Hex-a-poo on you." Minax has suborned some of them to her sinister service. When you fight an evil wizard, you must contend with his or her dangerous magic missiles.

Thieves are pickpockets, mostly human, and carry a sword in their left hand. Don't be deceived by the weaponry, they would much rather steal than fight. After each encounter with a thief, check your pockets with the 'Z' spell. Sometimes, if a precious object is gone, you'll do better to return to the place where you last invoked the 'Q' spell. You *could* go back and kill the thief and regain your valuables, but in towns this will bring the guards down on you so it is often very, very fatal.

Which brings us to guards. Guards are giant, musclebound humans who strut around with their fists clenched by their side. They are mindlessly loyal to the town, village, or king that they serve. If you break any of the rules, the guards attack you immediately and relentlessly. If you have a lot of hit points, you may (with luck and persistence) defeat one or two or three guards, but more will keep coming and wear you down. However, fighting a few guards can sometimes literally be a key to your success.

Merchants are small, mild, and unarmed. They stand with their arms hanging harmlessly by their sides. They are found in towns, often peddling apples to eke out a meager living. A few have managed to open shops of various types, and you'll deal with those for weapons, armor, food, transportation, and liquid refreshment in the taverns. Talk to all merchants, and be sure to tip bartenders. Some merchants also sell knowledge and have set themselves up as oracles (also known as seers). These latter are far more expensive than bartenders, but sometimes worth the cost.

In castles and at least one village, jesters caper around with their arms thrown up in happy abandonment. They are almost always simple buffoons, but sometimes they drop useful hints.

Castles house kings and sometimes queens. Royalty is larger than humans, but smaller than guards. Mostly they just sit on their thrones, take your money, and grant favors.

Learn to recognize these eight types of people, and respond to them appropriately. Your mission will go much more smoothly.

Magic

Unlike in the First Age, only wizards and clerics can use magic, and even they are limited to just a few spells. Also, spells work only inside towers and dungeons.

Both wizards and clerics can cast light spells, thus eliminating the need for torches in the dark towers and dungeons. They also can use Ladder Up and Ladder Down spells.

Clerics have three spells only they can cast. These are Passwall, which destroys the wall in front of you; Surface, which teleports you instantly out of the tower or dungeon; and Prayer, which *sometimes* calls down divine intervention to destroy your enemy.

Wizards also enjoy three spells unique to them. The Magic Missile is an offensive weapon whose destructive power varies with the strength of the wizard using it. Blink randomly transports you to a new location on the current level of a tower or dungeon. Finally, Kill attempts to destroy your enemy by magic. Its success depends on the relative strengths of the wizard and his or her enemy.

Necessary Items

Check your inventory with the 'Z' spell after each fight with a monster. You'll pick up all sorts of useful stuff. In fact, there are twenty different items you'll want to accumulate for various uses. These are torches, keys for regular locks (not to be confused with skull keys), tools, quick swords (which enable harder and faster striking than regular swords), wands, staffs, boots, cloaks, helms, viewing gems, red gems, green gems, skull keys, brass buttons, blue tassels, ankhs, strange coins, green idols, modern-looking power sources called trilithiums, and rings. Some of these are absolutely necessary to complete your mission.

Keep a close watch on these items, because they are very precious. Thieves just love to pick the pockets and plunder the packs of the unwary. Some of these items are especially rare and hard to obtain, so guard them well.

Various people and monsters are more likely to have certain items than others. If you meet someone who says he has one each of every item, take him up on his claim and offer him some money. He just might be telling the truth.

Transportation

Thanks to the many time gates, you can walk through time—from nine million B.C. to 2112 A.D., and a lot of places in between, such as 1423 B.C. and 1990 A.D. But you can't walk *every*where you need to go, so look into the four available modes of transportation.

Horses, as in the First Age, are cheap. Riding a horse is faster than walking. When you first buy a horse, you can ride it all over town, but from then on you'll not be able to bring it inside with you. However, don't worry. The horse will stay wherever you leave it, munching on the grass contentedly, and will be right there when you return, even if it is months later.

Frigates are sailing crafts usually manned by pirates. As an adventurer you are authorized by law to commandeer frigates for your own use, assuming you have blue tassels, the proper proof of this authority. If you do, then you can sail anywhere you want. If you can enter a port, you can steal frigates. Like a horse, they will stay wherever you put them and may thus be used again at any future time.

Airplanes, when you find them, can only be stolen. You'll need brass buttons and skull keys to fly them. There are no runways out in the field, but these little planes will land on grass very nicely. You can even taxi these planes through time doors and fly around in nine million B.C. or any era you like!

After your experience and hit points have increased sufficiently, rockets are available to you. If you have vacuum armor to survive space travel, your own fuel, and an ankh, you can steal and use rockets. In fact, to win, you'll have to!

Your Challenges

Now that you know how to define your personal traits, how the planet is laid out, and how to obtain what you need to eventually rid the planet of Minax's monstrous ministrations, you're ready to learn more specifics about the challenges facing you.

Dungeons and Towers

You do not have to enter dungeons and towers (which are nothing but high-rise dungeons) to complete your mission. You won't get any hit points for fighting in them, as in the First Age. All you will gain is gold and perhaps an occasional secret message, both of which you can obtain elsewhere.

If you do enter a tower or a dungeon on a whim, keep a map. If your torch happens to go out, you're trapped in the pitch black and your only hope of escape is to have a good map so you can retrace your steps exactly to the entrance. Otherwise, you wander around bumping into walls until you are killed by an unseen monster or until you starve to death.

The minute you enter, get to the top or bottom level as fast as possible, that is, by using Ladder Up or Down spells to reach the desired level. Grab whatever you can grab, and immediately escape by using a series of the opposite spell. On the other hand, the items you find show up outside reasonably often. Also, you need only four or five trilithiums anyway, if you've listened to the philosopher who gives the coordinates on where to go in space.

Unless you have time and resources to waste, the best thing to do with dungeons and towers is to stay out. The theory is that Minax created these somewhat superfluous places to be no more than a red herring and a waster of your time.

Monsters

The Second Age of Darkness has many fewer monsters. While Mondain's rich, inventive imagination created many different types, Minax satisfied herself with only five kinds, four of which are extremely vicious fighters.

Her first creation was orcs. A genetic mating of human and boar, orcs are very stupid and more of a pest than a threat. They are huge, hulking humanoid figures with what appears to be horns on their heads.

Daemons are smaller but also horned. Their upraised palms look as if they're signaling you to stop, and indeed they are, because they can stop you in your tracks by magic, paralyzing your arms or your legs.

Devils, horned as well, carry tridents in their left hands.

The feared balron is a genetically enhanced version of one of Mondain's most feared monsters. Minax has augmented its Herculean strength and given it a sleep spell to use against its victims. Balrons are recognizable by their great, leathery wings.

Finally, there are sea monsters, which look like huge reptilian swans. They delight in chasing and sinking any frigate that dares to venture out onto the oceans.

Some towns, like Port Boniface, have tame sea monsters. Leave them alone. Not only are they fierce fighters and almost impossible to kill, but the guards all come running to attack you for molesting the poor, "defenseless" monsters.

We cannot emphasize enough that, although they are fewer in type, the monsters of Minax are generally much harder to defeat than those of Mondain. You definitely should carry as many protective devices as you can find.

Space

Space travel on this mission has a different purpose from that in the First Age: to find Father Antos. You do not have to fight enemy starcraft, change ships, or even leave the solar system. There's no docking with space stations, but you do land on various planets—which can be a real bear.

Your adventurer's kit includes a map of the solar system with coordinates. The location and terrain of all nine known planets are given. Each leg of a trip, including getting into Earth orbit, takes one unit of energy—that is, if you go from Earth to Mars to Venus and back to Earth, you use up four units of energy, plus what you needed for takeoffs and landings. In other words, either know where you're going, or be sure to have lots of energy available—or you'll get stranded in space.

Earth's coordinates are 6, 6, 6. It's OK to enjoy visiting and exploring the other eight planets of the solar system, but just remember that space travel is very dangerous. Anyway, your final destination in space will yield an extremely helpful ring.

At least there are no time doors on any other planet to worry about.

Figure 6.3 *You have to provide your own fuel when traveling in space, so be sure you have plenty. Dungeons and towers can be a source if you are unlucky in finding it in safer places.*

Your Strategy

Your strategy in this adventure is similar to that used in the first mission: build up strength and other resources; search and explore to obtain the items and information you need; and finally, you're off to off Minax!

The First Stage

When you first arrive in Sosaria, you are on a grassy plain with no weapons and no armor in the year 1423 B.C. Your approximate location is somewhere in North America. Action begins immediately, and you are subject to attack at any moment.

Although you lack weapons and armor, you start with more resources than on your first mission: four hundred hit points, four hundred units of food, and four hundred pieces of good, yellow gold. All this largesse may seem wonderful at first, but it's not really. Your food will dwindle quickly in the exertion of exploring and of fighting for your life. Having no armor means your hit points drop rapidly as you beat ineffectually at your attackers with bare hands.

Your first goal, then, is to get weapons, armor, and food. From your point of entry, walk west until you find the land bridge between North America and Eurasia. Walk across Asia and Europe—the trip will go quickly—then south to Italy where you will find Towne Linda. Enter the town, shop for weapons and armor, but save some money for food and drink. If you shoplift, do so carefully. Enjoy a few quick ones in the tavern—and listen carefully to the barkeep. Talk to everyone else as well.

Leaving Linda, journey down through Africa until you find the village of Le Jester. Plenty of food here, so stock up for some long-range adventuring. Again, talk to everyone and listen for clues.

After each achievement, be sure to go outside and invoke the 'Q' spell to make a record in case you lose something and need to refresh your memory. As in the First Age of Darkness, you can invoke the 'Q' spell only while you are in the open and dismounted from any vehicle or horse you might own.

In this initial building stage, you want to thoroughly explore 1423 B.C. and fight all the monsters you can find (there will be plenty of those). Use the 'Z' spell after each combat to check your inventory. You'll start picking up useful items from the beasts you kill.

Hit Points

Watch your hit points and don't let them get too low. The only place to get additional hit points is from kings. The closest king to you now is Lord British. You can see his castle in England across the channel but, alas, right now it's out of reach because you have no way to traverse oceans.

If you stay in 1423 B.C., your problem will become very severe in a hurry. Luckily there are two time doors which pop in and out of existence just on the other side of the Alps, the mountains north of Towne Linda. Catch the one on the left to get to England in 1990 A.D. There you can visit the castle of Lord British and the village of Port Boniface.

Lord British is in the throne room of his castle. He'll grant you three hundred hit points for fifty gold pieces. You can offer him tribute as often as you please.

England, 1990 A.D.

Lord British's castle in 1990 A.D. is a place you'll visit often, as it's the easiest source you will find of renewing your hit points. Feel free to explore the castle and talk to everyone. Brother Antos in the chapel has a very significant hint for you, as do others.

Stop to buy food in the village of Port Boniface in England.

Near the castle is the time door. Walk through it to return to 1423 B.C. By now it should be sort of a home base for you.

Nine Million B.C.

Take the time door to the right of the one that takes you to England in the present time. You'll arrive in the prehistoric mists of nine million B.C.

You'll find yourself on the eastern peninsula of the single huge continent. Go all the way to the western coast and down to the southern part of the continent down to Baradin's Village. Talk to the oracle there if you have the money. Buy some food.

Gather all the clues you can in the one village. Kill all monsters, thus gaining valuable items, more experience points, and additional gold. Other than continuing to build yourself up, there's nothing to accomplish here or in 1423 B.C.

The Second Stage

The first stage of your strategy blends into the second stage somewhat, but by now you should have enough resources that you can be more daring and venturesome, and you can consider yourself in the second, or searching and exploring stage.

You must acquire a plane at some point. After you've accumulated the items needed to fly one, visit New San Antonio in North America in 1990 A.D. Be sure to have three keys to get into it. Once you're inside the airport, only one fighter acting as security officer tries to stop you. The runway looks short, but if you have the buttons and keys needed, you can take off easily. Once you have the plane, you can taxi it through time doors and use it in other periods also.

You absolutely need a spacecraft, which you procure in 2112 A.D. in Pirate's Harbour by the time-honored adventurer's procurement technique—stealing. This craft enables you to search known (and unknown) space for the final thing you will need before facing Minax in the climatic battle. As with flying planes, you'll need to have certain items in your possession, especially extra power sources.

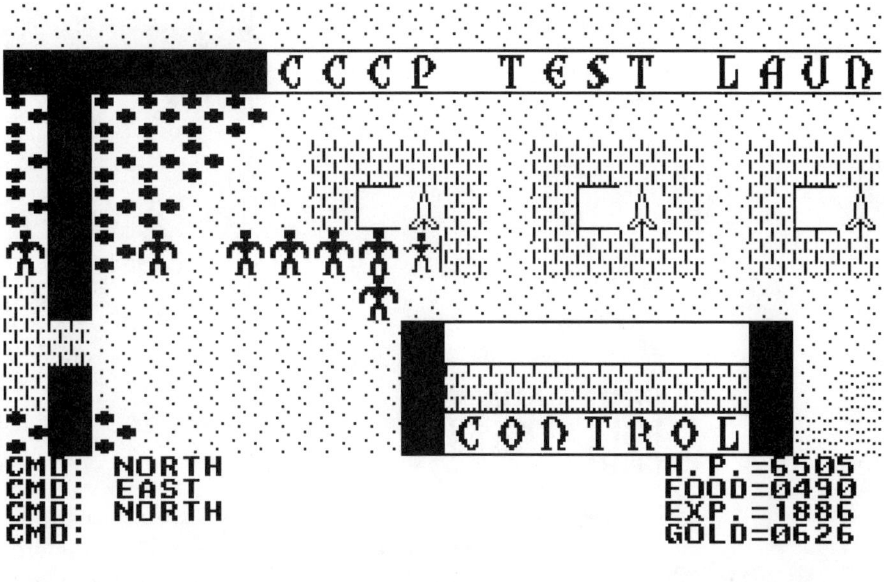

Figure 6.4 *Stealing a rocket is a snap, except that the whole KGB is chasing you.*

When searching out in space, watch the people you meet on the various planets. They don't much care for Earthies. Even in town you'll get attacked, or have items stolen if you're not very, very careful.

Eventually, of course, you need to journey to Minax's land. Employ a gradual approach to undoing her forces; do this by invading Legends a bit at a time. As soon as you feel strong enough, venture forth slightly from the signpost area where the four time doors are located and kill a few monsters. Don't go very far, though. These are Minax's prime troops, and you'll face balrons and their sleep spells, wizards throwing magic missiles, and the paralyzing attacks of daemons.

Knock off a few bad beasts whenever you can, and return to England in 1990 A.D. to purchase more hit points from Lord British. It's a slow process fighting your way into the interior of Legends, but it has to be done.

Finally you arrive at the center of the continent and find Minax's castle surrounded on three sides by water and mountains. Additional demonic troops protect the castle, and you'll have to fight your way in. This, again, may require you to retreat now and then to get more hit points.

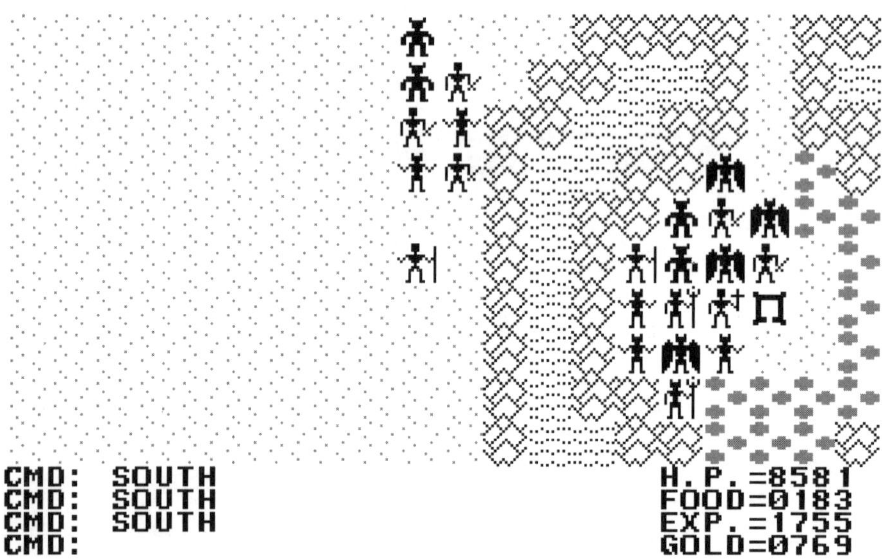

Figure 6.5 *By this time, you've fought your way to the center of the Legends continent and have only a few more monsters to contend with before entering Minax's castle. Just a few more monsters. Good luck (you sure need it!).*

The Final Stage

After your return from space, assuming a lot of preparation beforehand, you should have all the items and information you need for your final invasion of Legends, when you actually seek out Minax for the final, climactic battle. Be sure you have the strange coins, which you may have been carrying for good luck; they will stop monsters in their tracks and effectively "freeze" them so you can get past.

Finally, however, most of the outside troops will be out of commission and you can enter the castle. You can't get at Minax easily. Numerous force fields that blast you down a thousand hit points at a time dot her castle. Since you will be passing back and forth through these force fields a lot, you'll be glad you accumulated all those miscellaneous items.

Minax's palace is large and full of fearsome beasts and weird gadgets that help her to rule time and space. Moreover, she is hard to find and refuses to die politely.

Because killing Minax is very hard, I will give you a more explicit briefing than usual here. She likes to hang out in the upper right of the castle, in Chamber One. When you attack, she fights briefly and moves down to Chamber Two, all the way down on the left side of the castle, and a heck of a long walk. Each time you attack, she fights briefly, then moves to the other chamber.

This is easy enough (although, granted, a little boring), but that's not all you have to contend with. Balrons, devils, wizards, and daemons make your life miserable at almost every step and protect Minax in her chambers. Don't try to fight all of these assistants, because they will wear you down very quickly.

Instead, use the strange coins. Just rubbing them negates time more than one square away and leaves Minax's minions frozen while you chase her. You'll need more than one coin, too, to say the least.

The death of Minax does not come easily, but if you are persistent and very, very careful, it does come. Once you are victorious, this evil enchantress and all her works will be destroyed.

Now read the story of a good wizard, the great Nimsman, who traveled the way you now must go. May good luck ride with you and protect you.

7 Nimsman, Master of the White Magic

Nimsman stood forlornly on the almost endless grass plain, the pain of arrival still racking his body.

He had wanted to be a wizard in the worst way, and now it looked as if he had achieved that goal. He had no weapons, no armor, knew no spells—you couldn't get much worse than that, could you?

Suddenly nervous, he whirled around to look behind. There was nothing in sight, but the plain undulated away for miles in a series of small hills and hollows that could be hiding an army of monsters. It sure wasn't as flat as it looked in the computer simulations at the Adventurers Academy. There was the hint of mountains in the far, blue distance. A faint rustling came from the grass as a hot, fetid wind sporadically stirred it. Otherwise, a deathly silence. Danger and evil seemed to hang in the air like heavy smoke from the burning of some foul substance.

"Well, dummy, are you going to just stand there moping forever?" a voice asked. With a start, Nimsman realized that it was *his* voice.

He grinned ruefully and looked up at the sun. Getting on into the afternoon, time to start adventuring. He oriented himself and started walking northwest, trying to visualize the layout of the continents in 1423 B.C. He was aiming for the land bridge that would take him from North America over to the Eurasian land mass.

Nimsman was but a youth at this time, freshly graduated from the Adventurers Academy. This was his first campaign. He had been too young to take part in the glorious victories of the First Age. He was of medium height with a high forehead and alert brown eyes denoting the intelligence required of a wizard. Yet his arms and chest were well-muscled. His hair was black and a little long, but a leather sweatband kept it out of his eyes. On his feet were the standard issue brown adventurers boots.

Nimsman reached the land bridge as the late afternoon shadows were lengthening toward evening. He recalled learning that time and space were much compressed in the Second Age of Darkness. He was sure not looking forward to spending the night out here. He started across the small strip of land only to see a hulking figure jogging toward him from the other side.

The bulk of the body and the hornlike protuberances on top of the head alerted Nimsman immediately.

"Orc," he told himself and clicked into a fighting stance. He was well trained in unarmed combat and held the proper stance even though his heart was pounding in fear.

The orc was close now. It stopped about five feet away and glared at him out of piggish eyes.

"Hi," Nimsman said, knowing it was useless. Orcs were just too dumb to carry on any kind of conversation.

"Arrrrr!" the orc said, the sound rumbling up angrily from its throat, and charged.

Nimsman waited until precisely the right instant, grabbed two solid handfuls of fur on the thing's chest, let his body go limp so that he hung down, then jackknifed so his feet shoved into the orc's chest. It was a perfectly executed maneuver, using the orc's own momentum and weight. The surprised beast sailed over the young wizard and landed on the ground beyond in a thump.

It was quick to get back on its feet, however. It stood for a second gazing off in the opposite direction as if wondering where its enemy had disappeared to.

Orcs are really dumb, Nimsman thought in amusement, his fear forgotten. Why, even his old weapons instructor, Rolf, could take this moron.

The moron turned quickly, so quickly that Nimsman could not have run away if he had wanted to, and charged again. Nimsman reached out to repeat his previous demonstration of the martial arts and suddenly saw stars as a huge, hard paw hit him on the side of the head. Trying to clear his mind, he felt himself lifted into the air and *thrown* for a considerable distance. He hit hard and it hurt a lot. He could feel himself losing strength fast.

Coughing with pain, he rolled to his feet and lashed out in a neat kick to the orc's right kneecap. The monster screamed but kept coming, so Nimsman let the orc have another kick. Again there was a scream, and the thing slowed down some.

Nimsman dashed by it, getting in a good elbow jab to the neck and three power kicks to his spine before the orc could get turned around. From then on, although he took additional blows, it was just a matter of wearing down the orc and finishing the battle.

By the time darkness had arrived, Nimsman limped proudly away from his first combat victory.

Stiff from spending the night in a tree for safety, Nimsman walked westward across a large plain. To the south he saw a high range of mountains, which he identified as the Alps. He had just come out of an extensive forest.

In front of him, suddenly appearing from nowhere, was a large, brilliantly shimmering portal.

"Time door," Nimsman said aloud, a habit he was getting into from spending so much time alone.

He detoured around the time door, having decided that he would have enough trouble just surviving in 1423 B.C. without adding the problems of another era just yet. He curved around the western end of the Alps. Just to his northeast from here, he knew, was the island of Britain and the castle of Lord British, but there was no way to cross the English Channel from here right now.

After a long hard walk that felt as if it would never end (even though his well-trained intellect told him it would) he reached Italy, or what would become that country in something over two thousand years from now. The Towne Linda was in sight, and he gratefully entered. At least he wouldn't have to worry about orcs or something worse while he was inside.

"Pay your taxes," a guard snarled as Nimsman strolled by.

"Buy my apples," a merchant pleaded.

"Believe!" a cleric preached to him.

Nimsman smiled and talked politely to everyone he passed. You never knew—some pearl of wisdom that could shorten the mission by months might come your way.

"Psst, wanna buy a watch?" a thief asked, hand sliding slyly toward Nimsman's coin purse.

Nimsman slipped past him, and finally found the weapons shop. He'd heard stories from the old vets of the First Age campaigns, like Rolf, that high tech weapons were not offered right away, but that was not the case here. He had his choice of eight weapons, from lowly dagger to a powerful phazor. The latter was beyond his means at the moment, and guards were patrolling to prevent shoplifting, so he bought a mace instead and went in search of armor.

Wearing new leather armor proudly, Nimsman stopped in at the pub for a couple of dust-cutters. The bartender was in a talkative mood, especially after getting a five-gold-piece tip. Nimsman made careful note of what he had said and moved on. He bought himself a horse and rode it out of town.

He headed next for the village of Le Jester down in Africa to stock up on rations. He smiled happily as he cantered along, idly swinging his mace with one hand and hoping to find an orc or three.

Several months passed, mostly long periods of boredom separated by moments of sheer terror when under a monster attack. Nimsman had used the eastern time door in Europe several times to visit England in 1990 A.D., paying tribute to Lord British and always feeling much stronger after his visits. He also hung around in Port Boniface. Like most seaports, the village was a good source of useful rumors.

His forays across Eurasia, North America, and South America in 1423 B.C. had brought him several helpful victories over monsters, and he had added more to this by venturing cautiously through a few time doors into other periods. As his gold supply and store of experience had grown, he bought better weapons and armor; now he carried a phazor and wore a reflective suit.

Even better, he had accumulated a clutch of interesting items from the monsters he had vanquished. These included torches, tools, wands, staffs, boots, cloaks, helms, blue tassels, ankhs, red gems, skull keys, more normal-looking keys, green gems, brass buttons, viewing gems, strange coins, green idols, and a couple of futuristic power sources called trilithiums.

Being smart, as wizards naturally are, Nimsman invoked the 'Q' spell after each new acquisition to make sure he would not lose it.

One thing bothered him during his trips to towns, villages, and castles. Various locked doors in towns and villages blocked him occasionally from getting to places he wanted to go. In castles he could see through the bars of windows into Lord British's armory, where there were racks upon racks of weapons and protective gear. All he had to do to lay his hands on them was get past the locked door. And in the castle prison, he could hear snatches of interesting-sounding conversations and noises of people and beings held behind locked doors. He'd wager there were some useful tips there if he could just get in.

He *had*—just *had*—to find a way to get into these places. He racked his brain, but no ready answer came.

Then one day, by accident, he found the answer. He was in the village of Port Boniface to restock on food. As he passed down the streets as usual, he felt a pickpocket steal something. He looked quickly and found that his single green idol was missing from his pack.

Nimsman didn't know yet just what green idols did, but he suspected they would be extremely useful later on, and he did not want to lose the only one he had. He had no idea of when he might find another, so he thumbed his phazor onto 'kill' and let the thief have the full force of the weapon. As he retrieved the small idol, he heard the pounding feet of the guards.

Without preamble, they hemmed him in against a wall and started swinging. Killing, even the wiping out of pickpockets, was against village ordinances and, like shoplifting, death was the penalty.

Nimsman was not so eager to cooperate. If he could win his way past the guards, by outfighting the one right in front of him, he could make a run for the village gate and escape. He turned his phazor on that guard and started firing.

It was a hard battle, but he managed to down one guard and made it out of the village. That was when he found he had a couple of keys.

Ah ha, he thought, it's natural that the guards of locked places would also be the custodians of keys to these same places. He reentered the village to find the guards had already forgotten him. He picked a fight with one near the edge of the village and, after winning, now had four keys.

He left the village, invoked the 'Q' spell and came back again.

"Pay your taxes," a forgetful guard snarled, and waved him on by.

Nimsman's first visit was to a locked room in the village restaurant. His key fit easily and opened the door, but stayed firmly in the lock. He now had only three keys. There turned out to be no worthwhile information in the room, unfortunately.

Well, how about the port itself? That too had a locked door in the gate, and over the fence he could glimpse three frigates docked there.

The key unlocked the door okay, but alarms went off. Several thieves attacked him, and he could hear the heavy boots of the guards clomping his way. He wiped out the thieves and jumped on the nearest frigate.

"Not so fast there, matey," a grinding voice said. It belonged to a sailor guarding the gangplank. "You're boardin' this scow withou' havin' th' proper authority."

The guards were thundering across the pier; there was no escape. Nimsman fumbled in his pack and started pulling out its contents.

The sailor just sneered until he glimpsed the blue tassel. Then he tugged his forelock. "Guess we're commandeered, matey."

"Set sail, *now*," Nimsman ordered. The ship glided quickly out into the harbor basin. "Open sea, set course for the coast of France," he added.

"Think we're havin' a problem, matey," the sailor said. He jumped overboard and started to swim back toward the pier.

Nimsman, unable to swim, could only watch in horror as three gigantic sea monsters bore down on the port side of the frigate. He took the helm and desperately sailed around and around the basin looking for an opening to the sea, but kept seeing only shore! The guards waited on the piers in overwhelming force. His only hope was to somehow blast his way through them, so he sailed to the dock and jumped off the frigate kicking.

He fought brilliantly and valiantly but soon went down into darkness and death.

Nimsman came back to awareness outside the village gate. It's true, he thought, restoration is a little confusing. He recalled hazily what would happen if he tried to steal a frigate in Port Boniface. So he decided not to do that again and retained his four keys to try in Lord British's palace nearby. He felt satisfied that if a frigate passed close to the coastline, he now had the authority to commandeer it and sail across the oceans wide.

Since he had built up a lot of hit points by now, Nimsman began venturing back into the interior of Legends occasionally. From the spot where the four time doors flashed in and out of existence he could walk up a narrow mountain valley and soon find all the combat anyone could ask for.

The first line of defense that he encountered was a large army of balrons, daemons, wizards, devils, and orcs. Nimsman didn't try to take them all out at once—that would have been suicide. Instead he would fight two or three, then escape through a time door, not to return until he had seen Lord British and replaced his hit points.

These battles were rough, not only due to the physical strength of his foes but also due to all the magic being thrown around. Wizards launched highly destructive magic missiles, balrons gloried in using their sleep spells, and occasionally he found his arms or his legs paralyzed.

Sometimes, under the influence of an immobilizing spell, he just stood there and let the monsters hack away, presumably to their little black hearts' delight. After a few minutes he would recover, so that he could get in several good licks before retreating. He tried a few of the spells he had collected by now but found them useless.

It was during this time that Nimsman begin to find out about some of the items he carried. The magical boots restored his arms and legs to working order, but disappeared into thin air in the process. The green idols helped him to stay fully alert at all times. Also, if he was about to be overwhelmed by several monsters, rubbing the strange coins could help him make a timely withdrawal.

Legends certainly offered the most intense combat of any place he had yet found. He knew it would take him quite a while to work his way inland, but at least the monsters he was killing in this initial army of

Minax's were not being replaced all that fast. So he figured he stood a good chance, over time, of wiping it out.

New San Antonio, Texas, North America, 1990 A.D. Well wahoo, partner, Nimsman thought as he entered. As he walked around, he noticed that it was a very colorful town, due to its interesting mix of Tex-Mex, medieval, and high tech culture. The sounds of both bards and country music singers wafted out of the taverns, and many of the people spoke with a pleasantly lilting Hispanic accent.

He spotted a few thieves around, so he kept close watch on his pack. He was not sure what such things as brass buttons and skull keys did, but he wanted to hang on to them until he found out.

After wandering around town talking to people, Nimsman finally came to the airport. Through the chain link fence he spied a plane on the runway, which looked all fueled up and just begging to be stolen. True, it was just a single-seater prop job with an open cockpit, but it seemed sufficient for his needs.

Security at the airport was moderately tight. There was a watchman inside, but he was just a fighter and not one of the hulking guards. However, Nimsman was positive the guards would come running to help the rent-a-cop in there if need be. There were also two locked doors between him and the plane.

Nimsman rubbed his chin thoughtfully as he considered. Surely by now he had all the items needed to fly a plane. Also, he felt certain he needed a plane to get further along in his mission. He knew that up the line in 2112 A.D., North America was empty (even New San Antonio was gone). Maybe there was something useful left over in Europe, but he had seen no frigates on the seas in that era, so a plane seemed to fill the bill.

Of course, first he had to get it.

He unlocked the two gates and was forced to leave his keys in them. The fighter yelled at him to halt and charged forward. Nimsman let the fighter have it with the phazor, but the guy was really tough and kept on coming. Alarms were going off, and he heard with a chill the thump of running guards.

"Ugh, me tough!" the fighter yelled, but howled in pain as he took another phazor burst.

The fighter got in a mighty blow to Nimsman's stomach. It hurt even through his reflective armor.

Still, the fighter was no match for Nimsman and his phazor, and finally succumbed. Yet, the duel had bought time for the guards. An especially mean-looking one had reached Nimsman and was flailing away with his sword at the left side of Nimsman's back.

Ignoring the pain, Nimsman hopped into the cockpit and looked helplessly at the instrument panel. There wasn't much there—an airspeed indicator, a turn and bank indicator, an engine RPM dial, and a rudimentary altimeter were the sum total of what he would have to deal with. He saw a label reading 'Start Engine,' with a bare spot beneath it and an adjacent keyhole.

Whap, *clang* went the sword of the guard against his helmet. Fighting off dizziness, he tried the keys he had taken from other guards, but they would not fit.

Ah, but he had another set of keys, didn't he? Nimsman put his pack on his lap and fumbled them out. A perfect fit!

"Pay your taxes!" the brutal-looking (and moronic) guard demanded, and hit him again.

Press the starter, press the starter, Nimsman was telling himself through a haze of pain. The button, press the button!

"There is no button!" he exclaimed.

Whack! Nimsman slumped forward from the force of the blow, spilling the items from his pack onto the floor of the cockpit. A glint of yellow caught his eye. Of course!

He put the item into place, pressed hard, and the engine of the little plane roared to life. Not waiting to give the guard another chance to land a blow, Nimsman gunned the engine and released the brakes.

The plane surged forward down the short runway. Uh-oh! It was heading straight for the high walls. There was no time to pull up and clear them.

"Oh, hell," Nimsman said, bracing for the crash, but just as the propeller touched the wall he was suddenly outside the town and the little engine was roaring lustily.

"Up, up, and away," Nimsman yelled giddily and aimed the plane into the sky.

Lack of sophisticated controls means lack of control. Nimsman found that he more or less aimed the plane instead of flying it. The craft was very fast, and the ground whizzed by below at an astounding rate.

A huge grass plain was coming up, so he quickly landed and got out of the aircraft to check things over. While he was outside, he invoked the 'Q' spell just for safety's sake.

Obviously, judging by the minimal landing gear, he could land only on grass. To try anywhere else such as forests, swamps, or mountains would be a sure way to crack up. Ah well, at least he had good transport now.

He taxied the plane through the nearest time door and experimented a little, buzzing around to the various eras. Flying turned out to be a great way to recon the continent of Legends, because he could fly over Minax's armies and find the exact location of her palace. Now he would be able to bypass a good many (or should he say, "a bad many"?) of her monsters on his way there.

But he wasn't quite ready for that. From tavern gossip, he knew that he needed a blessing from a certain Father whose son he had met in Lord British's chapel. That blessing, so the rumors went, would earn him what he needed to best Minax. The rub was that this Father Antos lived on some other planet. This adds new dimension to the term 'otherworldly' when applied to a cleric, Nimsman thought dryly as he banked the plane through the bumpy air and away from Minax's palace complex.

He headed back to the coast. He would taxi the plane though the door to 2112 A.D. and go find the good Father somehow.

As Nimsman approached the village of Pirate's Harbour in 2112 A.D., he could see signs of the great battles between nations that the evil enchantress Minax had set off years before. Shattered buildings had not been repaired, and there was still rubble piled haphazardly here and there.

The guards all called themselves 'KGB,' and looked just as mean and as large as guards anywhere. However, as Nimsman noted, there seemed to be a lot more of them.

As he searched the village and talked to people, Nimsman found two types of inhabitants: pirates and people who spoke reverently of the good old days in Moscow. He also saw two places of interest, both behind locked doors (naturally). The first was the Pirate's Club, where frigates were docked. Next to the club was a launch facility with not one but *three* spaceships.

Unfortunately, he couldn't just unlock the gate and walk into either place. The KGB station next to the launch facility was jam-packed with guards. Also, a pirate stood staunchly on guard just inside the entrance to the pirate's club.

It was a thorny problem. He was positive the KGB were there to guard the launch pad facility, and the moment he unlocked its gate they would swarm him! He was not sure what to do, but he was certain that he *had* to do something soon.

Maybe the pirate's club offered a better chance. He unlocked the door and went in fighting. He wasn't too surprised when he immediately heard the alarms go off in the KGB station.

The pirate was not much of an opponent. Nimsman later surmised that he was much more used to keelhauling enemies or making them walk the plank than to fighting on land. Nimsman went right through him and outran the guards to a frigate. He sailed around the harbor lagoon, firing the ship's cannon to fend off a couple of sea monsters and visiting an island, where he found some pirate weapons and armor. Fortunately, *this* harbor had an exit to the open sea, so he sailed out and left the frigate moored there for his future use.

He had noticed, as he was raising the sail and tacking out of the harbor, that the launch facility's frontage on the harbor was unguarded. This, then, would be his way to steal a rocket!

He went back into the village and found that the KGB now ignored him. The door to the Pirate's Club had been repaired, and a new pirate was on guard. No matter, Nimsman unlocked the door, took care of the pirate, and again managed to steal a ship just ahead of the vengeful KGB.

This time, after killing two sea monsters, he beached the ship at the launch facility and casually strolled over to the first rocket. Across an arm of the harbor, he could see the KGB gesturing futilely on the pier from which he had left.

Inside the spaceship, Nimsman opened his pack. His good luck ankh was on top, so he took it out and placed it on the control console. Down at the bottom of the pack were the heavy power sources he had been accumulating. These he removed and fed into the appropriate places. The control console lit up and he blasted off.

Orbiting Earth, he saw that the instruments of the spaceship were even simpler than those in the airplane: a button for engaging the hyperdrive, one for landing, and a set of three numbered wheels to enter coordinates. It was now reading '6-6-6,' obviously the coordinates of the nice place to return to that was called Earth.

Nimsman wasted no time. A philosopher he had met in his travels had told him the exact coordinates of the planet that Father Antos was on, so he set those three numbers. Engaging the hyperdrive, he was immediately on his way into deep space.

Landing the spaceship on Planet X was tricky, very tricky. It was a jarring landing but Nimsman managed to get down in one piece. To the north was a castle and to the south was a town.

Nimsman found the inhabitants of the planet to be very hostile and tricky. Thieves were especially virulent in Basko, and he had to fight his way out of town a couple of times.

A king and a queen ruled the castle Barataria. The king gave him hit points in return for tribute, just like Lord British would back on Earth. The queen seemed to know something about his mission, for she mentioned that Father Antos awaited him. (Being a king or queen is good clean indoor work with no heavy lifting, but openings are rare.)

This castle was not so open as that of Lord British. Burly guards prevented Nimsman from exploring beckoning hallways. He would have to find a way around them if he was to get anywhere.

Behind the thrones of the king and queen were two locked doors. His keys from Earth fit them (he assumed that the locks had all been mail-ordered from the same manufacturer). He entered a hallway that stretched away to the right and left. Exploring to the right, he found the king's bedchamber, which contained nothing of interest. A door in the king's chamber led to an extensive maze that ended up only wasting a lot of his time. All the exits from the maze were guarded except for the way he had originally entered.

Down the hall to the left side, however, was the queen's chamber, and beyond that, the prison. Nimsman passed through the prison carefully, because one of the inmates was pitching spells at him. Beyond was a courtyard graced by a pond, and after that, a chapel. He entered the chapel and finally found Father Antos!

"I give you my blessing," the father intoned, dashing a little holy water on his head. Nimsman thanked him, mindful of a previous conversation that had the ring of truth to it and did even more so now.

Nimsman felt triumphant on his way back to Earth. It was all over now except for the defeat of that diabolical dame Minax. He maximized his hit points with the help of Lord British, overflew a good deal of Minax's armies, and fought his way to a palace door. As he did so, a searing force field flickered across his path. Too bad there was no doorbell to ring. But he walked through the destructive energy field unscathed.

With satisfaction he heard the strange coins that he had been collecting clicking against each other in his pack. Nimsman was very intelligent, of course, as is required for wizards. He had correctly surmised that the very toughest and strongest of Minax's monsters would be those she retained to protect her person.

He knew it would be impossible for any single mortal to defeat the massed might of these select monsters, but he guessed that if he could render them ineffective long enough to get in his blows at Minax, he could eventually triumph.

Maybe.

The palace was huge and filled with many horrid displays. He passed a torture chamber and a morgue. He saw a room that had one of every type of transport available. Another large room had four time doors, but he could not gain entry. He suspected that this was the place from which Minax controlled time. Her death should solve a lot of problems.

There followed much terror, blood, and pain, as Minax's monsters brought him close to death often. Finally, fending off an attack of balrons with the strange coins, he cornered Minax in her primary chambers.

"Die, fool!" she screamed, launching a blast of magic missiles at him.

Nimsman got in a good hit, and she suddenly disappeared. He was dead certain she wouldn't give up the ghost *this* easily—she must be using her black arts to run from him.

The chase was on!

It was a long jog all the way across the palace to Minax's secondary chamber, and he had to contend with occasional monsters on the way, avoiding some and negating others. When he reached her, she looked very irked to see him. He negated the guards temporarily again, more than glad to see their frozen status as the time-stopping effect of the strange coins stopped all but those next to him. He got in another hit before she disappeared again.

Back once more he went to the primary chamber, negated the guards, struck at the leering Minax, and took a hit in return just before she faded out on him.

"This is more exercise than I bargained for," Nimsman said to himself, puffing, as he went all the way across the long palace and back to the secondary chamber.

Another negating of the balrons before they could get off sleep spells and another strike at Minax. Did she seem to be weakening? She almost knocked him off his feet with a counterblow, but did not stay around to pursue the advantage.

After a few more back and forths, Nimsman was out of strange coins and feeling very weak. He made a final desperate lunge at Minax, pushing his phazor into her stomach and holding down the firing button for all he was worth.

She struck out, screaming, and he almost passed out. One more blow from the evil enchantress and he would be defeated.

The balrons were stirring and coming forward. Any moment now, they would cast sleep spells.

His phazor spluttered and quit firing, its energy pack depleted.

"Too bad, fool," a weak but now triumphant Minax sneered. "You almost won. Now you die!"

Nimsman knew it was all over, but he still did not give up. With a quick flip, he reversed the heavy phazor in his hand and swung the butt of it as hard as he could onto Minax's skull.

She screamed, and her eyes rolled up, but she kept struggling. Nimsman felt a claw tearing into his left shoulder.

He struck again.

And again.

And raised the phazor to hit her another time, but it was unnecessary. Minax was dead. He had won! The evil castle walls were collapsing around them.

Thus passed the great Nimsman into glorious and victorious legend.

PART

4

Ultima III—Exodus

8 Offspring of an Unholy Union

You are not alone this time, adventurer. Three stalwart companions are to stand by your side and guard your back. This era is very different from the first two ages of darkness. This era, the time of Exodus or the Dawning of Darkness, as some historians have called it, is too complicated and too dangerous for a single adventurer to risk his or her life, even considering how expendable adventurers are. Land, seas, skies, all are disrupted. To find and eradicate the great evil responsible for the new devastation, to restore the planet to peace and productivity, Lord British is calling upon you and your party.

Background

For twenty years after the fall of the evil enchantress Minax, peace reigned in Sosaria. Lord British used the time wisely, continuing to build his empire and to improve the prosperity and well-being of his subjects.

A few, Lord British among them, realized that the all too short era of peace was coming to an end when a dreadful manuscript came to light, an evil, cryptic document bearing the mark of the dead enchantress.

The document was rambling and obscure in places, a product of the insanity of its authoress. Yet one horrible fact seemed certain: the relationship between apprentice and sorcerer had been more intimate than was previously thought. And that unholy alliance had borne fruit! Somewhere the hell-born progeny of Minax and Mondain lived and perhaps plotted to avenge its parents. As to where this demon-thing-child might be now, or what its appearance might be, there was no clue.

Disquieted by the document, Lord British was soon to notice other omens of trouble. Raids wiped out all outlying settlements; pirate fleets scoured the seas of commerce and raided the seaports. Many cried out that the end of the world had come. Comets flashed across the sky, and deep rumbles came from the ground as if the very earth were being tortured.

These rumbles, to the mystification and fear of all, continued for some days, and the seas grew high with waves. Later came a report from sailors who had, in midocean, seen an island born of fiery lava and created in a single day. The hellish heat and steam of the volcanic eruption kept all from approaching the island closely, but a few mariners claimed they had glimpsed a huge castle through the drifting mists of steam surrounding the island. Most people rejected this later intelligence as merely the imaginings of drunken sailors, but Lord British and his scribe made thoughtful notes when the reports came to their ears.

Finding the evil wizard enemy of Lord British and the entire world is not to be an easy task. The only clue was the word 'EXODUS' written in blood on a wall in an abandoned and undamaged merchant ship. Small help for you and your fellows, but you must save the world from the living death it is now suffering.

Your Characters

In your holy mission, as leader of this group of adventurers, you have increased responsibility. How you structure your party, the races and professions to which its members belong, and a host of other factors will determine whether the mission stands a chance of success, or whether the people you lead will leave their bleached, scattered, and shattered bones on the monster-ridden plains of Sosaria.

In general terms, you designate a party by choosing the race, sex, and profession of yourself and your three companions. Also you get fifty points to distribute among four attributes for each party member: strength, dexterity, intelligence, and wisdom.

There have been some minor changes in the races since the campaigns in the First and/or Second Ages of Darkness, and some major ones in the numbers and types of professions available to you. These changes necessitate a different strategy from those employed in previous missions.

First, race and sex.

Race and Sex

The races now are five, instead of the four present in the first two Ages. They are human, elf, dwarf, bobbit, and a never-before-seen race, fuzzy. Each race has a set of maximum limits on the various kinds of points it can possess, top values beyond which each characteristic cannot rise.

Humans are still the ruling class. They are of average ability in every quality. The maximum points for a human, as measured on the Adventurers Competence Scale (ACS), is 75 across the board in strength, dexterity, intelligence, and wisdom. They start out with fewer points.

Elves move quickly and are slight of build and very agile. Their natural abilities make them excellent thieves (although shoplifting is still dangerous). An elf tops out at 75 in strength, 75 in intelligence, and only 50 in wisdom, but can reach as high as 99 in dexterity.

Shorter than elves, but usually outweighing them because of their stocky build, are dwarves. They are strong and extremely courageous. They can attain 99 in strength, 75 each in dexterity and wisdom, but only 50 in intelligence. Dwarfs are dumb but faithful.

The bobbits have come back. The bobbits of the First Age evolved into hobbits, but have now returned to bobbits. They are still a small and gentle race, shorter than dwarves and not nearly so strong. Bobbits have more innate wisdom than other races; this quality can go as high as 99. Their strength and intelligence maximums are 75, and dexterity, never rises above 50. The devolutionary return to bobbits did them good in one respect; they now undertake adventures more gladly and are often a worthy addition to any party.

Fuzzies are the new race. Fuzzies are about the same height as bobbits, but totally covered in a soft, fluffy fur (hence their name). Fuzzies are very weak, and no member of that race rises above 25 strength points. However they make up for that lack by having the capacity to achieve 99 in *both* dexterity and intelligence, and they can attain a respectable 75 in wisdom. Obviously, because they combine high dexterity with intelligence, fuzzies are even better thieves than elves! They also make very decent wizards.

As for choosing the sex of your characters, males usually have an edge in strength, while females are more dexterous. In addition to these two choices, you may now choose to have a character whose sex is 'Other.' Little is known about this sex as yet.

Since you now have the luxury of four members in your party, as opposed to having to go it alone as did those hardy veterans of the first two Ages of Darkness, it is not necessary to compromise and select human. You can include members of various races for the marked advantages each can offer and to fit your overall strategy.

Profession

There are a total of eleven professions now, instead of only four as in the first two Ages of Darkness. I recommend the classic callings of fighter, wizard (also known as mage), cleric, and thief, but there are also paladins, barbarians, larks, illusionists, druids, alchemists, and rangers.

The new professions allow you to create character classes previously unavailable. Druids, for example, know and use both mage and cleric spells and regain magic (which gets drained) faster than any other profession. Paladins are warriors who can cast cleric spells. Barbarians are fighters that also have some ability as thieves. Rangers are fighters who can cast both mage and cleric spells.

A lark can use magic, illusionists have the power of clerics, and alchemists are casters of wizardly spells. These are interesting professions, but somewhat less desirable than those mentioned above. Only fighters and barbarians have no magic abilities at all.

You might think that choosing a ranger or druid for your party would free up the slots of cleric and wizard, since he or she (or it) would be able to perform all three functions—fighter, cleric, and wizard. However, there is an important drawback. Only the pure wizard or cleric can ever advance in ability to the point of being able to cast the highest level, and therefore most potent, spells in each category. The party makeup already suggested remains the best compromise.

Each profession has limitations on its weapons and armor. Fighters, paladins, barbarians, and larks can use any weapon. Clerics, illusionists, and druids are restricted to maces. Wizards and alchemists are able only to wield daggers. Thieves and rangers use swords, although the ranger's sword needs to be a +2 model. (Rangers do not have to use a sword, however.) All character classes can use exotic weapons.

Only fighters can wear all types of armor. Wizards, larks, druids, and alchemists are limited to cloth. Clerics can wear cloth, leather, or chain mail. Thieves, barbarians, and illusionists are restricted to leather or cloth. Paladins can wear all of the above plus plate mail. Rangers can wear all of the above and may also purchase magical armor (up to +2 plate). Fighters can wear magical armor up to +4 plate.

You'll use much more magic in this campaign and many fewer hack and slash tactics than you did in your two earlier campaigns. Magic works in many more places—not just in dungeons—and many more spells are available to you.

Therefore, at least two of your party should be magic users. In fact, it's wisest to have both a wizard and a cleric because they each use different spells. A little later in this briefing we'll give you the fundamental spells that are of great utility to wizards and clerics.

Be warned, though, that there is a point beyond which the multiclassed character cannot advance, and only the "pure" mage or cleric will ever be able to cast the highest-level, and therefore most potent, spells.

A good initial party would have an elf thief, a bobbit cleric, a fuzzy wizard, and a dwarf fighter. Elves are dexterous enough to be thieves and, although a fuzzy may be a better overall thief, elves are also strong enough to fight. In the early going, your party will be fighting more than shoplifting.

Bobbits, being more wise than the other races, excel as clerics, and fuzzies have the intelligence to be good wizards. Dwarves are the strongest of all and are fantastic fighters—they will just stand there and bang away fearlessly at whatever you order them to attack.

The order of march is important. Your two fighting members, the dwarf and elf, should be up front in any encounter. The two magic users, the bobbit and fuzzy, can hang back in the second rank, lobbing in fire on the enemy.

Running a group combat is a little confusing at first, so give your troops names easy for you to remember. Their having names as well as numbers enables you to issue orders as quickly as possible. This can sometimes mean the difference between life and death.

Group Strategy

Having more than one character means employing a more sophisticated and complex approach, in which you need to coordinate the various members of the group and to distribute all resources to the maximum benefit of the team as a whole. Here are some general principles.

Each person in the party has 150 hit points and is level one at the start of the mission. Hit points are tied directly to experience now. Every time someone slays a monster, his experience points go up. Unfortunately, only the one striking the actual killing blow or spell in combat gets the additional experience points, so try to spread the wealth around. If a monster is tottering, let your wizard or cleric finish it off to earn some points. The rule of thumb is, the tougher the monster, the more experience points you earn by killing it. (Of course, the greater the chance it will kill some of your party instead!)

Still, you can't do it all with just magic. Using magic drains magic points temporarily. When you're completely drained, you can't cast any more spells until you build your points back up again with the passage of time. Thus, the old hack and slash style of fighting with physical weapons remains the mainstay of combat. Use your magic to soften up your opponents, and send the fighters in to take and hold the ground.

The Lay of the Land

The cataclysmic events concurrent with the fall of Minax had fused the land masses of Sosaria into one large continent with a few islands off the coast. In another important change from the previous Age, moon gates have replaced time doors.

Moon Gates

Get to know the moon gates. Unlike the time doors in the Second Age of Darkness, moon gates only transport you (and your horses) to a different place. You can't reach these places by any other means and most often they are sources of important ancient knowledge. (Some moon gates are static, meaning they don't go anywhere.)

There are eight moon gates in all. One is far more important than the others since it transports your group to the dungeon of the mysterious Time Lord, who is of great help in your mission.

The coming and going of moon gates is linked to the phases of the twin moons Trammel and Felucca. The phases appear on the map that came in your adventurer's kit. Understanding these will help you predict when moon gates appear and disappear. (Also, you need to keep track of the moons' phases in your search for the City of Dawn.)

Numbers represent the phases of the moon. There are eight phases (0-7) for each. Zero to three stand for new moon to gibbous waxing, and four to seven for full moon to crescent waning. The moons aren't always in the same phase. The combination of both moon's phases is expressed as a two digit number.

For example, if the first moon was a new moon (0) and the second moon was a full moon (4), the phases of the moons would be '04.'

Here are the eight moon gates and their destinations:

Castle of Death	To the Time Lord's Dungeon (57)
	To North of the City of Moon (50)
	To the dungeon island (51)
Dungeon Island	To the south coast (13)
	To the south gate (14)
	To the Castle of Death (15)
East of Devil Guard	To the north gate (62)
	To southwest of the twin cities (63)
	To the south gate (64)
North of Moon	To the dungeon island (01)
	To the north gate (02)
North Gate	To Devil Guard (26)
	To the Time Lord's Dungeon (27)
	North of the City of Moon (20)
South Gate	To the Castle of Death (45)
	To Devil Guard (46)
Southwest of Twin Cities	To the dungeon island (31)
	To the north gate (32)
Time Lord's Dungeon	To the Castle of Death (75)
	To Devil Guard (76)

North Gate and South Gate are each located in a mountain dead end, and the only way in or out is by moon gate.

Your Resources

No matter the characteristics and identity of your party and no matter how well they know how to get around on the planet, it's a certainty you'll need to use every bit of help you possibly can to build up your points, cash, information, and necessary items. Nearly every part of Sosaria provides both traps as well as help; next you'll be briefed on the important resources available to you, as well as the critical dangers and challenges facing you.

Towns

There are ten cities on the continent during this period of Sosarian history, and you need to visit all ten:

City of Dawn	Dawn is a hard place to find. It exists only briefly in the forest to the southwest of the City of Lord British, but you definitely need to seek this city out. Remember to look for Dawn only during the proper phase of the moon; otherwise you will look in vain. It has the usual shops for food, weapons, and armor, and a cozy pub. Fine horses are in the stables. An oracle and a thieves guild also do business. The unique aspect of the shops of Dawn is the merchandise. You will want to bring many thousands of gold pieces to buy the advanced and exotic weapons and armor available here. Seek out the clerics in the southeast corner of town—they can explain much about these arms. Bribe the guards well, for you may have trouble with two of the clerics.

City of Fawn

This city is on an island off the coast to the northeast of the City of Lord British. There is a food shop, a healing kiosk, a tavern, and a thieves guild. You will want to find four clerics because they have significant clues.

City of Grey

Located to the south of the City of Moon, on the southwestern tip of Sosaria, this town has, besides the usual things to be found in town, a room with some interesting chests. Three people you definitely want to find and talk to are a thief, a fighter, and a cleric.

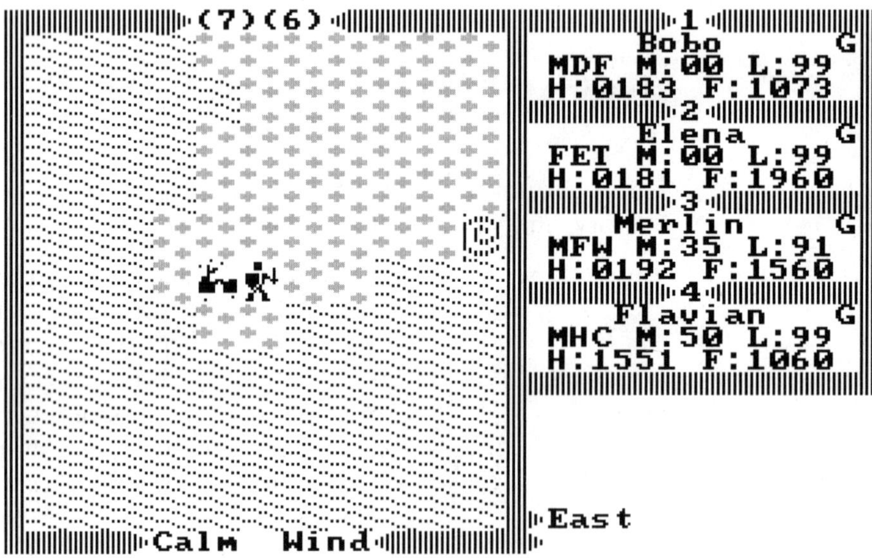

Figure 8.1 *Your party approaches the city of Grey. The Thieves Guild here is a source of four very important consumable items.*

City of Lord British

In the northeast of Sosaria, this city is located next to a fine harbor. There are normal shops, but be sure to talk with everyone who will stop and converse. This town is the easiest to escape from after unsuccesful stealing attempts because you can exit to most directions, not just the way you entered.

City of Moon	This small town southeast of Montor East has the usual shops and a healing kiosk. Search the woods in town for clues. Watch out for balrons!
City of Yew	A mountainous holy city to the west of the City of Lord British. It has an abundance of clerics. Watch out for the wall of fire while you're exploring the forest inside this town.
Death Gulch	Located on a large island southeast of the City of Lord British, Death Gulch lives up to its name. You will need lots of keys. There are a number of force fields and mazes and a rather nasty river of fire. No really great clues, but lots of chests to be had.
Devil Guard	This town is totally hemmed in by mountains, and you can only reach it through moon gates. Talk with six fighters and a thief. The latter can provide you with a clue that might very well assure the success of your mission. Don't try to steal horses here; you can only buy them.
Montor East	Montor East and West are twin towns to the south of the City of Lord British. The eastern city contains several valuable clues that various individuals will impart to your party.
Montor West	In the western city there are two thieves in the prison with whom you will want to have a chat. Bribe the guards first, or you'll have a fight on your hands.

Castles

During the Third Age of Darkness, there were only two castles in the whole of Sosaria.

The first is Lord British's castle, and you will visit it often to talk with Lord British and to buy cures and healings. You need to thoroughly explore the castle, taking along plenty of keys, and talk to everyone you find. The other palace is where Exodus lives. More on that later.

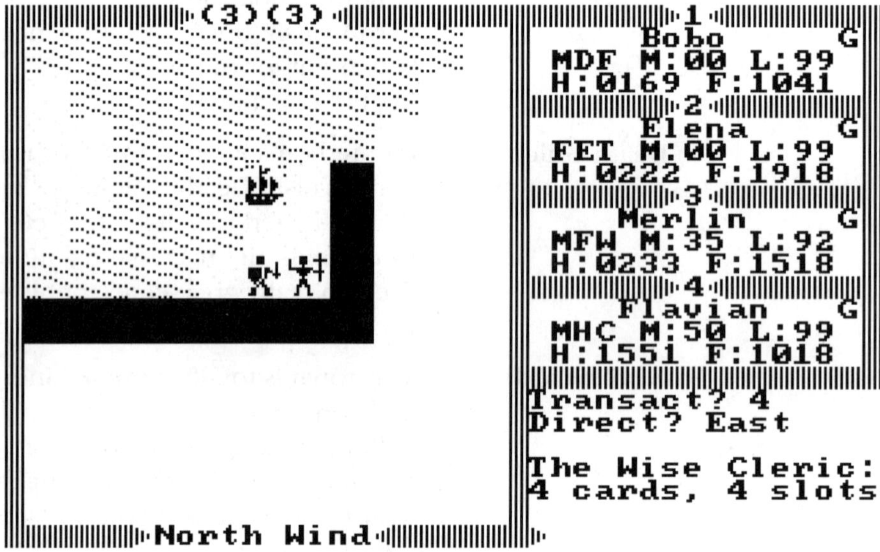

Figure 8.2 *Thoroughly explore Lord British's castle. Take the boat in the moat around to talk to the cleric on the little isolated hunk of land against the walls. He has some very good advice for you.*

Arms

Weapons are important. Some are *very* expensive. You can get and use everything from a cheap dagger (which is virtually worthless except for cleaning your fingernails) through a +4 bow (which costs 6,550 gold pieces) to some mysterious but highly desirable "exotics."

Even slings in the hands of a strong fighter can be delightfully lethal, and bows are fantastic. Long-range weapons make a tremendous difference in your party's fighting effectiveness, and therefore in their chances for survival.

Figure 8.3 *Your party engages in combat with a group of trolls.*

Armor

Armor ranges from cloth to +2 plate, which sells for a hefty 8,250 gold pieces but is well worth it. Only certain professions can wear the higher classes of armor, but get the best armor you can for everyone. The better protected a party member is, the longer he, she, or it will survive, and the longer they survive, the more experienced they become.

One method suggested by some tactical authorities as a way to raise your group's experience points rapidly, involves battling guards in a town. Don't try this until everyone is level five, but then find a town with only two sets of guards at the entrance. Attack and kill them, then leave the town and invoke the 'Q' spell. Repeat this process as many times as you like since you can immediately reenter the town to find the guards already replaced. Guards are powerful but do not throw fireballs or poison bolts. Each guard killed gives the party member dispatching him fifteen experience points.

Also, until you have long-range weapons, avoid thieves, brigands, and cutpurses. These villains will rob you blind if they get close. Once you have slings or bows, just stand back and let them have it.

The general rule of thumb is the tougher the monster, the more experience points that will be gained by killing it. Also, the greater the chance that it will kill some of your party instead.

Be careful.

Transportation

One thing you don't need this time around is skill in piloting and space navigation. No aircraft or space vessels are even available during this mission.

There are still horses, of course. You may buy horses in the City of Devil Guard and buy or steal them in the City of Dawn. Mount your party on horses so they can travel faster and use less food. Often, a weakened and wounded group of adventures on horseback can outrun monsters and thus live to fight another day.

A few frigates, manned by pirates, sail the seas. If you can get on board one and if your party defeats the pirates, then the ship becomes yours. Using a frigate does require more seamanship in this period than was necessary in earlier times. The vessels are all wind-powered, and you cannot sail against the wind, so the direction of the wind is very important. Keep a weather eye on wind direction, for it is most fickle and can change in an instant, with disastrous results if you aren't prepared.

Use a frigate to explore various important islands. Enter the mighty ocean whirlpool, which moves here and there across the waters. This powerful swirl of currents destroys docked and empty ships, but sail your ship into the whirlpool and it will be transported to the Lost Continent of Ambrosia. You have to go here to meditate at the four shrines to strengthen various aspects of your character and to retrieve four important items.

Money and Sundry Items

Money is something you need a lot of. Your overhead is high. There are constant expenditures for food and healing and for upgrading weapons and armor. Also, there are four items that you will need to keep good supplies of—torches, keys, gems, and powders.

Dungeons are dark and swept by strange winds that sometimes blow out torches. You need lots of torches to explore dungeons.

Keys, not unsurprisingly, are used to unlock doors. Look behind all the locked doors in the City of Montor West, Ambrosia, and most certainly in Lord British's Castle.

Gems are exceptionally useful. They show you a bird's eye view of where you are at the moment. This is the easy way to map dungeons, explore those hidden places in cities, and navigate through mazes. Buy lots of gems and use them often.

Powders are available only in thieves guilds. Whenever you find one in a city, stock up. Taking a powder can often relieve pain. That is, by stopping time in places more than one square away from your position, they can keep too much pain from being inflicted on your group during hot battles. You'll want to have some handy while exploring the Castle of Death also.

Magic

Magic is a tremendous aid. Hence, the importance of having a wizard and a cleric in your party and of knowing when to have these worthies unleash their power. For example, your wizard's Repond spell usually can wipe out monsters such as trolls, orcs, and goblins. A cleric's Pontori spell is excellent for turning away undead creatures like zombies, ghouls, and skeletons.

With experience, wizards and clerics develop their potential. As this potential increases, they will be able to cast various spells that perform helpful tasks such as Transport, Light, Heal, Cure, Map, and Resurrect. Their offensive spells include Wound, Negate Time, and Destroy.

Healing

War is not all glory; it is often pain and blood. *Your* pain and your blood, or at least that of someone in your party.

Fighting in Sosaria, I can guarantee you, is very bloody and dangerous. The members of your party will often suffer wounds, and even death. So provide for the medical necessities—and do so long before you need them. Troops fight harder when they know care is waiting in case bad luck befalls them and the blade of an enemy slips through their defenses.

Also, poisoning is a danger. Should one or more of your people be poisoned in some manner, he will waste away until receiving a healing antidote.

Clerics and more advanced wizards can administer first aid in the field. Even deceased party members can be resurrected to fight again. Unfortunately, the healing process drains magic points heavily, and, after a serious encounter, the wounds may be so severe that healing on the battle site is out of the question.

Luckily, many towns and Lord British's castle feature healing kiosks where, for gold coins, healers cure your wounded, remove the effects of poison, and resurrect those killed in action.

Spell points recover fastest on the surface. Do most of your healing there.

One other source of healing exists. Certain fountains in dungeons have healing properties, and a wounded adventurer has but to drink from one of these to have all the party's hit points restored. Unfortunately, some fountains are poisonous rather than beneficial, while others merely alleviate thirst and have no other properties. The only way to tell which is which is by drinking from the fountain. Exercise care and, as always, invoke the 'Q' or 'Save' spell before entering a dungeon.

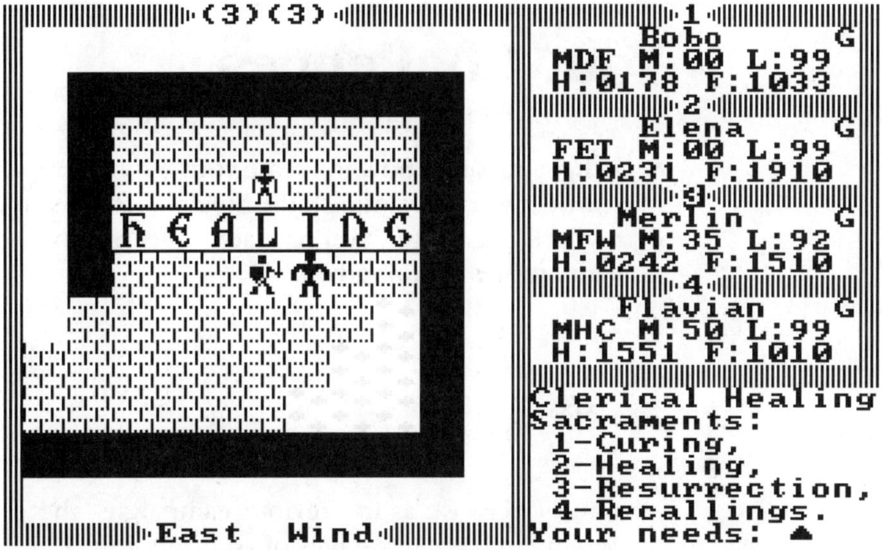

Figure 8.4 *The healing facility in Lord British's castle. You'll need a key to get into it.*

People

The people of Sosaria during the Third Age of Darkness are somewhat more varied also. In Lord British's castle and the several towns you'll find guards, merchants, jesters, healers, oracles, and bartenders. Also, there will be people of the adventurer professions such as fighters, clerics, wizards, and thieves.

As in the previous two adventures, transact with everyone you meet to get many valuable clues. Also, explore towns completely. There are numerous individuals with important data in wooded areas, behind shops, and behind locked doors.

Find and talk to everyone— that's the general rule of success.

Your Challenges

Now that you know how to create your team members, how to acquire what is necessary to vanquish the horrible Exodus, and a good bit about what you'll encounter, you're ready to learn more specifics about the difficult entities awaiting you.

Foes

First and foremost, as in previous campaigns, there is a lot of combat happening in the early stages of your mission.

As to enemies, there are lots of them, and they now usually attack you in groups. You'll find over two dozen species of monsters, plus various renegade fighters, thieves, clerics, paladins, rangers, wizards, and so forth. In the countryside, on the sea, and in the dungeons, constant attacks keep your party always hopping, and sometimes hopping mad.

Until your group has lots of experience points, there are many opponents you will want to avoid by moving away when they come into sight. Sea serpents, men-o-war, and pirates are a few that are just too strong for the inexperienced party. Also stay above level five in dungeons. Below that are wyverns, manes, devils, and other who will roll over your party like a poker through cream cheese. Once the group is experienced, however, defeating these monsters is a source of many thousands of experience points and gold pieces.

Dungeons

In the First Age of Darkness, adventurers had to visit dungeons in order to increase their finances and to fulfill those gems of quests from the various kings. During the Second Age of Darkness, dungeons were much less important—in fact, you could easily accomplish the mission without ever setting foot in one. Now, however, dungeons have taken on much more importance than they had even in the First Age. They are a resource as well as a danger.

The only way you can complete your mission is to explore all the dungeons. You need certain marks to progress, and these marks usually exist in a wall on the eighth level of dungeons, but sometimes higher also. For example, a character must have the Mark of Kings before Lord British will deign to increase his or her points above 2550. The Mark of Fire lets your party stroll coolly through fires. The Mark of the Snake is necessary to bypass the Silver Snake guarding the entrance to the Castle of Death, and the Mark of Force allows passage through force fields.

Use the same strategy you employed in the two previous missions to retrieve marks. Purchase plenty of Ladder Down and Ladder Up spells. Proceed to the desired level, get what you came for, and get back out as quickly as possible by using the Ladder Up spells in quick sequence. Alternatively, you could use gems to quickly map each level, then dash to the ladders. Whatever you do, do not tarry in dungeons—even if your party is as strong is possible, you will eventually be overwhelmed.

You will want to fully explore dungeons, but do that carefully, one stage at a time. Map thoroughly and only venture down when your party is up to its full potential, that is, when it has no badly wounded members.

Dungeons are very, very dangerous places, inhabited by a multitude of malevolent creatures. Traps, strange winds, poisoned fountains, gremlins, mazes, and dead ends plague the exploring party. They are decidedly nasty places, yet part of your job description as an adventurer is to search such territories of terror.

There are a total of seven dungeons in Sosaria:

Dardin's Pit	This dungeon lies to the northeast of the City of Lord British. A kingly reward is rumored to lie in two locations on level eight—the King's Mark, in fact.
Fires of Hell	Aptly named because it is surrounded by fire, this dungeon is in the mountains southeast of the City of Lord British. The Mark of Force and the Mark of Fire are on level eight, as are four fountains.

Doom	To the southwest of the City of Lord British, in a deep and dark forest, is the Dungeon of Doom. The Mark of Force is to be found there, and fountains of each type as well.
Mines of Morinia	To the north of the City of Grey, near the coast, are the mines. You can find the Mark of Kings on levels three and eight, and the Mark of Fire on eight also. Be ready to cast lots of transport and ladder spells to this dungeon because it is a bear to get around in.
Perinian Depths	Northeast of the City of Lord British is yet another dangerous dungeon. This one has the tremendous advantage of not one but two Marks of Kings on the first level, which even a weak party might win. The Mark of Fire is on level eight, as is a healing fountain.
Snake	This dungeon is on an island off the southeast coast of Sosaria. Be sure to thoroughly search levels two and three for clues. Level six has two healing fountains, and there is one on level seven also. Level eight hides the Mark of Kings and the Mark of the Snake.
Time	This very important dungeon is totally surrounded by impenetrable mountains. Your only method of access is to use a moon gate. Healing fountains are to be found on levels one (two of them), four, and eight. Be sure to converse with the Time Lord who lives on level eight.

Your Strategy

Your basic strategy in this adventure is similar to that of the first two missions: increase strength and all your other resources while searching and exploring to procure the items and information you need, and at last, venture forth to "X" out Exodus!

The First Stage

Your party of adventurers is injected stark naked onto the plains of Sosaria. In a party of mixed sexes, this always causes some minor embarrassment as everyone quickly dons their cloth armor and readies their daggers. Be sure each member of the party does these two things, because walking around Sosaria naked is not only unseemly, it is downright fatal.

Immediately look for a town. All four members of the party have sizable purses of gold. Use the gold to buy the best weapons and armor you can afford that are appropriate for the individual being outfitted. Be sure to get lots of daggers for your cleric and wizard. Consult again the earlier portion of this briefing on what types of armor and weapons each profession can wear and wield. You don't need to worry too much, however, about buying the wrong type of armor or weapons because any merchant who sells a given type will also buy it back.

Be sure to save money to buy food with, and do so. The towns are far apart and starvation will quickly overtake an improperly provisioned party. Don't forget to talk to bartenders and oracles; tip bartenders varying amounts and you will get differing bits of information.

Your party always gets to strike the first blow, and thus is very fast on the trigger; you should obtain bows or other long-range weapons as soon as possible to take advantage of this fact. Spell casters can use only one ranged weapon: the dagger. Buy as many as you can afford, and throw them at all targets. Once you ready the daggers, you can throw all of them until you exhaust your supply (which has a maximum of 99). Don't waste money on slings; anyone who can use a sling can also use a bow.

If you have any opportunity at all to steal a pirate ship, chase it down and grab it! These are very hard to come by.

Use the 'Q' spell frequently, and certainly after each significant victory or other achievement. If you have done so and the party is wiped out later, you can start again from the last place you invoked the 'Q' spell, thus saving you much retracing of steps. Bear in mind that the whole party must be wiped out. If a single member is left, the deaths of the others are recorded on your save disk, and you'll have to get them resurrected.

The Second Stage

Slowly branch out as your confidence and strength grows, visiting the cities and other places described earlier in this briefing, gathering clues and the necessary items you will need for the final victory.

Until your people pass level five, they can get additional hit points from Lord British. However, at that plateau, he refuses and tells you to "Seek ye the Mark of Kings." There are four of these marks, as explained earlier. When your party has one, Lord British raises the hit point limit of each member of the group according to experience level, with the absolute maximum being 2550.

This is a very complex mission compared to the first two Ages of Darkness. You will need to spend a lot of time acquiring what is needed. Don't rush the final confrontation.

The Submerged Continent

The only way to assure defeating Exodus includes a visit to the lost continent of Ambrosia. You get there by sailing into a whirlpool.

Points of interest in Ambrosia are four shrines: Dexterity, Wisdom, Intelligence, and Strength. These are located, respectively, to the southeast, northeast, northwest, and southwest.

Be sure to have a copious supply of gems and several keys. There are many mazes that would be confusing otherwise, and some doors that you need to enter. Also, as is generally true in this money-hungry age, you should have plenty of gold.

You will need to take two more frigates from pirates, since you can reach two of the shrines only by water. After you've visited all four shrines, you can return to Sosaria by sailing into the whirlpool again. Be very careful all the time you are in Ambrosia, since the 'Q' spell cannot be invoked here.

The Final Stage

There comes a time when your intrepid group girds itself for the last great battle and journeys to the Castle of Death to confront Exodus.

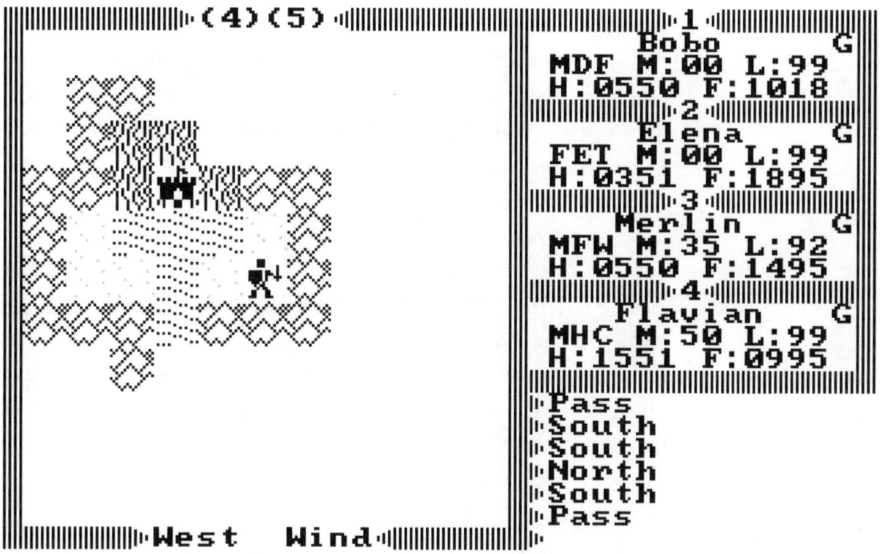

Figure 8.5 *Exodus hides out in the Castle of Death, which can only be reached via moon gate or boat. Don't go here until you have the utmost in weapons and hit points.*

In the Castle of Death lives Exodus. You'll find it on an island southwest of Sosaria. To get to the castle, you must sail past the Silver Snake. It is rumored that Exodus's headquarters is against the northern wall of his castle. Do not even think of trying to enter here until you have followed all the clues, found what needs finding, and built your party up to an awesome strength. And, even then, the final battle will be a tossup.

Exodus has an army of hellish monsters plus a continuous stream of fireballs for protection. The monsters are extremely hardy, and only the exotic arms dug up from the uninhabited islands have any effect against them.

Even the very floors of the Castle of Death will fight you! These weird, invisible floors keep attacking and attacking until they are completely destroyed. One suggested strategy to deal with them is to have your cleric cast an 'O' spell followed by a 'P' spell from your wizard. Then advance step by step while attacking in all directions. It's not easy, but in this manner you can overcome the floors. And don't hang around outside too long, or you'll have to fight the grass in the same way.

Exodus, you will find, is a thing—more of a machine than a monster. Its evil powers are mighty, but victory is in the cards if you insert them in the proper order.

In fact, after the horrible battles it takes to get to Exodus, you can perform the final dispatch rather placidly. Still, victory is most satisfying as you triumph for Lord British and save the world from the evil fate that Exodus had attempted to impose on it.

Although this briefing surely has helped you, nothing can substitute for the words of one who has actually been there. Therefore, read the next scroll, which bears the tale of the cleric Flavian the Good. Pay close attention to the valuable information that the scroll of this noble hero provides.

9 Flavian the Good, Cleric and Hero

Flavian looked around and shuddered. They stood on a slimy wharf before the Castle of Death. A dank, fetid wind moaned out of its entrance as if the lost souls of some adventurers were clawing an agonized, incorporeal way out into the sunlight again from their final torture. Scattered bones lay on the floor inside next to some bloodstains. Further back in the darkness were a multitude of eyes fiercely glowing red. Flavian the cleric could hear claws scratching on stone back there too.

"Is safe to go in?" Bobo the dwarf asked.

Elena rolled her eyes in exasperation and sighed. Bobo was a fearless fighter and had been a boon companion to them all during the long campaign to reach this destination, yet, like most dwarfs, his intelligence was not outstanding. She shook her head, smiling at the short, squat fighter. It was hard not to like Bobo.

Merlin, the small wizard of the fuzzy race, chuckled merrily and checked his belt pouch once more, undoubtedly to make sure that the all-important cards were still safely there. He gave Bobo a thumbs-up signal and Flavian nodded in satisfaction.

Flavian grinned down at the dwarf.

"Of course it's not safe, Bobo, but when has that ever stopped us?"

Bobo nodded. Apparently all he needed was confirmation that he was to fight. "Bobo fight hard," he said, flourishing the exotic weapon they had found for him a few weeks before.

Flavian gave him a gentle punch on the shoulder in acknowledgment, smiled reassuringly at the other two, and peered further into the castle. Daemons, balrons, huge guards, evils not imagined as of yet—all these things were in there waiting for them. They had survived many chilling dangers so far in their quest to rid the planet of the evils that festered on it, but could they survive this final peril, much less triumph over the enemy lurking inside?

He took a deep breath and cast one last lingering look out over the lake in front of the castle. This might very well be the last time he would ever see sunlight. Far across the lake there was a glint of reflected light as the huge silver snake which guarded the exit to the sea stirred restlessly.

Flavian turned back to the Castle of Death.

"Well, who wants to live forever?" he said, "Let's go get it over with."

The others followed behind him as they started into the castle's depths. They readied their weapons while the monsters inside screeched and whined with eagerness to taste their life's blood.

It had all started months before when four novice adventurers, scared out of their wits, had materialized naked on the plains of Sosaria. That this would be and why had been well explained at the Adventurers Academy but, because of his clerical background, Flavian was the most embarrassed.

Elena was the first to don one of the four coveralls that had appeared beside them and to pick up one of the four daggers. She hefted it experimentally and smiled her satisfaction while the others also dressed and did the same. The only other item was a standard adventurer's pack for each. Inside were 150 food rations and 150 gold pieces.

Of the four, Merlin was by far the least embarrassed. Since he was totally covered by soft fur, it hardly mattered whether he had clothes or not.

"What fun!" Merlin said. "That was some ride, eh?"

"Bobo not like much," Bobo said, kicking at the grass. Discomforts he did not understand always made him slightly irritable back at the Academy.

"They need to work on that transfer process," Flavian contributed, while warily scanning the horizon for enemies. "Looks like we could at least arrive fully clothed."

Elena giggled. "Don't you remember the physics of it? We're lucky they had enough power left to send our clothes and daggers right behind us, or we'd be running around Sosaria fighting monsters in our birthday suits."

"Yuck," Bobo said, chewing on a food ration taken from his pack. "Food ration as bad as Academy cafeteria." But he kept on eating.

Flavian noticed that he, too, was hungry. Ravenously so, in fact. He took out food rations. The other two did likewise.

Flavian decided that it was time to assert his role. Before they had left for the mission, his group had elected him leader. He wasn't certain of the reason, although he had emerged from his circle of friends as the most studious and had helped them all get through the class work, as they had helped him to master weapons, fighting techniques, and magic—the things they individually excelled at."OK," said Flavian, "the first order of business is to restock on food and to see if we can get some better weapons. Let's find a town before orcs or skeletons find us."

"Turn around," Elena said.

Flavian grinned as he saw a town and a castle at the bottom of the long, gentle slope they were on. "OK, that was fast."

"That's the town of Britain and Lord British's castle," Merlin said, confirming what Flavian remembered from the briefing sketches. Flavian derived some comfort from the fact that their starting point was so close to the benevolent monarch who had in effect called them to this land. He also was aware that Lord British would provide aid to them in more material ways as they prepared to face the destroyer and disrupter of the planet.

"Tavern," Bobo said. "Bobo buy all drink."

"We have to get there first," Flavian said. Conscious of the need to continue to assert his leadership, he added, "Bobo takes the point, since he's the fighter and the strongest. Elena, you're a good fighter, too, even though you are primarily a thief—you go second. It doesn't matter whether Merlin or I take the third slot, but we'll let Merlin do it and I'll guard the rear." He hoped they would notice he was taking a slightly more dangerous spot than Merlin.

They started walking. Flavian's mind wandered back to his childhood. He was unusual among the many adventurers who had answered Lord British's call in that he was actually a native Sosarian. He had been raised in the town of Yew in the peaceful period before the troubles now besetting the realm.

His father and mother were both clerics, and Flavian spent long, placid years in the study that had made him also a cleric. He had reached young manhood and his life seemed ordained to be spent quietly among the sacred groves of Yew, but then came the Troubles.

His mother and father were caught outside the town by a roving band of balrons and were killed. Flavian had been beside himself with grief, unable to continue his duties as a cleric for weeks. But he had come to terms with his great loss, turning it from self-pity into a burning determination to fight the evil that now stalked this once-fair land.

He had communicated this desire to his superiors in the Order. After much discussion, during which it became evident that his commitment was genuine, the clerical Order sent a petition to Lord British requesting that Flavian's service be accepted in the fight against the diabolical menace tearing apart Sosaria.

Soon thereafter, a weary, travel-stained wizard arrived in Yew. He told Flavian that the young cleric was now in the service of his emperor. Before Flavian could reply, he cast a shimmering powder into the air.

Flavian smiled as he walked, remembering that his next sight had been of the dusty surface of the parade ground of the Adventurers Academy as he had stumbled into existence there. When he looked up, he saw the rough face of a huge drill sergeant close to his own.

"Cadet, that is the absolute WORST materialization I've even seen! Drop and give me fifty pushups. NOW!"

Suddenly the walls of the town loomed before him. They were just outside the town now. Flavian pulled his attention back to reality. His four years at the academy were over. Classroom work and theory were finished. It was live or die time.

Bobo was already entering the town, grinning at the guards.

"We'll go into town first," Flavian said, ignoring Elena's snicker and Merlin's chuckle. He knew that most of his leadership would have to be earned and now was not the time to make anything out of Bobo running off ahead.

"Good day," one of the guards said, eying them stonily. "You break even the smallest rule, adventurers, and we'll chop you to bits."

Elena winked at Flavian while flexing her limber fingers.

"Just be very careful," Flavian whispered to her.

Naturally, they found Bobo in the tavern. He was sitting at a table drinking from a frosted flagon. There were three others in front of him, and he pushed one to each as they sat down.

"Bartender say to Bobo, 'Ambrosia, ever hear of it?' Sound familiar to Bobo."

"Yes," Flavian said, pausing to let a stream of delicious coolness trickle down his parched throat. "Ahh! Ambrosia is some sort of submerged continent I read about in several premission intelligence reports."

The other three nodded respectfully.

"Good work, Bobo," Flavian added, pleased to see how the dwarf fighter basked in even minor praise. "Let's stay together now. We'll stock up on food and get a weapon or two if we can afford it."

"There are other ways of getting things," Elena said knowingly.

Flavian shook his head. "Not just yet, Elena. It would be best for us to do our business, then go outside town and invoke the 'Q' spell before you try stealing anything."

She shrugged, but acquiesced.

The grocer seemed glad to sell them fifty food rations each. They stowed the food in their packs and went to the weapons shop.

"Bobo needs a bow," Flavian said to his friends, "but he doesn't have enough gold to buy one."

Merlin handed Bobo more gold and he transacted with the shopkeeper for a bow.

"Bobo like long-range weapon. Bobo want to go kill orcs!"

"Soon, Bobo," Flavian said, trying to unobtrusively pull Elena away from where she was staring at one of the gold chests behind the shopkeeper's counter and flexing her fingers.

"Not *now*," he hissed.

They went outside the shop and sauntered along the cobblestoned street.

"Talk to everyone who will talk, and take good notes," Flavian ordered. "Bobo, you might want to ready that bow now so you won't forget."

"Yes, teacher, we'll all do as you say," Elena said, but tempered the sarcasm by fondly patting him on the arm.

They roamed the town for several days, frequenting shops and taverns. Flavian noticed that Merlin seemed to have the most luck at gathering information. Not only was he cute, but also highly intelligent. He seemed able to worm more phrases out of the people he talked to than the others did from the people they met.

During the next week they stayed close to the town of Britain and the massive castle of Lord British nearby, meeting ghouls, balrons, orcs, and other dangerous creatures on a more than daily basis.

The first combat, the tenth day of their stay, was not too bad. Bobo, the point man as usual, had been the first to see the party of orcs charging their way. He had unlimbered his bow and dispatched three orcs before they were within striking distance. There were three orcs left. Bobo stood back at the ready, covering them with his bow, while the other three each killed an orc apiece.

After the battle they found a chest. Elena opened it easily and took the gold.

That night as they were sitting around the campfire, they had only minor scratches. Nonetheless, Flavian did an after-action critique. It was favorable because they had all performed flawlessly as a team. He reminded them that only the party member actually killing a monster got the experience points, so it was important for them to spread out the kills as much as possible so that they would all make progress and grow stronger evenly.

"Bobo deadeye shot with bow," Bobo said proudly.

"Yes, you are," Flavian agreed, "and that's the key to our survival in these early stages. With your bow, you can whittle large parties of monsters down to a reasonable size before they get close enough to overwhelm us by sheer numbers."

"Skeletons—out of the trees!" Merlin shouted, jumping to his feet.

Just like that they were into their second combat, which went as successfully as the first, with another chest of gold appearing afterwards.

"They won't all be this easy," Flavian warned them.

And in fact they weren't. During the next six days alone, Elena nearly lost her right arm to a greedy troll, which would have been disastrous from an acquisitions standpoint as well as a strategic one, and Bobo and Flavian both suffered numbing blows to their backs that incapacitated them for several hours.

However, the group's frequent encounters with monsters increased their strength and experience dramatically. Flavian was glad of this because during each visit to a tavern he felt an increasing sense of fearfulness and nervousness in the townsfolk, as tales of more and more disasters circulated.

Two months passed. They visited the castle of Lord British often. Transacting with the monarch was beneficial. As they gained experience, it seemed the increases in their strength intensified too.

They also explored the castle as much as possible, but were often stymied by locked doors.

One day in a certain corridor a force field blocked their way.

"We have *got* to get some keys," Merlin frowned. "I bet there are lots of important clues behind those doors."

The only reply he got was, "Bobo see boat in moat."

At this, as a unit, they dashed off, hurrying through corridors down to the door leading from inside the castle to the strip of land at the edge of the moat. But it was locked!

Flavian sighed and racked his brain.

"Elena, you're a thief. Use your profession. Where can we get keys?"

He saw an expression he hadn't seen since the Academy cross Merlin's face. He hoped it was one of respect. He knew that a leader had to *earn* respect and it seemed that he was on his way to achieving it.

Elena thought for a moment. "I guess the only way is to buy them from the Thieves Guild. I think there's a shop in Grey, but it's way over on the southwest coast."

"That's OK," said Flavian. "It'll be worth the time and the expense of the food."

They left the castle, invoked the 'Q' spell, and went into Britain to stock up on plenty of food for their first long journey. Elena insisted they pass through the weapons shop and slyly showed off her skill by swiping some gold from a chest.

"Good, good," Flavian said, "just don't try it too often, though. Or when we haven't done a 'Q' spell in a while."

"OK, OK," Elena chanted. "I know what's wise and what isn't."

The town of Grey was not much different from Britain in design, but the people were very different. There were more thieves and brigands, furtive figures who slipped away down dark alleys as the party walked between buildings. The guards looked meaner and hungrier as if they got to practice their profession here fairly frequently. Also, Flavian heard more chattering and louder laughter in the pubs here; he knew that meant these folks were becoming uncomfortably aware of the dangers surrounding them.

The foursome explored the town, finding a pub, a grocery store, a weapons shop, and an armory. They had conversations with a thief, a fighter, and a cleric that contained information that Flavian noted down carefully.

"Look in there," Elena whispered suddenly, pointing to a narrow passageway.

Several treasure chests gleamed faintly. She started to go in, but Flavian grabbed her arm. "Brigands in the shadows," he said. Elena gasped.

Flavian went on, "We'll come back when we're stronger. I have a feeling the guards would be really upset if we took any of that gold."

He motioned them toward the pub. Elena followed reluctantly, castling longing glances back at the treasure cache.

In the pub they had a cold one each. "Good thing you noticed those guys back there," Merlin observed. Flavian was complimented, because at the Academy and on their journey thus far Merlin had been the most observant one of the four.

"Bobo no see them, but you did."

"Yes, Flavian, thanks," said Elena. "I—we—could have been a goner."

A few minutes later, Merlin leaned over and asked Elena what was going on in the back room. She turned around and watched for a few moments as people entered and left a small door, then snapped her fingers.

"That's where the Thieves Guild is!"

They quickly finished their beverages and went to the back room. Elena looked over the selection of merchandise, nodding knowledgeably.

"Keys, torches, powders, and gems," she said, "All tools of the thief's trade. The torches are cheap, so we all should stock up on them. We need a bunch of keys and as many of the powders and gems as we can afford. All of us can use them, so buy what you can."

"Good work, Elena," complimented Flavina. "These are fairly—no, might as well not downplay it—*absolutely* crucial if we're going to find everything we need to get Exodus."

Merlin had picked up a gem and was rolling it around on the palm of his hand.

"Pretty. What does it do?"

He started to look at it more closely, but Elena quickly stopped him.

"Don't peer into it until you are ready to make use of the information it gives."

"But how do I know this?" queried Merlin.

"You don't. It was not in your curriculum," said Flavian. "It gives you a bird's eye view of a town, maze, dungeon, castle, or continent." Unlike the others, he had studied not only his profession, but that of the other three as well. "What you are shown depends on where you are. Each gem only has a one-time use, consuming itself in the process."

"They are not cheap," Elena confirmed, "so use them wisely. The powders are expensive also. They negate time, stopping attackers and giving you an immense advantage. One-time use here also."

Merlin smiled, seeing the merits of having some of each. "I think we'll come back here often," he said, buying a couple of gems and a bundle of torches.

For another month they continued exploring, talking to people, and fighting. They visited the locked areas in the castle of Lord British and took the frigate in the moat around to where a cleric stood on a small spit of land. He gave them an important clue. Flavian liked seeing his list of clues grow longer and longer.

The party made many forays up and down and across the single large continent. Their combat experience kept mounting, though not without cost in aches, bruises, gashes, broken limbs, gaping wounds, and many even more serious injuries. Flavian was careful not to take advantage of his supervisory position to spare himself any danger or pain. Luckily the healing facility in Lord British's castle was available to them now that they had keys and could get in. The town of Moon had a handy healing shop also.

The latter healing shop came in very handy five months to the day after they arrived in Sosaria. The party had been fighting a party of balrons when, to the horror or the other three, Merlin received a mighty swipe to his head that killed him! Tearfully they carried the torn little body to the healer at Moon. He asked a stiff fee, but Merlin was restored to life. They all hugged in great relief.

Two days later, Elena discovered that the guards could be bribed and would then disappear, making theft of the gold chests from merchants easier and safer. She was becoming more and more adept at purloining those shiny yellow coins. Flavian complimented her on her discovery and her agility and observed that both were very useful because everything on Sosaria was so darned expensive.

"Thanks, boss," she returned, straightening her shoulders a mite.

The next afternoon Merlin received a compliment too. In a combat with six orcs, he cast a Repond spell and destroyed all six before they even got close to the party.

"Great work, Merlin," Flavian smiled at him. "Your magic seems to work better and better after each fight."

Flavian noticed his cleric spells beginning to work also. His healing spell was especially handy out in the field when it kept a sorely wounded comrade alive during a fight.

Bobo thrived on two things, combat and visiting the taverns. Although not the brightest in the world, he kept his ears open and always related to the party what he heard the bartenders say. In the sixth month of their stay, they were all in a tavern in Montor East. Bobo told Flavian he had just heard the bartender say, "The conjunction of the moons finds a link."

Flavian took out the paper he had jotted earlier notes on and added this latest.

"Let's see what we have now," he said and read: "Ambrosia. Ever hear of it? Dawn. City of Myths and Magic! Nasty creatures, nasty dark, sure thee ready, fore thee embark. None return so I'm told, from the pool, dark and cold. Shrines of knowledge, shrines of strength, all are lost into the brink. Fountains fair and fountains foul, all are found in dungeon's bowel. Seek ye out the Lord of Time, and the one way is a sure find! The conjunction of the moons finds a link!"

"Good poetry it isn't," Merlin commented, "but there must be some good clues in there."

"Yes, I've been thinking about them a lot," Flavian said, tapping the paper. "It's almost like a road map for us. As I see it, there are three places we're going to end up having to find and visit: the lost continent of Ambrosia; dungeons; and the mysterious city of Dawn. I think this last clue refers to finding it."

"Why?" asked Merlin.

Elena snapped her fingers. "I overheard something as I passed the table in front of us to the effect that 'dawn comes with each new pair.'"

Flavian smiled. "Exactly! When the two moons are both zero, Dawn appears."

"Appears where?" Merlin asked.

"That, we still have to find out," Flavian said. "But let's get back to the castle and see if Lord British will raise us yet another level. We're sure to need more strength wherever it is."

It was a shock to the party when Lord British, for the first time, did not acknowledge their accumulation of experience by strengthening them. "Seek the mark," he told them.

"Mark who?" Bobo asked, but his question went unanswered.

Disappointed, they left. It was obvious something needed to be done before Lord British would help them again. But what? What kind of mark? Something to do with kings maybe??

"Well, let's check out the moon gates first," Flavian said, scanning the copious notes he had been making. He had seen a moon gate flickering in and out of existence north of the town of Moon, and that's where they went first.

"This one appears," he told the rest of the group, "when the moons are zero-zero, zero-one, and zero-two." He paused and showed them the pages in his notes describing the phases of the moons.

Bobo looked into the sky. "Bobo see moons right now becoming zero-zero."

Sure enough the gate popped into existence and they quickly stepped into it, but nothing happened. They went nowhere.

"OK," Flavian said with a shrug and making a notation, "this one is static. We'll wait for zero-one."

A few minutes later, they stepped out of the gate to find themselves on an island with a dungeon entrance just in front of them. Flavian cautioned them not to explore it because they weren't strong enough yet, so they waited for the moon gate to reappear and stepped back through it.

In the following week, they found the other moon gates by simply entering the ones already discovered at different phases of the moons. Each gate appeared during three phases, and each had a unique series. Flavian carefully noted the location and moon phases at which each gate occurred so that they could use them on a regular and reliable basis.

The second place they found, to their horror, was the Castle of Death. Even Bobo recognized it, their instructors had shown them so many pictures of it.

They stood in a small area totally surrounded by mountains so Flavian concluded it was accessible only via the moon gate. "That's it! There's where Exodus is!" Merlin shouted excitedly.

"Well, what are we waiting for?" asked Bobo. "Let's go!"

"But we're nowhere ready for the final battle," protested Merlin.

"I know," Flavian reassured him. "I want us to see what we'll be up against so we'll be as thoroughly prepared as possible when we do come back."

"Good idea," Merlin replied, that same look crossing his face.

A small lake was between them and the castle's entrance. On the other three sides, constant ribbons of fire flared up between mountains.

"Very well protected," Bobo offered.

"I would say there has to be another way in," Flavian commented and led them back through the moon gate.

"Oh, I guess you're right," replied Elena. "I was looking like mad for an opening, but there could be another way altogether."

A few days later they discovered another place also accessible only by moon gate—the town of Devil's Guard. There, Merlin and the others elicited invaluable clues from six fighters and a thief. Flavian conscientiously wrote them all down and read them aloud to the others at night around the campfire.

"Listen to this," he said after their visit to Devil's Guard. "We were told: Hot metal leaves a mark! 4 marks, 4 uses! The King favors a mark!

Marks gained in dungeons! A mark helps invoke the Snake! Mark thee well! Seek ye the dungeon of fire!"

"Four marks," Merlin mused, absently playing with the fur on his face. "Found only in dungeons. Looks like we're going to be spending a lot of time in dungeons, eh?"

"Ugh," remarked Bobo.

"Looks that way," Flavian acknowledged matter-of-factly. There was a pause. Eyebrows raised, the others were looking at him expectantly.

"Well, leader?" This from Elena. "What words of encouragement have you for us now in this our six hundred and fifty-fourth challenge?" Flavian detected no sarcasm in her tone.

Merlin and Bobo continued to be silent too. Did they really have that much trust in him?

He realized suddenly that they had come a long way together, and that he had used his knowledge wisely to get them thus far. He smiled at them, too overcome with emotion at the moment to say anything.

They were lucky, very lucky. Their first cautious venture into a dungeon was the Perinian Depths northeast of the town of Britain. They were to later learn that this is the only dungeon with marks to be gained on the top and safest level. Better yet, they found the Mark of Kings!

Gaining the mark was painful for each of them. There was a piece of red-hot metal embedded in the wall. They each had to touch it, and a mark was left on their skin.

Returning to Lord British, the party was delighted to find that Lord British now would again reward experience with strength.

The exploration of the various dungeons took several days, but it was time well spent. Also they found additional clues and gold and gained more combat experience. They found healing fountains as well, which allowed them to recoup from battles and stay in the dungeons longer to accomplish their complete investigation of its dark depths.

The gems were absolutely invaluable to them, in finding their way around dungeons, and they always made sure to have plenty of torches so that they would not get lost in the dark.

Most irksome were the gremlin cities. Strange winds always blew out their torches, and the gremlins would steal food from them if they were careless.

After seven months in Sosaria, Flavian was experienced enough now to invoke his 'E' and 'F' spells, which would lower them a level and raise them a level in a dungeon respectively. Unfortunately, as did Merlin, he had to use spells sparingly since it took time between each spell to recharge magic points.

The climax of the dungeon campaign came while exploring the dungeon whose entrance was surrounded by impenetrable mountains, which they had first discovered while checking out the moon gates.

On the eighth and most dangerous level, they suddenly encountered a tall and awesome-looking gentleman. The mysterious Time Lord rewarded them for finding him by naming a certain sequence of cards that he assured them would be much needed later. Of course Flavian noted down the sequence.

Back in the pub at Britain, the party enjoyed a little rest and relaxation to recover from the long and arduous ordeals of the dungeons. Resting his boots on the bench, Flavian remarked on how the clues about the town of Dawn puzzled him.

"Yes, the mystic town of Dawn," Elena contributed. "We know when it appears, we just don't know where."

"Flavian, I just heard a clue about Dawn! 'Exotic clues found at Dawn,' " Merlin reported.

Flavian thrust his papers into his pouch. "Good, Merlin! And *I* just thought of something, gang. Now that we have the Mark of Force, we can go through that force field in Lord British's castle and see what's on the other side. Maybe some of these phrases I've jotted down will start to make sense."

Having explored the storage room behind the force field, they used keys to enter the castle's underground chamber.

Bobo the dwarf had wandered over to where a bright fire burned in one corner, a very large fire, reaching from floor to ceiling, and into which he was now peering.

"Hey! Bobo see someone in there!"

The others came closer. Sure enough there was a writhing figure chained within the fire.

"Wow," little Merlin said, "that guy must have been involved in something really dastardly."

Flavian carefully moved his hand toward the fire. It didn't feel hot at all. He stepped boldly into the fire and up to the fellow chained there. The Mark of Fire was a handy thing to have, he thought. The flames were all around him now, but he felt very comfortable, a lot more so than the poor wretch here.

"West 8 . . . South . . . and Dawn awaits!" the tortured man croaked.

"Thanks," Flavian said, and left the flames, feeling vaguely guilty that he could not help the prisoner, even though he was sure that he deserved his fate. He frowned hard as he thought of the immensity of the evil in Sosaria these days, but at the same time knew that the best way to get rid of it was to find and vanquish Exodus, whoever and whatever that may be. And he had the coordinates for Dawn!

The woods were dark. From the stars they had seen before entering the forest, Flavian knew the sun would be rising now.

"Are you sure this is the right place?" Elena asked doubtfully. "It looks just like all the rest of this lousy forest to me."

"No, I'm not dead sure, just dead tired," Flavian replied, leaning wearily against a tree. He was exhausted from traveling all night as well as from an orc ambush they had fended off. "I can only assume that the directions we got are measured from the castle gate."

Merlin was a few paces distant, in the only place were there was enough of a break in the dense forest canopy to see the sky. He was watching the twin moons.

"Now!" he exclaimed. "The moons are zero-zero!"

"There's nothing hap—" Elena began, but stopped as a large patch of mist appeared before them. It quickly solidified into a town there among the trees where nothing but underbrush had been before.

"Move fast," Flavian ordered. "It will only be here for a moment!"

Inside, Dawn was much like any other town. There were the usual shops—weapons, armor, food, and a tavern that they had to stop Bobo from heading directly toward.

"Not before breakfast," Flavian said.

"Bobo not want breakfast, Bobo want cold one." But he followed them into the weapons shop, and his interest was suddenly piqued by the display.

"Some nice but expensive stuff," Elena said, adroitly stealing a chest of gold while the shopkeeper had his back turned.

"Bobo want!" Bobo said, pointing to a +4 bow.

The party pooled their gold and Bobo bought the bow, selling his old one.

"You think these are the exotic weapons we heard about?" Merlin asked, peering closer at a +2 sword.

"I don't know," Flavian said, "let's check around town and see what else we can find."

They walked the narrow streets, which were really no more than wide paths of hard-packed clay and looked into the various buildings. They found an oracle and a Thieves Guild shop, where they purchased some more viewing gems just in case.

The armor shop also had more advanced protective garments than most armor shops they had seen, but the prices were high. Flavian realized they would have to stock up on gold, maybe making a few trips down into dungeons, and come back.

There were stables also, and they bought horses for the party so they could save on food costs. Their greatest accomplishment, however, came through conversations with various people encountered in the town.

"Dig up exotics!" one suggested, laughing when Bobo immediately begin scratching at the hard dirt of the street.

"Dig carefully!" another said, and an old man in a tattered cloak added that they should "Dig on the isles!"

"What does it all mean, Flavian?" Elena asked.

"Between our need to go to Ambrosia and the need for exotic weapons," Flavian said, "I guess we need a frigate."

"Bobo not want to go on ocean and get seasick," Bobo said.

They all nodded at that. Often they had stood on the beach and watched the huge waves buffeted by the ever-changing winds. A massive whirlpool roared unpredictably across the surface of the water. The seas of Sosaria were not a place for weekend sailors. Besides, up until now they had seen no ships at all. "Still," Flavian said, "that's what we have to do, but first I'd like for you guys to see where I grew up." He paused and saw questions on their faces, as he expected to.

"Actually, we are going to Yew, but the real reason is that the other day I heard someone say that one should 'Pray in the Circle of Light.' That just happens to be in my home town, and I just happen to know exactly where that is."

The city of Yew was located in the mountains to the west of Lord British's castle. It was difficult to find the small pass leading to the town. Flavian explained to his friends that the town discouraged visitors from coming since the onset of the troubles.

Because Yew was a holy city, they saw dozens of clerics. They also found a healing kiosk and a food shop, at which they restocked.

The place was heavily forested. Flavian met a few clerics he knew from the old days, but none could tell him anything of significance.

Finally Flavian led them to the Circle of Light, which was really more like a square with attendant clerics on each side. He entered and prayed. A booming voice told him to yell a certain word, which Flavian carefully wrote down. He wondered why the voice had specified "yell" but he was sure he had heard aright. He also was sure that it would be extremely important at the right time.

Somewhat reluctantly, Flavian led his band out of his hometown and birthplace. It was a relief to be here in familiar surroundings with people he knew and with little sign of the marauding monsters and general vileness corrupting the rest of the planet. But he knew that the world needed their services. He knew they had almost everything they needed to stop the evil at its very source. Remembering his fulfilling life before the Troubles, the fate of his parents, and his vow to himself, he strode determinedly down the road.

Their next visit was to the town of Montor West. Relaxing in the pub, the party listened as Flavian went over his notes. He had a feeling he should pay special attention to the ones from the two oracles they had found and consulted during their travels.

"Let me read these," he said, "and see if you guys can help me determine our next step. Some are pretty cryptic."

"Here goes. And so the sage said unto thee: If thou can solve my rhyme, you'll learn of marks and playing cards and hidden holy shrines. Of marks I say there are but 4, of Fire, Force, Snake, and Kings. Learn their use in Devil Guard or death you'll surely bring. Shrines there are again but 4, to which you go and pray. Their uses are innumerable and clues throughout I say. The cards their suits do number 4, called Sol, Moon, Death, and Love. Unto the Montors thou must go for guidance from above. To aid thee in thy cryptic search, to dungeons thou must fare. There seek out the Lord of Time to help you if he cares."

Merlin smiled. "A lot of that we already know, having done all that dungeon stuff. I would say, judging by this and the bartender clues, that we need to find and visit Ambrosia soon."

They also paid a visit to the small municipal prison there. Elena batted her eyes at the guards and managed to bribe them into looking the other way while the party entered. Inside were two prisoners, and they both revealed helpful information.

"Time for a little sea voyage," Flavian said.

"Avast ye lubbers, get away from those gangplanks!" a scruffy-looking pirate yelled. It had taken them two weeks of wandering along the coast, fighting monsters both seaborne and on the land, before the party had found this very scarce pirate ship. Flavian, for one, was not going to let it get away.

"Take him, Bobo," he ordered.

No sooner were the words out of his mouth then Bobo had used his +4 bow to put a shaft through the pirate's chest. The other brigands of the sea on board immediately launched a vicious attack, but the party fought their way onto the vessel and took it.

"Yo, ho, ho," Merlin yelled in glee as they slipped from land.

Bobo just grunted, because to him had fallen the hard work of raising and lowering the sails.

"Be careful," Flavian shouted above the flapping of the rigging. But he feared his words were lost so he decided to wait to give his directions till the sails were set.

He gathered the other three around him. "Be very careful. That whirlpool could pop up anywhere, so we need to avoid the open sea as much as possible. We'll hug the coast and explore those close-in islands."

On one of the larger islands, they found the city of Fawn. It had a healing shop, a grocery, a pub, and a Thieves Guild where they got some more of the ever-useful gems. Four clerics were kind in imparting information to Flavian.

Returning to the ship, they visited an uninhabited nearby island. Bobo, digging around in the scrub that covered the island, was the first to make an amazing discovery. Triumphantly he held up a metal device with several curves, artistically designed but still bizarre-looking, that could only be one of the legendary exotic weapons they had heard about. He decided that the weapons they were discussing earlier were not very exotic-looking, after all. The others quickly dug in nearby spots and made similar discoveries.

They sailed on around the continent of Sosaria, using the frigate's cannon to destroy some monsters and engaging in combat with others. Even Bobo was becoming used to sailing now.

South of the continent they found a large island completely guarded by high cliffs except for a steep inlet on its southern side. A vast silver snake was guarding the narrow water passage leading into the interior of the island.

"We've seen this before," Flavian said excitedly. He could barely restrain himself from jumping up and down with eagerness. "From the moon gate on the other side. This is how you get into the Castle of Death."

"Good," Elena said, "we have our exotic weapons and the Mark of the Snake which should let us pass—let's get in there and give Exodus a little what for!"

"No, we're still not ready," Flavian cautioned her. He pulled out his notes. "Listen to these three clues: Seek ye the shrines of truth! Search for cards! Search the shrines!"

"Right," Merlin contributed. "And remember what the Time Lord told us in his dungeon. Those cards in that sequence have got to be the key to defeating Exodus."

"But," Elena said, lounging comfortably against the rail as the ship bobbed on the gentle swell of the inlet, "we've been *everywhere* in Sosaria. Where are those blamed cards?"

"Seek ye the Shrines of Truth! Search the Shrines!" Flavian read.

"I've seen no shrines either," Elena said.

"Has to be in Ambrosia," Merlin said. "That's the only place left, but how do we get there?"

"I'm not sure, possibly by sailing into the whirlpool," Flavian said.

Elena shuddered. "I hope you're not going to try *that*!"

Flavian shook his head. "Not just yet. Maybe we can find some more clues. Raise the sail, Bobo. We'll go back up the coast to Grey and start talking to people again."

As they sailed out of the inlet, Flavian gripped the tiller and met the oncoming seas head-on. He was enjoying the exhilaration, the taste of salt in the air, and the sea breeze on his face when Merlin suddenly yelled and pointed behind them.

A raging swirl of water was rapidly overtaking the ship! Flavian pushed the tiller hard over, but it was too late. With a roar and a gurgle in their ears, they were sucked down into blackness.

They came back to awareness on the beach of a strange land. Other than a few scattered and broken boards, a small pile of tangled rigging and a few scraps of canvas, there was no sign of their frigate.

"Going to be a long walk home," Merlin commented, getting up and brushing the sand from his fur.

Flavian got to his feet and pulled out his notes. The paper was soggy but still readable. "Seek ye the shrines of truth! Search for cards! Search the shrines!" He read.

Merlin pulled out a gem and they all gathered around to peer into it.

"There, there, there,and there," Merlin said. "On the four corners of the continent, those four places must be the Shrines."

"Oh, no! Look at all those mazes we have to go through to get there!" Elena complained. But after she sighed she stood tall and looked ready for anything.

They started off, fighting monsters occasionally, and negotiating mazes. There were several locked gates and they were glad they had stocked up on plenty of keys before coming. After three days they reached the first shrine, the Shrine of Strength. Entering the shrine one at a time, they found, increased their strength.

Finally Flavian directed Merlin to search the shrine thoroughly, and he came up with a card! "Ah ha," he said. "One down and three to go."

Reaching each shrine did not offer any new types of challenges, but still presented many annoyances, to say the least. They met many varieties of monsters and had difficulty actually finding the shrines.

However, all the previous long months served them well because they fought expertly and used their resources wisely.

Reaching the northwest shrine did require them to cross a large lake. As good luck would have it, a pirate ship was moored on their side of the lake. A brief combat ensued and the frigate was theirs. They crossed the lake, walked to the shrine, retrieved the card there, and returned to the ship. Alas, however, search as they might, there was just no exit to the open sea to be found. Reluctantly they abandoned the ship and went to find the northeastern shrine.

During this period, images of destruction and death troubled Flavian's dreams. He felt haunted by the burden of knowing that Exodus not only was still operative but also seemed to be increasing in strength.

The southeastern shrine was a stroke of really good fortune. Again it was necessary to cross water, and again there was a fortuitous pirate ship. They took the ship, went to the entrance to the maze, got the card, and boarded the frigate yet again.

"Over there," Merlin said pointing, "what's that white blur in the distance?"

They sailed toward it and found a gate blocking the channel. Luckily, Bobo still had a key left and was able to open the gate. Beyond was the open sea and a stationary whirlpool.

"Hold on tight," Flavian said and steered them into the vortex.

This time the ship did not break up. When he regained consciousness, Flavian saw the familiar coastline of Sosaria. He knew they were near the inlet guarded by the Silver Snake.

"Bobo see whirlpool coming!" Bobo yelled from the bow where he was keeping a lookout.

Flavian pushed the tiller over hard and this time managed to evade the whirlpool and enter the inlet. Since they were out of keys, he definitely did not want to return to Ambrosia—they would be stranded there this time.

The vast Silver Snake regarded them with beady eyes and refused them passage. Flavian held up his hand with the Mark of the Snake on it, but the massive reptile was unimpressed.

"Didn't we hear a clue that had something to do with invoking the snake?" Merlin asked.

"Of course!" Flavian said. "In the Circle of Light in Yew. Thanks, Merlin."

He yelled the word that the booming voice had given him in the Circle of Light. The snake was instantly out of their way and they were in the lake facing the Castle of Death.

Inside the Castle of Death it was one major battle after another. The guards and other monsters were aggressive, mean, and very, very hard to kill. In fact, the only weapons that seemed to work on them at all were the exotic weapons they had dug up before their trip to Ambrosia.

Magic, of course, worked, too. But it took the strongest offensive spells that Merlin and Flavian knew to do any good, and then there was a long wait while their magic points recharged. So the four of them spent their time mostly in hand to hand combat.

Finally, in the northern portion of the castle, they found a larger force field than normal. They entered a room, only to find that the very floor itself was attacking them!

The battles with the floors were their hardest yet. The party found the only workable solution to be a technique of constantly attacking in all directions while Merlin and Flavian used their high-level spells whenever their magic points had built up to the proper level.

Several times they fought the floors, and finally they won. The rest was almost anticlimactic. Almost.

Against the north wall of the castle were four racks of equipment.

"Where's Exodus?" Elena asked. "After those floors nearly killed us, I thought sure he'd be here. Besides, we've used most of our objects and all the clues, we've done everything we should, so this has to be the end—doesn't it, Flavian?"

"You got it, Elena," Flavian confirmed. "This is the enemy."

"You mean *this* is Exodus?" Merlin asked, disappointed. "It looks more like a computer than anything else."

"That's no Commodore 64," Elena said, but the others looked at her blankly.

Soberly Flavian said, "It's hard to believe so much human suffering has emanated from a collection of hardware like this."

"Well, in any case, time to shut down Exodus for good," Merlin said. He stepped up to the nearest panel and took the four cards from his pack. "Now, let's see, according to the Time Lord, this is the first card."

He inserted the card into the panel. There was a blue flash and the fuzzy wizard immediately crumpled to the floor, dead! Elena and Flavian rushed to the little fellow, while Bobo stood guard.

"Can you resurrect him?" she asked tearfully.

"Not just yet," Flavian said. "My magic points are still low."

There followed an agonizing wait, until finally Flavian was able to cast a healing spell, and then the one of resurrection. Merlin sat up groggily.

"Make sure you use the right card this time, huh?" Elena said.

Merlin nodded, consulting with Flavian to make sure he fully understood the order in which the cards went in. Satisfied, he inserted the first card. Again he slumped to the floor dead.

After building his points back up, Flavian cast the resurrection spell. This time it failed, and the lifeless body of Merlin was consumed in flames, leaving only a small pile of ashes.

Elena sank to the floor crying. Even Bobo's eyes were not dry. Flavian gulped in determination and concentrated on building his magic points to their highest level. Finally he was able to cast the very strongest spell a cleric could ever obtain, the spell that would recall someone from ashes.

Merlin coalesced back into being. He sat up, this time holding his head and moaning about a tremendous headache.

"Something is wrong," Flavian said, baffled. "We are inserting exactly the right card."

"My head, oh my head," Merlin said, groaning while Elena gently massaged his neck.

Bobo had been looking at the racks of equipment making up Exodus and now spoke. "Bobo know he is dumb, but if Bobo was putting in cards he would start with first machine first."

Merlin groaned again and looked at Bobo in disgust, then suddenly it dawned on him that the dwarf was right.

"Want me to do it this time?" Flavian asked.

"No," Merlin said, letting Elena help him to his feet. "You might need to resurrect me again, and only a cleric can do that."

He walking unsteadily to the first machine, gritted his teeth, and quickly pushed in the first card. The machine beeped in despair and vanished.

"Yes! Yes!" Elena said, doing a small dance of joy.

"Go for it!" Flavian said.

"Bobo right! Bobo smart!"

Merlin grinned and inserted the second card into the second machine. *Poof*—it was gone. Then the third card into the third machine.

"Now," Merlin said, flourishing it, "for my next trick, the fourth card!"

Deep beneath them a vast rumbling began as the world, relieved of its mammoth burden of evil, began to rearrange itself.

"Let's get out before this crumbles," Flavian ordered, and they ran for the entrance past confused and dying monsters.

Outside, the sun was shining. A new world was being born. The lake was boiling from the subterranean movements, but Flavian and his party were safe. They had triumphed and once more evil had been defeated.

PART

5

Ultima IV—Quest of the Avatar

10 The Gypsy Woman Who Asks Questions

Greetings, Adventurer. Harken to this briefing. This new mission, should you decide to accept it, is harder than those you completed during the Ages of Darkness. Now, you will be expected to end the time of Darkness and to bring Britannia into the Age of Light. Only those of special moral fiber can even hope to triumph. Only those who follow exactly and rigorously the Way of the Avatar shall survive. Only those who scrupulously adhere to noble principles will achieve their goal and that of Lord British.

If you do strive constantly and if you do persevere to prove yourself worthy in each and all of the eight virtues of an Avatar, then and only then can the realm be saved. Then and only then will you be able to find and view the Codex of Ultimate Wisdom, and thus acquire the knowledge that will usher in the Age of Light for the people of Britannia.

It will not be easy. Listen carefully if you would live to return.

Background

After the destruction of Exodus by a small party of intrepid adventurers, a period of peace once more settled on the land, or at least what was left of it. The ravages that occurred during the three Ages of Darkness had been cataclysmic, with major geological changes to the very geography of Sosaria not once, but three times! Continents disappeared and were replaced by others. Oceans boiled from the molten lifeblood of the planet—the magma and lava that gushed up from the huge rents and wounds in the fabric of the world itself. Vast clouds of black volcanic ash hung in the sky for years.

Yet, through all this, people survived. Lord British's leadership and his dedication to raising the quality of life in these horrible times gained him the everlasting loyalty of his subjects. From the cinders of Sosaria, a new land came into being. Britannia was its name, called after their beloved monarch. Slowly the countryside was reclaimed and the ruinous effects wreaked by the Triad of Evil came to be alleviated.

Lord British caused major public works to be constructed to better the lives of all. Three of these have major significance. The Lycaeum, wherein lay the great observatory, is one. Another is the Empath Abbey with its oak groves where wise men and women meditate upon the teachings of the ancients. The third is the great castle of the Knight's Order of the Silver Serpent. Only the flower of Lord British's chivalry is invited to join this order, which as Kyle the Younger, the erudite historian of the era, wrote, embodies "the highest ideals and exemplary bravery."

Each town is committed to cultivating the study and advancement of its own particular virtue. Numerous small satellite villages dot the landscape between the towns.

But even after Lord British made these improvements, all was not peaceful and idyllic. While the "point men" for all that was bad—the Evil Triad of Mondain, Minax, and Exodus—had all met a well-deserved fate, pockets of their legacies still existed. Marauding orcs and hill giants, places where explorers did not return from, traps for the unwary—all these and more were still in the realm. Worse even than that was the baseness that yet lurked in the human heart. Neighbors coveted the fields of neighbors, no merchant's goods were safe from the thief, and those with hate in their hearts struck out at their fellows and did grievous harm, even murder.

The wise philosophers at the Lycaeum, under the direction of Lord British, considered and probed this situation. They concluded that the next era of human growth would come not from territorial expansion, in which there is always a loser, but from within the human psyche. For survival and enlightment, only the living of virtuous lives by all of society could insure lasting peace.

Complex systems of laws and ethics were constructed, analyzed, found wanting, and discarded. The philosophers spent many years doing this and in fact would have gladly continued for all of time, sitting in their ivy-covered halls at the Lycaeum debating this fine point and that tiny nuance. But they adjourned after they had formulated eight major virtues and postulated the perfect person typifying the new order of society. They called this theoretical enlightened individual an Avatar. When the people saw one person who was a prototype of these ideals, they would be able to lead virtuous lives themselves.

A sharp debate raged over whether anyone could achieve the status of an Avatar.

As always, it remained to Lord British to find the answer. He determined that the right adventurer could achieve the status of Avatar. It would not be at all easy, but it could be done, and such a long-shot success would be the salvation of Britannia. He then issued a call to adventurers across time and space, saying that he and his people needed an individual who would become a beacon, an example of highest virtue to guide the populace into a new age full of light and enlightenment. The individual would need to search the hearts of the people and the land for all the parts of the mystery, and gather them together to solve the Quest.

This will be *your* mission when you are transported from your present position in space and time and materialize in the Empire of Britannia. You also will look for the Codex of Ultimate Wisdom, a legendary and powerful document that can assure the triumph of virtue.

Your Character

Before I cover choosing specific personal characteristics, you need to know certain new principles applying to all persons in your party. As you know, the Hero or Heroine who undertakes this mission must possess good moral fiber. This is not something you can just pay lip service to. If you steal, if you lie, if you cheat, if you kill for the sake of killing, a price will be exacted. You will fall behind. Too much wrong behavior, and there is no hope left of eventual success.

I realize, for those of you who are veterans of the three earlier campaigns, that in those eras a certain degree of unlawfulness was tolerated, even encouraged. To survive it was sometimes necessary for an adventurer to steal food, or gold, or weapons and armor. Lord British, in those desperate times, often turned a blind eye to what adventurers had to do.

This is no longer true. You will be in Britannia to serve as an example. You are there to progress along the Way of the Avatar, to master the Eight Virtues, and to save the realm from evil. No flouting of the rules will be tolerated. Believe me—the penalties are automatic and there are no appeals.

Specifically, do *not* touch the unguarded chests you will often find while exploring towns. Stealing is wrong and most detrimental to your progress along the Way of the Avatar. Don't give in to temptation.

Before you begin the mission, a message will be given. It says: "You read the Book of History." The Book of History referred to is *The History of Britannia* as penned by Kyle the Younger. There is a copy in your adventurer's briefing materials for this mission.

I highly recommend that you do so. While this briefing covers much *not* in the book, lack of time prevents me from totally repeating what *is* in it.

During your travels, if you survive, you might find others who are willing to join themselves to your party, and you can have up to seven other members. Some people who might look favorably upon joining your quest if you are advanced enough are Dupre, Katrina, Shamino, Jaana, Geoffrey, Mariah, Julia, and Iolo.

Race

All, including yourself, will be of the human race. Sadly, the other races of the old Sosaria—the elves, bobbits, dwarfs, and even the cute little fuzzies—have succumbed to environmental pressures and ecological disasters. They are, alas, no more.

Professions

Before entering into the mission, there is a certain gypsy woman that you must visit. She will ask you seven very important questions. The results of this test will determine your profession and your entry point into Britannia. There are eight professions and eight entry points.

Figure 10.1 *You must visit the gypsy woman in her caravan wagon. She will test you and determine your character.*

Here is a listing of the Eight Virtues and the professions and cities associated with them.

Virtue	**Profession**	**City**
Compassion	Bard	Britain
Honesty	Mage	Moonglow
Honor	Paladin	Trinsic
Humility	Shepherd	Magincia
Justice	Druid	Yew
Sacrifice	Tinker	Minoc
Spirituality	Ranger	Skara Brae
Valor	Fighter	Jhelom

Now, to the questions, that all important test of your moral fiber.

The gypsy woman will turn over cards and ask you questions about them. You will have to carefully consider each of the seven questions and weigh the answer you give in light of the virtue you desire.

After the questioning is finished, the virtue that you most favor will be apparent, to her at least, and your character thus defined. The closer your answers are overall to the ideal state of your dominant virtue, the higher the class of the character. Instead of being a rank beginner, for example, it is possible to be a third-level Fighter or a second-level Druid, and so forth.

Whatever the virtue that results, you will have to master it and the other seven as well. That is the Way of the Avatar.

Successful adventurers, which is to say *live* adventurers, know that it is wise to maximize the odds in their favor. Since you will be the leader of the party, and therefore always first in the order of combat, you want to have the greatest chance to survival possible.

Perhaps the best profession, in that light, is to be a Paladin. Paladins have the highest levels of physical and magical combat abilities.

Paladins espouse the virtue of Honor. If you would be a Paladin, you must always answer the gypsy lady's questions with the thought of Honor foremost. Choose the answer that most typifies Honor, even if it is not the logical answer.

The Lay of the Land

At all stages of the development of your character, it is important to understand the geograpical makeup of the planet and the types of terrain you'll be crossing.

Geography

The destruction of Exodus unleashed mighty geological changes. Almost all of the surface area of this world fused together into one large continent, now called Britannia. There are a few islands, some of which pay homage to Lord British, and some of which do not. Beyond the known islands lie fearsome shoals, pockets of evil, and various mysterious places.

Terrain and Vegetation

Moving around Britannia is somewhat more difficult than it was in Sosaria. For one thing, Britannia is sixteen times larger. The only certain way to tell where you are is to use the system of coordinates developed by, of all people, pirate cartographers. Unfortunately, the only instrument capable of accurately reading this system is a sextant, and these are only available at shops of the Thieves Guild. Obtain one as soon as possible.

Terrain determines the speed of your progress. The easiest and smoothest traveling is on grass. Large areas of brush and scrub growth also exist. These will slow your party to three quarters of its normal speed.

Forests make for even slower going. You can achieve only half of normal speed as you seek a way through the dense trees. Visibility is almost nonexistent because the thick canopy of leaves cuts off almost all sunlight from the forest floor.

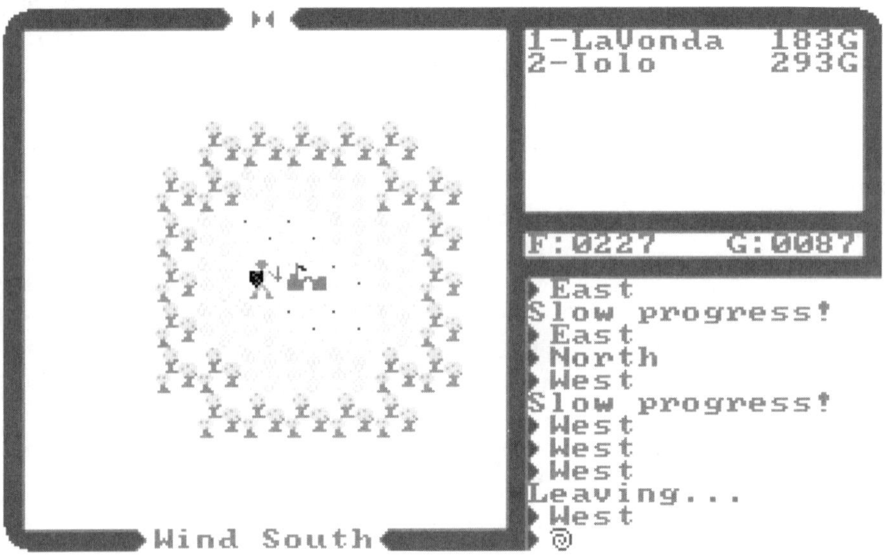

Figure 10.2 *Forests are hard going and drastically limit visibility. Here your party stumbles upon the city of Yew, which is hidden completely within a forest.*

Hills are abundant and slow you down dramatically. While you can travel through a hilly area, it is often faster to go completely around it.

Marshes and swamps are excellent places to stay *out* of, since the muck and mire slow your travel. Then, there are also the poison gasses released from the mud by your feet. These gasses can cause severe harm or even death.

Finally, there are mountains. The art of mountaineering is unknown in Britannia, so your only option is to bypass the mountains. Mountains also hinder visibility, since it is impossible to see over them.

Your Resources

Your party will be fairly well balanced with regard to abilities and skills, but you still need to take advantage of all the resources that you and your party are able to, to increase your knowledge and of course build your characters in the eight virtues. Britannia offers clues and essentials in almost every region. So next you'll be briefed on where to go, what to look for when you get there, and how not only to stay alive but also to progress on the path to Avatarhood.

As for the resources you are used to thinking about from your previous missions, you'll be glad to know that on this mission you don't have to bother with purchasing food for each member of your group, because it is divided automatically among your party. Shops, arms, armor, and taverns function similarly to how they functioned in the previous mission.

Castles

There are four castles to find and thoroughly explore. You'll want to converse with everyone, and each castle holds several pieces of important information—some of which I will help you with, and others of which you will have to find out for yourself. I strongly urge you to take very good notes. Make a list now of all the castles, towns, and villages and write down the individuals you meet in each place. Often you will be referred back to someone for additional (and usually critical) information, and it's very helpful to know where to find that person.

The coordinates are given for each location in longitude and latitude. You will need a sextant from a Thieves Guild shop to make use of these coordinates. Ask about sextants at the pub in Jhelom. Or, if you find a guild shop, purchase item 'D' in their standard inventory.

Britannia Castle (G'L", F'G")

This vast, rambling pile of stone is the home of Lord British, and the seat of his power. In a magnificent throne room on the second floor you will find the liege lord of Britannia. Talk to him of virtue and he will impart much valuable information, and also define your quest, providing important information about it.

As he did in the Third Age of Darkness, Lord British graciously raises the levels of you and the other members of your party as they gain in experience. Therefore you will want to visit him often. Be sure to ask him about his health. If there are any wounded or ill people in your party, answer 'no' when he inquires of your health. He will raise all your hit points to their maximum at no charge. You may avail yourself of this service at any time.

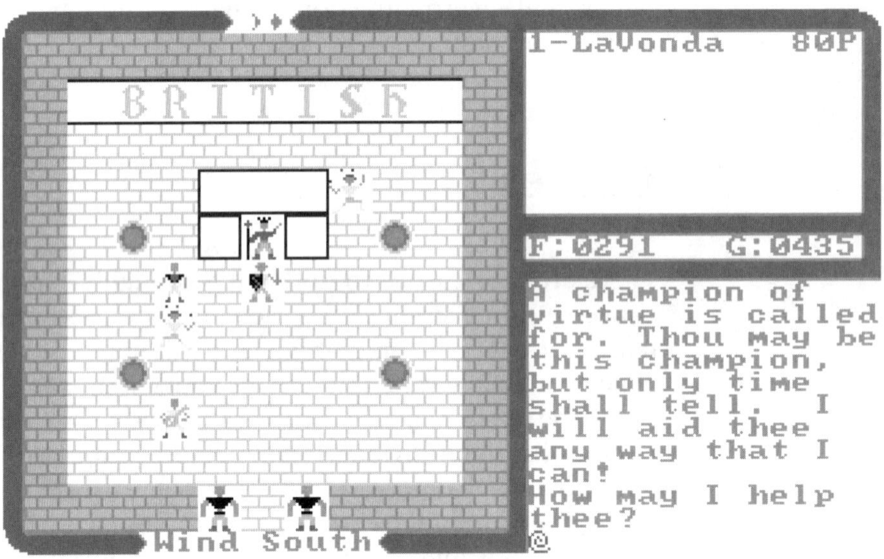

Figure 10.3 *Lord British is very helpful. Visit him often. Here he explains the quest to a new adventurer.*

Also in the castle you will want to regularly visit the seer Hawkwind, who will inform you how far you have progressed along the Way of the Avatar. You may check your status in each of the Eight Virtues.

Others in the castle have good information. Converse with Sheesha the injured fighter and Shawn the Shepherdess. Finding the secret of Shawn's location in the castle may require the passage of some time. Try walking through some brick walls, because they conceal secret passages.

Empath Abbey (D'C", B'M")

The Empath Abbey is where wise men and women meditate on various truths among stately groves of oak trees. There are many people here to talk to—at least fifteen of significance. You will need keys to enter an important oak grove within the Abbey.

Some of the things to inquire about include the candle of Love, the Silver Horn, the White Stone, the Bell, and the Skull.

Lady Marcy and Lord Robert know a single syllable of the word needed to gain entrance to the chamber housing the Codex of Ultimate Wisdom. Suzanna will tell you who can lead the way to the Silver Horn. You'll also learn a significant clue about a three-part key and altars, among other items of information.

Explore the Abbey completely, and look for secret passages. Talk to *everyone* and note their responses.

The Lycaeum (G'M", N'K")

Here is where the great philosophers hold endless debates. There are only four items of truly significant data to acquire. A charming lady has another syllable of the word of passage. You'll get some good advice and a formula for an important spell. And talk to the injured fighter about dungeons.

Serpent's Hold (P'B", J'C")

Only four pieces of information are here, but again they are significant. You'll learn of a sailing vessel, the *HMS Cape*, and how its hull was strengthened. Listen for the third and final syllable of the word of passage, and get some training in the use of stones as well.

Towns

As a candidate for Avatarhood, you need to visit all eight towns and search them thoroughly. Talk to *everyone*. Some of the information you can find out is given in the following; some is not. Be meticulous in approaching all individuals, and in exploring the town and its hidden places. Only then can you hope to succeed.

Britain (G'K", F' C")

Many are the things you can find out in the town of Britain. How to increase your compassion is one, and where the Shrine of Compassion lies is another. The end of a hallway may also bring compassion in a secret way, as will a certain mantra. You will hear of the Skull and the yellow Stone's location, in the dungeon Despise. Meditations, runes, and the great Stygian Abyss are all subjects for discussion.

Jhelom (N'O", C'E")

Items from a Thieves Guild shop will unlock secrets in this town. You will hear a mantra providing bravery and learn where to seek the Shrine of Valor. Be sure to ask Nostro of the Rune, and hold a strange conversation about the red Stone. Induce a wounded fighter to speak of what he learned in Dungeon Destard.

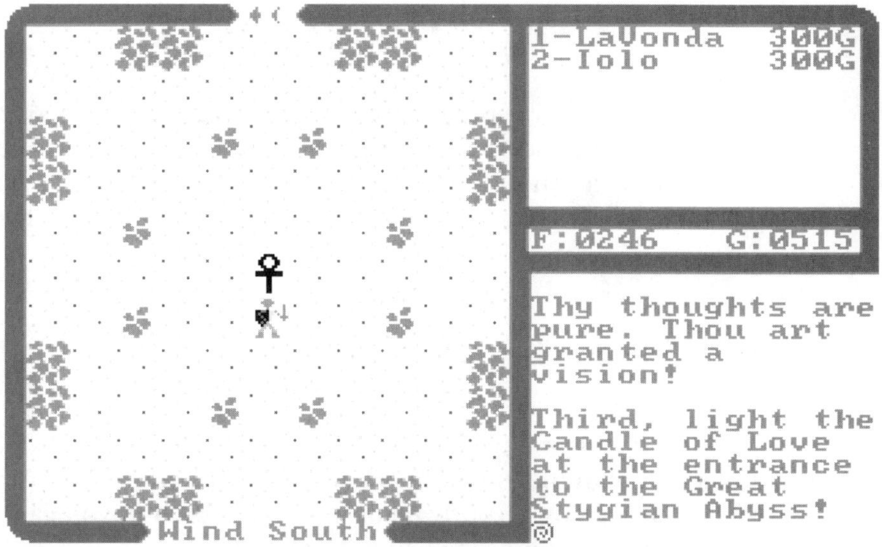

Figure 10.4 *In Britain, find out about the Shrine of Compassion and what to do when you get there.*

Magincia (K'J", L'L")

Nate the Snake knows were you can find out more about the black Stone. Casperin speaks of humility, and when you hear a proud mantra, mull it over, and remember that the reverse of pride is humility. Some notes on the Silver Horn might become yours as well.

Minoc (B'E", J'P")

Interesting and many are the facts and rumors you will garner in Minoc, the town of Sacrifice. A orange Stone will help you with spirituality, and you can locate the Skull. The Shrine of Sacrifice is not far, and you can hear a mantra from a hidden shepherd. Listen to tips about mystic weapons and armor and the requirements to obtain them. You find out where to obtain the Rune of Spirituality and learn where the Candle of Love is hidden, among other things.

Moonglow (I'H", O'I")

Moonglow is the seat of honesty. You'll find directions to the Shrine of Honor, and where the stone of Honor may be found, in the dungeon Deceit. An elderly woman knows a nice recipe, you'll hear a mantra leading to honesty, and now you'll be able to find the Rune of Honesty.

Skara Brae (I'A", B'G")

All you have to do is ask for the white Stone and it is yours; find out how here in this town, the center of spirituality. Hear about magic missiles and enjoy a saintly mantra. From a teacher, you can learn of the Abyss and the additional study you need.

Trinsic (L'I", G'K")

Trinsic, the seat of honor, has several knowledgeable persons. You'll talk about the purple Stone of Honor, and discuss navigation with a scruffy merchant. You can learn much information about the virtue of Honor. You hear a mantra leading to honor and the location of the Shrine. A skeleton knows of the purple Stone, and the old hermit might speak of the white Stone. You can learn the location of Nightshade, if you can avoid the poison.

Yew (C'L", D'K")

The people of Yew are just, and withhold no information. You learn where to listen for a mantra of justice. The location of the stone is in the dungeon Wrong. You'll hear discussion of mandrake root and a quick mention of blood moss. The rune is hidden well; ask Talfourd about it.

Villages

Villages are smaller than towns. In Britannia, they are quaint places, full of the bucolic placidity of rural life. Yet, just as strong currents sometimes flow under still water, very useful and critical information exists in villages. Approach the exploration of them in the same painstaking manner as you do that of towns and castles.

Buccaneer's Den (J'O", I'I")

Actually, this place has the least information of any town or village. You will, however, learn a very good way to reach out and touch monsters, and how all your virtues might be lost if you misuse the Skull.

Cove (F'K", I'I")

Cove is a busy place. Lots of folk to talk with. You'll hear about the Word of Passage and how to enter the Chamber of the Codex. Visit a shrine of peace, and write down the story about the ghost of Isaac and the white Stone. Learn how to spell 'gate' using various ingredients. To triumph, you need to combine virtues, and hear the truth about how to straighten ship hulls. Antos will speak of bells, books, and candles, and you can now find the black Stone.

Paws (J'B", G'C")

Sir Simon and Lady Tessa have a great secret, and they will tell you that they have a great secret, but not impart it until you are an eight-part Avatar. At that time, you can obtain mystic power and protection. You'll learn where to get mandrake root, and about secret entrances, and obtain a rune without bending yourself too much out of shape.

Vesper (D'L", L'H")

In Vesper, find Traveling Dan, who tells you the world is round. Learn how and when to visit the Shrines. You'll learn that you can combine three principles of virtue in eight ways, and how to find out the mantra of humility. You'll hear of an impediment to getting to the Shrine of Humility.

Transportation

At first, use your feet for their intended purpose. Later you'll find places to purchase horses, which speed your travel and make both journeys and boots less wearing.

Eventually you will need to make a voyage by sea. As in the Third Age of Darkness, you can obtain ships only from pirates. Seamanship is important again as well, because these vessels travel according to the prevailing breeze. Be sure to have a few wind spells because they can make life easier.

You'll encounter the mysterious moon gates you saw during the campaign against Exodus too. Consult the map supplied in your adventurer's kit to find out where they are and during which phases of the twin moons they appear. For example, one gate, called the Gate of Both Moons Dark, is indicated on your map as a solid black circle. It's on an island on the right side of the map. You should find a moonstone after the gate disappears.

Magic

Only spellcasters such as mages and paladins can perform magic. And even they must have certain natural substances called *reagents* to make a spell work. Look at *The Book of Mystic Wisdom* by Philpop the Weary, magician to the court of his most sovereign majesty Lord British, included in your adventurer's kit, for a detailed description of the reagents. To put it concisely, they consist of sulfurous ash, ginseng, garlic, spider silk, blood moss, mandrake root, black pearl, and the very scarce nightshade. You will want to stock up on these whenever possible.

If you prepare these ingredients in the proper proportions (you can pick up some very good recipes in the towns), you can cook up the following spells: Awaken, Blink, Cure, Dispel, Energy Field, Fireball, Gate Travel, Heal, Iceball, Jinx, Kill, Light, Negate, Open, Protection, Quickness, Resurrect, Sleep, Tremor, Undead, View, Wind Change, Xit (exit), Y (up), and Z (down).

For most spells, the use is obvious from the name. For full descriptions of each, refer to *The Book of Mystic Wisdom*. The most useful of these in the climactic visit to the Stygian Abyss are Awaken, Cure, Heal, Dispel, Negate, Protection, Sleep, and Tremor. I recommend that you have at least thirty of each available.

Healing

Adventuring is a dangerous profession. You and your fellow questors often take grievous wounds in the horror of combat. There are several ways to heal these wounds and to restore your hit points. Certain reagents have healing properties, and spellcasters can use them to effect first aid.

Since such reagents are very rare in the early going of your quest, another method of healing is to camp out. You can hole up for the night every one hundred moves; this restores most hit points. The drawback is that you chance being ambushed while you sleep.

Medical practitioners are not cheap, but healing booths exist in all towns. Expect to pay two hundred gold pieces for each patient, however.

Inns are another healing resource. Sleeping in an inn is safe and almost as effective as visiting a healing booth. Everyone can stay in the same room for one price (which varies widely, but is usually under one hundred gold pieces).

The best method of healing, if you are in the vicinity of Lord British's castle, is the monarch himself. He heals everyone completely and without charge.

Resurrection

Should you and *all* the members of your party be killed, this is not the end. Lord British will resurrect the party again, with part of its possessions and wealth. You start again from his castle, which could be very inconvenient. It is better to have invoked the 'Q' spell and restore yourself to reality from that state, with possessions and position intact.

Your Challenges

Now you know how to form the characters you start out with. You know a lot about the planet and where to obtain critical information, spells, and other items. You're ready to learn more specifics about the challenges facing you as you journey to the hiding place of the Codex.

Dungeons

There are eight dungeons you must visit. The hints you receive in the towns, castles, and villages help you to know what to look for in each dungeon. Here are their names and locations.

Dungeon	Location
Abyss	O'J"/O'J"
Covetous	B'L"/J'M"
Dasterd	K'I"/E'I"
Deceit	E'J"/P'A"
Despise	E'D"/F'L"
Hythloth	Behind Lord British's Castle
Shame	G'I"/D'K"
Wrong	B'E"/H'O"

By far the most important of the eight dungeons is the Stygian Abyss. It is here that the conclusion of your quest will occur, assuming you live that long. More on it later.

Figure 10.5 *The entrance to the Stygian Abyss is in the midst of a fiery lava cross.*

Combat

You will often engage in combat, especially in the early stages of your quest. Before fighting, make sure that every member of the party is properly equipped with appropriate weapons and armor. Ready the weapons and wear the armor. Each member of the party will be offered a selection of those available in the group's common inventory. A special permanent spell prevents you from selecting items not allowed for their profession.

When your party is adjacent to an enemy, you can attack. The field of battle will unfold before your eyes. If you don't attack an evil monster or monsters, they will gladly take the initiative and attack *you*. If you wait around trying to decide what to do, your opportunity to act will pass. If you've decided to cast a spell but don't know which one yet, press (C)ast to buy some time.

Combat is structured in turns—each member of the party has his or her turn either to move or attack. Attack can consist of using a weapon or casting a spell. Only those spells for which reagents have been prepared will work. Use missile weapons such as slings and bows often because they are very effective in letting you kill the enemy while staying out of the reach of its claws and fangs.

Once the battle is concluded, that is, once all of the monsters have been destroyed or the survivors have fled, you will often find that they were carrying chests of gold. Open these chests carefully, for some are booby-trapped.

Be wise: learn how to husband your forces. If the battle is going against you, there is no shame in making a tactical withdrawal to the rear. If just one of your party is near death, then remove only that one from the arena of combat and let the other members of thy party finish the job.

Use terrain to your advantage. When confronted with greater forces, occupy the obvious defensible positions such as between rock outcroppings, so that the enemy can hit you from only one direction instead of three or four.

Killing just to be killing is not acceptable anymore. You do not have the right to slay every monster, even if you are able to. Rather, before killing, ask yourself whether the monster is truly evil. If it's not, then just stand your ground until it retreats. Otherwise your progress along the Way of the Avatar will be retarded. The safe rule of thumb in combat is that if it attacks you, it is fair game.

Your Strategy

If you wish to complete the Quest within your normal lifetime, you need to employ certain strategies. Many paths lead toward the final solution, and there are many puzzles to unravel. You don't have to do all of this in any particular order, so proceed at your best pace. Just be thorough.

The First and Second Stages

As a Paladin, you materialize first in the city of Honor, Trinsic. You are armed with a sword and wear chain mail.

But before even starting, be sure to read *The History of Britannia* and *The Book of Mystic Wisdom*—both are included in your adventurer's pack. Don't start the Quest without this background information. Period.

Really, read the books before you start.

Don't say you were not warned.

Figure 10.6 *Lord British really means it. Read the book or your character will not live to regret it.*

Conducting conversations to gather information and exploring take place pretty much side by side, as the first and second thrusts of your mission overlap a lot in this adventure.

Conversations

The art of conversation is very important in this mission. Almost all of the clues you need to complete it will be imparted to you by various people in the castles, towns, and villages, if you just ask them the right questions. It will usually take three or four questions to hone in on the information you want. Here's an example:

You meet a tall bard.

When he asks, "Your interest?" respond "name?"

He replies, "My name is Smith."

When he asks, "Your interest?" ask "job?"

He replies, "I sing of quests."

As you might guess, the answer to your question about jobs gave you the key word 'quests,' which is what this person *really* knows. Continuing,

Your interest? quests

Are you on a quest? yes

Then ask Rudolf of the stone!

Obviously, the next step is to find Rudolf and question him. Talk to everyone in this manner and write down their answers.

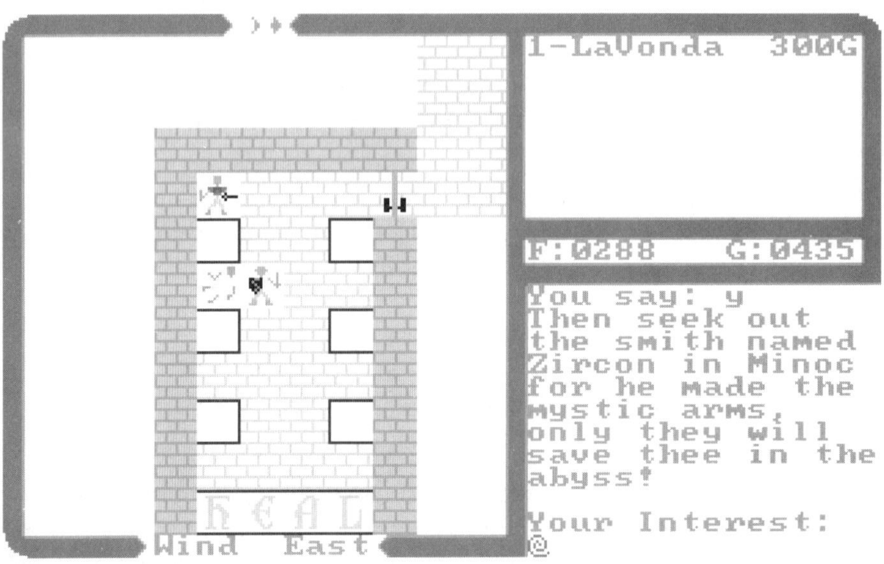

***Figure 10.7** Talk to everyone and note what they say!*

Write It Down

Which brings us to note taking. You are on an extremely complex mission with scores of pieces of important information to keep track of, and to act on in various ways at various times. It is absolutely crucial that you make a record of everyone you talk to, their location, and what they said, *even* if it seemed like an unimportant contact at the the time. It is quite possible that you asked the wrong questions and will eventually need to find this person again and query him or her more specifically.

Explore, Explore, Explore

Thoroughly investigate castles, towns, and villages; they are often larger than they seem at first, and full of dark and hidden crannies. You may conduct many of the minor quests undertaken to complete the larger one, entirely within a town or castle. Totally search the areas within the walls, and especially those dark nooks behind shops and other buildings.

Don't neglect the area outside the walls either. In some places you can walk completely around the outer perimeter of the walls without being forced out into the countryside. In this narrow strip of area that most do not even know exists, you will find a few well-informed and talkative people. Listen to them.

Most of the places you visit will have secret doors. Look for what seems to be an extraneous rectangle in brick walls, one which does not fit in with the pattern of the bricks. This is a secret door. Simply walk through it.

If you find locked doors or places where a magic field of force prevents you from entering, just make a note of their location and return later to enter when you have keys for the locks and the means of walking through force fields.

Virtue

I was not kidding earlier when I warned you about morals in this mission. Do not steal. Donate to the poor, show compassion, give blood, and build yourself in all of the Eight Virtues.

Adhere to the golden rule. Do unto others as you would have them do unto you.

The Final Stage

You can reach the Abyss only via water. A fiery lava cross marks it. Do not even *think* of coming here until your party has the maximum number of spell mixtures, all eight Stones, and all the other special items and information detailed in the many hints from the multitude of persons you have conversed with.

Throw the skull of Mondain into the Abyss now. There are eight levels in all, with an altar on each level. To go down a level, you must locate the current level's altar, answer a question, and use the appropriate color Stone.

Your final goal is to reach the chamber on the eighth level of the Stygian Abyss, which contains the Codex of Ultimate Wisdom. Keep your mind on that goal and do not waste time, for the Abyss is a very, very dangerous place.

In contrast to previous adventures, in which you could invoke the all-important 'Q' spell only out-of-doors, most likely you'll find that it now works inside this dungeon.

The viewing gems from the Thieves Guild are a necessity. Be sure you have plenty, because some of the altars are very hard to find. Watch for hidden triggers—there are often more than one to a room.

You'll be attacked by many powerful and horrid monsters. Conserve your resources as much as possible. If it looks like you're losing, run!

Although the monsters here look the same as they did in the Third Age of Darkness, conventional weapons and armor are ineffective against them. In the Castle of Death, where Exodus existed, only exotic weapons were effective. Here in the Stygian Abyss, you need to use mystical armor and weapons.

Level eight is the critical one. Be prepared with your answers or you will be kicked back to the surface and have to reenter the dungeon. Make sure you know the Word of Passage and the twelve answers (eight of them are the Virtues).

Good luck—you will really need it in the Abyss!

Use viewing gems generously to find the shortest and quickest route to the altar on each level. Avoid combat whenever possible, and remember that there are no penalties for running. Often careful use of spells will get you through a room in the shortest amount of time.

Sometimes, of course, you will have to stand your ground (or at least your dungeon stone floor) and slug it out toe to toe (or toe to claw) with monsters. This is especially true in the room with the secret door leading to the altar room. It is very unwise to search for that door while monsters are pummeling you. Deal with them first.

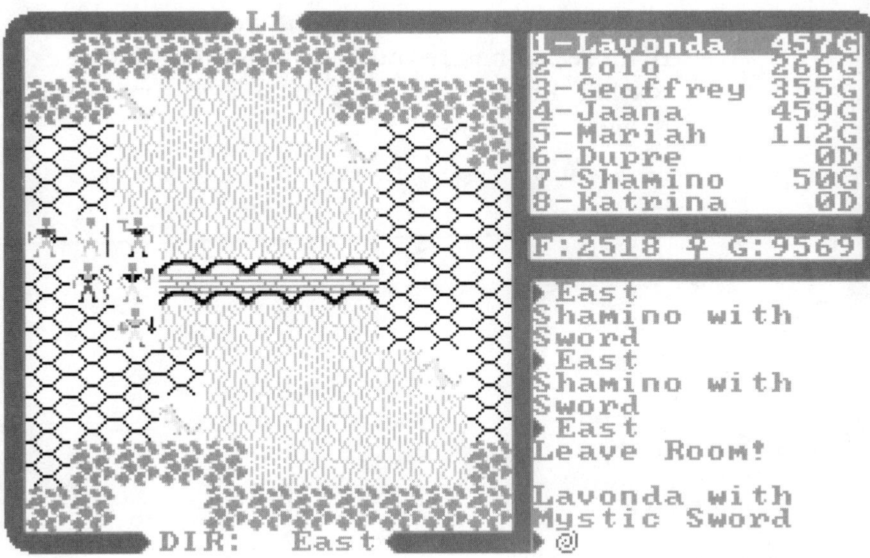

Figure 10.8 *Your party is starting to have trouble in the Stygian Abyss. Two of your team are already dead but can be resurrected. Perhaps you need to retreat and regroup.*

Each altar requires you to do something involving the right color stone, and to answer a question. An eight-part avatar should have no trouble with the questions.

It is possible to camp out in the dungeons, so hole up occasionally to restore hit points.

When you finally descend to level eight and reach the Chamber of the Codex, you will have to answer twelve questions in order to read it. Here you must be *extremely* careful. You must spell each answer exactly right. The slightest slip can be disastrous! So take your time and be very deliberate in your answers. The Abyss does not have a spell-checker.

If you answer all twelve questions correctly, the symbol of the Avatar will appear (if you read *The History of Britannia*, you will recognize it). Now, at long last you'll be permitted to read the Codex of Ultimate Wisdom. I won't tell you what's in it, but it is a good read, a very good read!

Now, listen carefully to the words of one who has walked the Way of the Avatar before you. Pay close attention, for experience is the best teacher. Lavonda will help you also to survive this most arduous and dangerous of tests.

11 Lavonda, Paladin of Great Beauty

Excerpts from a speech presented by Lavonda Da, Avatar, to the Adventurers Academy, Class of 2304. Full transcripts of this and other presentations in the series are available at Scrolls 'r Us shops throughout the realm. Discounts to qualified adventurers.

They have asked me to tell my story to you would-be adventurers.

I am not a teacher, I am a Paladin and an Eight-Part Avatar. Of course, as such, I cannot refuse. Avatars do good deeds, and saving the lives of young adventurers, despite what your drill sergeants and professors may say, is a good deed.

Yes, you laugh. I remember drill sergeants, too. Years ago, I was a student here at the academy. We studied the great campaigns of the Ages of Darkness. I read, it seemed interminably, of the heroics of Rolf the Warrior, the excellent ideas of Nimsman the Wizard, and the platitudes of Flavian the Good.

Series Editor's Note: Lavonda Da's name is legend. Her many successful quests earned her membership in the prestigious Adventurer's Hall of Fame. In highlights from this rare speech, she talks about her first mission.

You want to know the truth? I was not impressed. It was all just so much dry history. I was more interested in having fun, slipping down into town with my fellow students to carouse in the taverns. Coming here today, I was delighted to see the Bucket o' Suds is still open.

The academy was hard then. They had us up and running laps around the drill field at five A.M. A meager breakfast, then classes and exercises all day long, and supervised study at night. Boring, tedious stuff; it was hard for most of us to realize its benefits. We had joined up for glory and adventuring, and we wanted to get on with the program!

You probably feel the same way.

Well, let me tell you, out there in the field it's hell. Even if you *do* pay attention to your classes here at the Academy, you will be ill-prepared for the reality of the blood and guts spilled, the stench of combat, the pain of your wounds, the black despair, and the fear.

YOU WILL DIE, PEOPLE!

Or you will if you ignore what's taught here, and what I say today. Treat your quest like a game, and you'll not survive for long.

I am going to tell you about that turbulent and violent period between the end of the Ages of Darkness and the beginning of the Age of Light. Many of you, so I'm told, have volunteered to be injected into that period to perform the Quest of the Avatar. That, too, was my first mission.

By the way, I'm glad to see so many women present. In my day, I was one of the few. We took some harassment, but I like to think I've contributed a little in proving that females can succeed in the Way of Avatars just as well as males.

When my journey began, I remember, I was looking down at my palm and the ankh lying on it, that funny cross with the loop on top I had found in the circle of stones. When I looked up a fair had appeared in the valley below.

It was a beautiful spring day. Bees buzzed among the blooms, green grass reached up toward the sun and rustled gently under my feet as I strolled down to the fair, the mysterious-looking ankh still in my hand.

The ticket-taker took one look at the ankh and waved me past his ticket window. I wandered the fairgrounds, noticing nothing special among the crowds and the booths, when suddenly I found myself in front of a fortune teller's wagon. The wagon, I remember well, was dark and barely visible through the gathering dusk. I felt impelled to enter and slowly climbed the steps.

Eerie oriental-sounding music floated from inside somewhere. The deep mellow voice of a woman bid me to enter, and I dared not disobey.

Inside was sudden blackness. A small round table covered with green velvet glowed dimly in front of the woman, lighting her face only enough to give the barest hint of her high-cheekboned features. Her skin was ageless, her garments dark and mysterious-looking. Obviously she was a gypsy. The smell of incense hung heavily in the air.

"Ah, Lavonda," she said, her voice sending chills up my spine. "Long have I waited for thy arrival."

I stepped forward, feeling very much like the novice graduate from the Adventurers Academy that I was—nothing but a snot-nosed kid with no idea of what it would really be like and scared to death at this final test before being injected into my first mission.

"Sit down," the gypsy woman commanded.

I quickly did so, putting my hands between my knees to hide their shaking.

"Thou hast studied the Eight Virtues?" the gypsy woman asked, knowing full well such was required knowledge for AA graduates.

"Yes . . . yes, ma'am," I said and named them a little triumphantly. "Compassion, Honesty, Honor, Humility, Justice, Sacrifice, Spirituality, and Valor."

The gypsy woman was unimpressed. "Easy enough to name them by rote, Lavonda Da—to live them is another." Her slender finger tapped a deck of cards on the table. "The answers given here test thy true character. The answers given here could very well determine the success or failure of thy mission. Thy answers are extremely important."

"Yes, ma'am," I said, twisting nervously in my seat.

The gypsy woman sighed and placed two cards on the table before me. They were the cards of Honor and Humility.

"Consider this," she said. "Thou art at a crossroads in thy life. Dost thou A) choose the Honorable life of the Paladin, striving always for Truth and Courage, or B) choose the Humble life of the Shepard and a world of simplicity and peace?"

I lifted my right hand, pleased to see that it no longer shook, and reached out to tap a card. I wanted to be as strong as possible, which meant doing well on this test. Above all, I did not want to botch it all!

How you begin your quest was something we had discussed often, both in class and late at night in the dorms.

My decision on which profession to try for was a hard one, one I debated strongly within myself right up to the moment of the test. I was greatly swayed toward choosing the same as Clarin had.

Clarin was my idol at the Academy. He was a mage who had served in Britannia. Although he didn't succeed at his quest, all veterans were at a premium so he became an instructor.

I fell for him like a ton of altar stones, although I don't think he ever knew it. He later volunteered for another mission and was never heard from again. At the time, however, I could conceive of no profession more romantic than that of mage. I imagined taking long walks with him, talking of our calling. Oh, the secret lore that Clarin and I would exchange! (Such were my daydreams, that is.)

Sitting before the gypsy woman changed my thinking. This was *serious*. To survive I would need the utmost in advantages. I knew that only a paladin would have such advantages since they start with the highest class of armor and weapons. From that decision, it was merely a matter of knowing that Paladins espoused Honor above all and of carefully tailoring my answers to the gypsy's test so that Honor was foremost.

My index finger firmly tapped the card of Honor.

The gypsy nodded and presented two more cards, the cards of Honesty and Compassion. I was asked to choose between delivering a purse of gold untouched to its rightful owner or whether, in Compassion, I would give a coin to a needy beggar, knowing the owner would never miss the purse. Looking at the question from the viewpoint of Honor, I chose the card of Honesty. The other questions I answered in the same manner, putting Honesty first in all of them, even though the question did not mention that virtue at all.

When she had reached the last card in the set, the gypsy woman smiled. Instantaneously I found myself a level three Paladin in front of the town of Trinsic, the town of Honor.

I know it's hard to get started. As a novice adventurer during my first visit to the town of Trinsic, I was very shy. It was hard to bring myself to approach the first paladin I met—a big rough and gruff veteran who towered over me. His name was Rigamore. He was a very strong and gentle man as it turns out, but I will never forget the courage it took me to make that first approach. My heart felt as if it was beating ten times a second! It's funny, but fighting orcs and daemons has always been easy for me, and the art of conversation with total strangers something else entirely.

"Information about the Virtue of Honor," Rigamore said after my first few fumbling questions, "is found throughout Trinsic. There are two requirements to enter and use the Shrine of Honor."

That was all I could get out of him, but it was the basic facts I needed. In this town I could find more about Honor, the first of the Eight Virtues I had to master on my way to Avatarhood.

I had to cultivate the art of talking to people. Dergin, a soulful fighter that I met also in Trinsic soon after I began my mission, is a good example. He had much useful information, but I had to draw it out of him. Here's how it happened.

Dergin looked very weary, leaning against the check-in counter in the Honorable Inn.

"Job?" I asked him, making my language terse and staccato.

"I seek a place to rest," he said, beckoning the clerk closer.

"Rest?" I asked.

"I have quested long and hard."

"Quest?" I asked.

Dergin nodded in his earnest way. "I seek enlightment at the Shrine of Honor."

Ah, now we were getting somewhere! I was trying to formulate my next question, when suddenly he asked me one of his own.

"Art thou enlightened in Honor?"

"No," I admitted honestly.

He smiled, erasing the tired lines from his face for a moment. "The Shrine lies to the south and west beyond the swamps."

He then turned to the clerk and engaged a room. I asked him a few other questions, but he had no more information to impart. I then went looking for others to converse with, determined to keep asking them questions until I hit the right key words to get their knowledge.

The next person I spoke with in Trinsic was a sleepy fighter named Publius. "Seek the purple Stone of Honor," he told me in reply to my use of the word 'Honor.'

A searching paladin, who called himself Kline, was very forthcoming. He told me where both the Rune of Honor and the Shrine of Honor were located and, hearing me ask "Mantra?", he said "Summ."

In the dark forested area of the town, I found a child cowering beneath a bush. He was crying. I managed to calm him down enough to determine that the poor little tyke had been chased by a bull.

I comforted him as best I could. When the tears and sobs stopped, this youngster gratefully told me where the Rune of Honor was buried.

That reminds me—before I forget, I'll advise you not to overlook children. They often are wise beyond their years.

I got a lot of other good information from the people of Trinsic. I was slowly learning not to be scared when approaching a stranger. Gradually I was learning how to form my questions. From Trinsic, I was able to travel to the Shrine of Honor, enter, and meditate properly. That was the first part of Avatarhood I achieved.

I felt joy and fulfillment. If there had only been some way that I could have let Clarin and my friends back at the Academy know.

In the first few weeks of my stay, when riding between towns, with the high rocks on one side of the path and the dark forest on the other and the stars seeming to glare down malevolently, I felt very much alone. I even almost wished for an ambush (I couldn't believe I was thinking this way!) just so I could have contact with some other living being.

At other times, when I wasn't feeling lonely, I feared some extreme hardship such as running out of food and having no idea where a town was. Starving and lost, I would blunder around in an ever-weakening state until something killed me or I starved to death.

I also feared bands of orcs, bears, or other monsters would overwhelm my defenses and bludgeon the life from my body. I feared I would be unable honorably to complete my mission, or even to get back.

Yes, those are some of the things I experienced when I was going it alone. But I soon realized I was not trained at great expense and put into this mission to die gloriously for Britannia. I was put there to *live* and succeed in the Quest, while making the minions of evil die for *their* cause.

I had been granted certain leadership abilities. I began to realize—indeed to hope—that if I was on the right path, and advancing sufficiently, others would flock to my standard. I knew I needed to find these people and see if I could convince them to join me.

So, over a period of several weeks I visited all the towns of Britannia, the castles, and the villages. I met and recruited seven of the finest individuals it has been my privilege to know. To them I owe the success of my mission.

There was Geoffrey the fighter from Jhelom. Iolo the bard, who I found serenading a children's party in Britain, was only too happy to find a real job. Jaana was carrying out her duties as a Druid in the forest-bound town of Yew. Julia was a tinker by trade, fixing pots and pans in Minoc. Katrina was a shepherd from Magincia, Mariah an honest mage from the town of Moonglow, and Shamino a ranger from Skara Brae.

I imagine these people or possibly their sons or daughters might be inclined to join your party as well. They are all great fighters and staunch companions.

I took care that all my party members were of professions other than my own, to balance the party. For example, in Trinsic I met a fine young paladin by the name of Dupre. Had I not been a paladin myself, I'm sure he would have been an excellent addition to my party. We parted on friendly terms. For those of you who become mages or rangers, he might be amenable to joining a party of yours.

Oh, I remember my party affectionately. We were a ragtag bunch at first. Katrina, Shamino, Jaana, Geoffrey, Mariah, Julia, Iolo, and myself. All of different professions and backgrounds, and me with the added disadvantage of not even having been born in Britannia.

There were some arguments about who should lead. Iolo, for a while at first, seemed to think he could do a better job than I could. Certainly he did not always follow my orders. Then came the day that melded us together into a single, cohesive unit. It was an unexpected ambush and the resulting desperate battle that accomplished this feat.

The Serpent's Spine is a great, towering mountain range not far from the town of Britain. It always looked more like the teeth and fangs of serpents to me, actually. Sharp crags of naked rock tearing at the sky in a permanent snarl. A dreadful place, inhabited by dreadful creatures.

We were skirting the range closely, moving through a narrow valley in the foothills. A defile opened up into the mountain's side. From this shadowed area sprang a bunch of ettins intent on having us as a late breakfast. Other ettins tossed boulders down at us from above.

If you've ever seen an ettin, you never forget it. These two-headed perversions of nature are huge, mean, and *always* hungry. Shamino screamed as a boulder impacted his shoulder and his left arm hung limp and useless.

"Julia, Iolo," I yelled to the two bow-carriers. "Pick off the ones on the rocks!"

For once Iolo didn't argue. There was a double *twang* as he and Julia loosed arrows. Above us an ettin suddenly grew a single feathered horn in each of its two heads and tumbled lifeless down the slope.

I had my sword ready and led the others at a charge toward the ettins on our level. Jaana, as I had instructed her earlier, held back some and readied a fireball spell. The fireball whizzed by us, leaving a stink of brimstone in the air, and impacted the lead ettin on its chest.

Now close enough to smell the acrid odor, I plunged my blade into the smoldering beast and finished it off.

"Britannia forever!" Shamino yelled, taking a great one-armed swing of his sword at an ettin. The blade sank deep into one of the thing's heads and the other snarled as if in surprise at the pain.

Mariah tossed flaming oil over my shoulder, saving me by hitting the ettin about to leap on my back. My sword skewered the one clawing at Mariah, and Geoffrey got the one that was trying to bypass us to get at Iolo and Julia.

Meanwhile, their bows sang busily and Jaana kept getting off fireballs as our long-range weapons began taking a heavy toll. The rest of us formed a circle in the midst of the attacking horde, protecting each other's backs and hacking and slashing in a desperate bid for survival.

The battle seemed to last forever, but at last we felt and saw no more ettin movements. We stood gasping for breath. We were all wounded, blood dripping from holes ripped in our armor by the claws of the beasts that now sprawled lifeless around us, but we were *all* still on our feet because of teamwork! Each of us had saved the lives of others not once but several times.

Iolo laughed, and suddenly, there in the midst of death and the litter of the battlefield, we were all laughing and crying and hugging in happiness. We were one! We were a party!

Now WAKE UP and listen to this!

BUT, don't think that all you have to do is just defeat a few monsters and visit a Shrine with the right two prerequisites and meditate for three cycles. Any fool can do those things, and many do. You do *not* get virtue that easily, you have to *earn* virtue.

By the way, speaking of fools, don't ignore the jesters you see capering around in towns and castles.

I remember a visit to the town of Britain. More or less through boredom, I struck up a conversation with Gweno, who was currently between engagements but still practicing his prancing, gibbering trade. Among the silliness he said: "Beggars are thankful for small donations; show compassion."

"Give me gold and I'd be thankful, too," Shamino said with a grin, and we all laughed.

Not long after that, I met a beggar who asked me for help. Naturally I was all too glad to share with him from my meager store of gold. This showed my compassion and made the road to Avatarhood just a little less rocky. I began to look for ways to do similar acts for the other virtues.

A few days later, we were wandering along a hallway on the first level of Lord British's castle. "What's in here, I wonder?" Julia said, indicating a doorway.

"One way to find out," I replied and led them inside down another hall. We stopped as we were confronted by a tall, dignified man in the robes of a sage.

"Name?" I asked.

"Hawkwind," he answered.

We soon learned that Hawkwind could tell us how we were progressing in the cultivation of the various virtues.

"Thou art ready for the Shrine of Compassion," he told me.

I thanked him and we left. We were to return often.

We took a long sea voyage to Verity Isle, and was that trip rough! I was glad to see land, as were the others.

When we left our boat and trudged to the Lycaeum, Jaana exclaimed, "Look at all these wonderful books." There was a lot of knowledge there on the thousands of scrolls. Yes, the Lycaeum is definitely the seat of learning for all of Britannia. Unfortunately, the pressures of our quest were such that I didn't have much time to dally at the Lycaeum, but I did pick up some useful information there, as you can just about everywhere in the realm.

I was most fond of old Nigel, the noble wizard who lectures on pharmacology at the Lycaeum. Let me check *my* notes. Ah, yes. "The Resurrection spell consist of one part each of ash, ginseng, garlic, spider silk, blood moss, and mandrake root."

The telescope is what I liked best, though. I would gravitate back to it and back to it even after I knew a good deal of the terrain by heart. I loved to view the towns, castles, and villages of Britain, Britannia, Buccaneer's Den, Cove, Empath Abbey, Jehlom, Lycaeum, Magincia, Minoc, Moonglow, Paws, Serpents Hold, Skara Brae, Trinsic, Vesper, and Yew. I still like to say their names like that.

I didn't much want to draw a map but I made myself do it. Was I glad I did! I saved myself much time that way when I visited those places in person. The rest of my party were always amazed at how I seemed to know exactly where we were.

When we finally got to the Stygian Abyss, from the first it was obvious that it was vastly different from other dungeons. Not that we had much time to reflect as we were attacked by monsters from every side, fangs bared, flames spouting from their mouths.

Obviously staying there would have been fatal.

"A bridge!" Shamino said, pulling his robe closer to ward off the more severe effects of the flame and peering through the smoke. "There's a stone bridge there!"

I plunged my weapon into the gut of a monster, taking a face-full of flame but dispatching the beast. A soothing coolness washed over me as Jaana cast a healing spell.

"Follow me," I shouted and led a charge onto the bridge.

We ran across, only to be ambushed by another horde of monsters. Most of that day—or maybe it was night, there was no way of telling down in the Abyss—we fought agonizing inch by inch toward the altar room. Katrina died twice and twice we resurrected her before getting her hit points built back up to a decent level with healing spells.

The stench of burning sulfur filled the rooms. Flames seemed to spout from everywhere.

Finally we won our way to the altar room. I had the right Stone and properly answered the question. The way opened down to the next level.

"And this," Shamino said, gasping wearily from where he leaned against a wall, "is just the *first* level?"

"It was a bear, wasn't it?" Jaana said, her irrepressible grin still present but now strained.

"Only seven more to go," I said, to their groans, but all followed me willingly down the ladder to the second level.

"We'll hole up here to rebuild hit points," I said, and we set up camp.

We peered into a gem to map the second level and pinpoint the altar room. Then we endured another fierce fight and descended to the third level. Again we holed up to lick our wounds.

And so forth, from the third level on down.

It seemed to take forever, and it was an exhausting experience. The down spells had no effect here. Regular weapons and armor were useless. There was no option other than to fight our way through.

Finally, at the eighth level, when our strength seemed all but gone, then, and only then, was I permitted to read the Codex of Ultimate Wisdom and complete my Quest in glorious style.

My sense of accomplishment was incredible, yet I also felt a deep peace. I had saved Britannia and done my duty as the full-fledged Avatar I now was. One could not ask for more than *that*.

As to the contents, if I told you that, there would be no need for the Quest, now would there? Besides, you really do need to have achieved full Avatarhood to read the Codex.

Now, I leave you with a salute, which you might find useful later: Truth, Love, Courage, Infinity.

Good luck, adventurers.

PART

6

Ultima V—Warriors of Destiny

12 The Avatar Prepares Again for Battle

Greetings, Adventurer! Tomorrow you become a Warrior of Destiny. This briefing is to prepare you for the most important mission ever assigned to any adventurer yet. As you well know, Lord British is missing, a minister of abhorrent agents of evil rules the realm, and foul play is most definitely suspected. Unrest is everywhere, and time is of the essence.

Once again the call has gone out for adventurers, and great numbers have responded. The number of veteran Avatars who have signed up is gratifying, since anyone who completed the previous mission is granted special privileges for this campaign. Only a great Hero or Heroine, only a truly mighty Avatar can set things aright once more. Harken now to this briefing.

Background

In the fourth great crisis in Britannia's history, Lord British had issued a challenge for an individual to show the people the way of virtue and lead them out of moral darkness. He desired a Hero or Heroine who could unravel the concepts needed to become an eight-part Avatar, the human embodiment of the supreme virtues of Compassion, Honesty, Honor, Humility, Justice, Sacrifice, Spirituality, and Valor. Only such a paragon, this ultimate of blessed warriors, could and would find the Codex of Ultimate Wisdom.

So it came to pass.

Once the Codex was found, Lord British ordered that it be raised from the depths of the Great Stygian Abyss so that its teachings might be studied by the wise men and women of the realm. This was done, but moving the Codex created a mighty karmic imbalance in the very fabric of reality. Both the physical and the spiritual landscape of the world changed dramatically.

A fiery new island, the Isle of the Avatar, sprang forth from the murky bottom of the Great Sea. The cataclysmic bulging up of the world's surface to form this island opened a mammoth hollow far beneath, an immense underworld chamber.

On the island, once it had cooled, a shrine was constructed to hold the Codex for all time for the common good of all who dwell within Britannia. The learned flocked to this shrine, and the consensus was that a new Age of Enlightment had dawned. Alas, far below, under uncountable tons of rock, evil was once again aborning.

You see, the unfortunate side effect of Britannia's successful victories against evil is the fallout and pollution that can sully parts of the world for generations. Pockets of evil lie under the new continents forged by the death throes of wicked wizards like Mondain, Minax, and the diabolical conglomeration called Exodus, pockets of evil that fester like abscesses—waste of the most hazardous kind.

It was one of these pockets that was disturbed when the Isle of the Avatar rose and the vast and mysterious Underworld formed. From that pocket rolled three broken slivers, remnants of Mondain's black jewel of immortality that a heroic adventurer had rendered ineffective just before destroying Mondain. Shards that, far down there in the Stygian blackness, glimmered in a ghastly light of their own making. Shards that pulsed threateningly, then grew into three sinister Shadowlords. Shards that performed the bidding of the curse placed on them by a long-dead wizard and poured forth his revenge on the world.

The three Shadowlords—born full grown and possessing malevolent intelligences of considerable size—wasted no time in plying their trade of trickery and deceit on the world. What an all-out frontal assault by millions of monsters could not have accomplished, they did rather easily with the use of subterfuge. When Lord British was on an expedition to explore the newly discovered underworld, they captured him and removed him from the scene. They replaced him as King with Lord Blackthorn, a once good man now twisted and perverted into a tool of the Shadowlords.

Lord Blackthorn has declared martial law; violence reigns over the land. Even the very law of the realm, adherence to the rules of the Avatar, has been distorted and used by the human agents of the Shadowlords to oppress and manipulate the people of Britannia.

You are desperately needed.

Your Characters

The character you choose to be, as well as the party you choose to help you, is very important to the success of your mission. You probably are already an Avatar at the start of this game, because it is possible to carry over your character from the previous adventure (and to begin at fifth level). If so, you will begin your mission right away. On the other hand, if you are creating a new character, first you will answer the gypsy woman's questions and form your character. (If this is your first mission, read the section on virtue in *The Book of Lore* provided in your adventurer's kit.)

Your mission has three major thrusts. You need to kill the Shadowlords, but you have to wait to attempt this 'til you are ready, because you should never fight a Shadowlord until you can pick the time and the place, and have the right shard to destroy it. Also you must retrieve three of Lord British's emblems of power. The three emblems are the Sceptre, which can dispel magic force fields; the Crown, which absorbs all magic regardless of how powerful it might be; and the Amulet, which helps you to find the entrance to the dungeon Doom, and to see in otherwise blinding darkness. None of these three symbols is readily available until you have sufficient strength and resources. Of course, you also rescue Lord British, which can't be done until the other two parts of the quest are completed. To accomplish these challenging goals, you explore, search, talk to people to gather information (including eight words of power), build up points, and retrieve items. Be sure to take thorough notes, because many related clues and objects do not occur together in space or time.

This mission is, in some ways at least, a little easier than the last one. Because you come in as an Avatar, there is no need to "prove yourself" in the various virtues. However, it is important that you continue acting in good ways, or some people will not give you important information. If your actions are really bad, you could be penalized by not being raised in level. There is no Hawkwind in this game to give you advice, so it is up to you and you alone to decide if you are acting as an Avatar or not.

Profession

It is possible, by following one virtue when answering the gypsy's questions, to control the profession that is yours upon injection into Britannia. For example, always putting Honesty first makes you a mage. Which profession you are is not quite as critical as in the previous campaign, when being a paladin was of considerable advantage. There are now only three professions—Mages, Bards, and Fighters. Also, you will be recruiting at least five others to join your party, whose strengths will of course help you.

The only real advantages of one profession over the others are minor edges in intelligence, dexterity, and strength at the start. A mage is the most intelligent and therefore the best user of magic. Bards are dexterous and agile and moderately good at magic. Fighters are strong but lousy magic users because of their somewhat low intelligence.

I recommend you start as a mage. Intelligence does more for you in this mission than sheer strength, and you can always recruit fighters to serve you.

You don't need to consider arms and armor when choosing a profession, because there are few limitations on the use of weapons and armor. If a character is strong enough, he or she can wear any armor and use any weapon. This even includes magic bows and axes.

Strength is, in fact, the only factor that limits the arms and armor a character can handle. Someone who can wield a halberd while wearing leather armor, for example, might not be able to in plate armor. As a good leader, you will naturally experiment to find the best combinations for your people to maximize offense and defense.

You do need to consider magic-using ability in choosing a profession, because of its importance in this mission. The highest level you can hope to achieve is eight. The first level is granted at 50 experience points, and each following level requires double the previous level, with level eight requiring 6400 points. As a magic-using person, such as a mage, reaches a new level, a new circle of spells becomes available. Consult *The Book of Lore* for a listing of the spells according to the circles of proficiency that they require.

Your Party

I do not expect you to effect the rescue of Lord British and fulfill the other requirements of this mission alone. Not even that famed warrior of the First Age of Darkness, Rolf, could do that in this much larger, vastly more complex world. And, in fact, I encourage you to recruit help.

Such help is readily available. There are numerous people willing to sign on under your leadership. These include all eight of the characters that you veterans met in the last campaign: Dupre, Katrina, Shamino, Jaana, Geoffrey, Mariah, Julia, and Iolo.

Unfortunately, due to circumstances beyond our control, this time you may have only a total of six in your party, which includes yourself. There are some hard decisions you have to make on whom to accept and whom to reject. However, it is possible to recruit more than five, "park" one or more members temporarily, and use others in their stead to take advantage of their particular skills and abilities.

The optimum party for success includes as many magic users as possible. Perhaps the only non-magic user you should even consider having is Shamino, the fighter. Take bards like Toshi and Julia, and magic users such as Mariah. You will have five out of six who can cast spells, while faithful Shamino is there to do the heavy duty hacking. Maximize your magical "firepower."

Some caution must be exercised also from the viewpoint of loyalty. Due to the evil manipulation of society by Lord Blackthorn and the Shadowlords, some people have been duped into being on the wrong side. You certainly do not want any of them in your party sabotaging its chances of success. The best way to determine a character's trustworthiness is to talk with him or her and carefully analyze the replies. Be careful!

Vast responsibility rests on your shoulders as leader of the party of heroes. Only the strong live to return.

The Lay of the Land

Because you and your party have to do so much traveling, it's essential that you understand the layout of the planet and the types of terrain that will be between you and whatever it is that you need.

Geography

Britannia consists of a large continent, which is broken up by natural features such as mountains, rivers, swamps, and forests, and several islands.

Terrain

The largest portions of land areas are grasslands. Grass offers no impediment to travel, but also no concealment from enemies. Areas of brush usually exist next to grasslands, consisting of taller grass and dense shrubbery. This slows down travel dramatically, while also not offering concealment. Avoid brush areas.

Forests are extensive and very dark. The close spacing of the trees gives you little warning of enemies. While they can't see you either, your party is apt to stumble on them too quickly to escape. On the other hand, if pursuit is hot, forests are great to hide in.

Hills are beautiful, but they slow travel almost to a crawl. Mountains are tall and rugged; however, you can scale some of the lower peaks with the proper equipment. Mountaineering has finally reached Britannia! In fact, there are two mountain keeps that you have to climb some peaks to reach.

Swamps are still poisonous, although certain useful herbs grow in them. You have to cross them from time to time, so be sure to learn An Nox, the spell to cure poison very early on, and stock up on its ingredients. An Nox is a first-level spell.

In the northeast, there is a large dry lake bed that is now a desert. You need to venture out into this desert, but do so with care.

There are several rivers and streams and two major lakes. The oceans are large and, as you venture out from the shore, far too rough for any transportation except a large frigate. Unfortunately, the frigates draw too much water to come in close to shore except at a few deepwater ports. Skiffs are the best method of traveling on rivers, lakes, and the strip of shoal-filled water along the shores that frigates cannot enter. Skiffs can also go out moderate distances as long as you are careful to stay in smooth water. *Do not* go into choppy waters with a skiff; you may not live to regret it.

Your Resources

Numerous enhancements have been added since the last adventure to make the your lot a lot easier.

Your sight is better; you can see the details of things better and their colors are brighter. You can invoke the 'Q' spell in more places. People are even more talkative than in the previous mission, which means you need to question them more precisely. Castles are larger, with several stories (Lord British's castle has five). The world is much larger, twice the size as it was during the *Quest of the Avatar*. There are now lighthouses and huts and keeps also. As in your previous mission, food is divided automatically among your group. You and your party do not consume food so quickly, and there are plenty of healers.

Lord British is more accessible. He visits your party as an apparition when you are camped for the night if any party member has enough experience points to advance a level. He also heals your wounds.

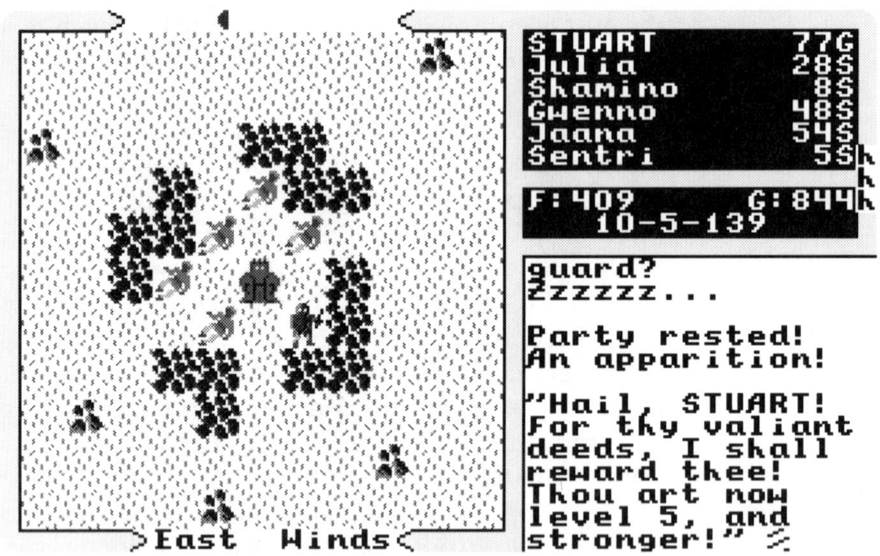

Figure 12.1 *Camping out restores your hit points and gives advancement by means of Lord British's apparition.*

Travel on land has been made somewhat easier by a rudimentary road system, and a few scattered bridges. There is, for example, a road going south from Lord British's castle and the town of Britain, passing by the village of Paws and ending at the town of Trinsic. A road has been built mostly through forest from Empath Abbey to Yew. At other places there are bridges over streams. Often trolls live under the bridges and demand a fee for passage, which is where the somewhat corrupted modern-day term 'toll bridge' originated.

Lord British's Castle

The castles here are larger than in previous missions. There are two important castles—Lord British's and that of the evil usurper, Blackthorn, which you'll hear more of later.

Veterans of the previous mission will recognize the location of Lord British's castle. It's on Brittany Bay, in exactly the same place as you found it before. However, in the intervening years, the castle has been much enlarged.

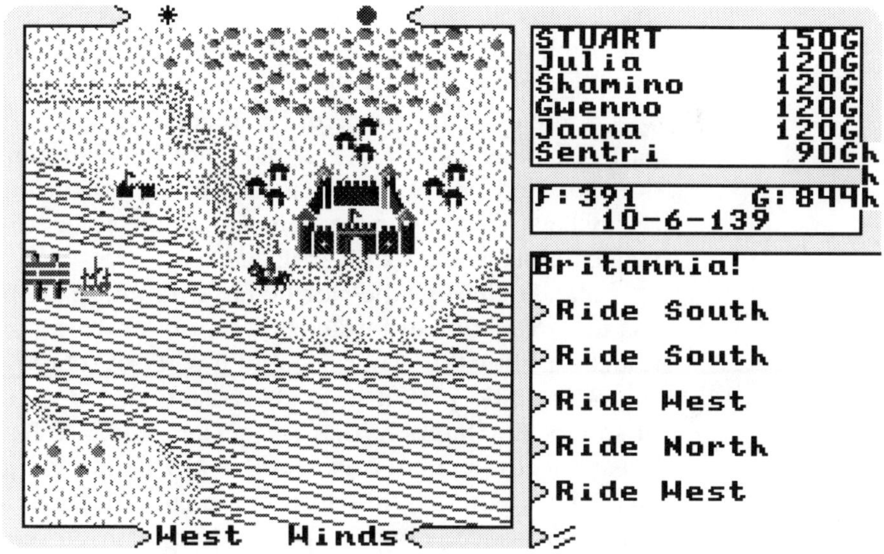

Figure 12.2 *Lord British's castle on Brittany Bay. Also present is the town of Britain and the three villages of East, North, and West Brittany. Your party on horseback travels toward the frigate they own, which is docked at the pier in the bay.*

Main Floor: While it's extensive, there is not a lot to be gained on the main floor of the castle. You'll find a kitchen and a table. The stable girl, Treanna, can help you later, but won't do so during the first part of your mission. You are free to borrow horses from the stable *if* one of your party can unlock the door to the outside (across the corridor from the stable entrance). If you don't have keys yet, forget it.

In the center of the corridor along the north side of the castle is another door that leads outside. This one opens onto a small patch of land bordered by the moat. If you have access to a magic carpet, this is a good way to escape from the castle if necessary. Unlike the previous mission, there is no dungeon behind the castle. On each corner of the castle there are towers. The towers have ladders up to the higher levels and down to the basement.

Basement: The basement is devoted mostly to storage. Keep trying to gain access to the storage rooms. There are several useful items secreted in the various containers. It's OK to take them. In fact, because Lord British is being held prisoner, he has given you special dispensation to use any of his special stocks to help effect his rescue. Some of the items even replenish themselves, so the next time you are in the castle, search that place again.

Some doors are locked. If a regular key just breaks, it means the party member using it either does not have enough dexterity, or the door is sealed with magic. So, getting at some of the items requires either a skull key (which opens most locks), or the ability to cast the fifth circle magic unlock spell, IN EX POR.

Max Engle runs the North Star Armoury in the basement, also. He has some very fine examples of weapons and armor, but his prices are not cheap. Buy the magical shield if you can scrape up the gold.

The castle prison is in the basement, as well. This is for local prisoners. (If it happens that *you* get arrested, you'll not serve time here but at the government prison and justice center in the town of Yew.) As far as I know, there is little information to be gained in the castle prison. A surly prisoner is behind the middle of the three doors. You'll get nothing but a fight from him. The cell on the right is empty, and the door on the left opens onto a stone wall. If you determine the secret of this wall, please inform us here at the Academy, because we haven't been able to, nor have any of our intelligence sources.

Second Floor: Above the main floor, without too much surprise, you find the second floor. It's large and there are lots of rooms, including another kitchen, banquet room, smaller dining room, barracks for guards, and an empty throne room. There is a secret passage through the center of this floor, with outlets to the main throne room, banquet hall, and kitchen. The only person with valuable information you might find on this level is Desiree. Talk to her about food.

Roof: There is a terrific view from the battlements. You find several cannons, which you can move around and even fire by invoking the 'F' spell. In the center of the southern or front side of the castle, a walkway leads toward the center of the roof. Lord British's penthouse is located there. Unfortunately, there is also a guard. While you could move a cannon around and blast him, this is not recommended. Remember, you are an Avatar and an Avatar does not attack someone who is only doing his job and not attacking you. The thing to do is to wait patiently until the guard is not blocking the walkway, then zip by him. He won't chase you.

Lord British's Apartment: The door to the penthouse, as befits the private apartment of a king, is magically locked. Only a skull key or an IN EX POR spell can open it, and you had better have two, because you might have to unlock it from the inside to get out again.

The apartment is nice, especially the rug on the floor. Take it as a souvenir, because you'll find it very handy. There are few furnishings here, although the harpsichord is very nice. A fire burns in the fireplace. Walk through it (and find out just how hot it is) and explore the small hidden room behind. Nothing there, but it's neat.

Back in the main apartment it's time for a little music. Sit down at the harpsichord and play. If you've already visited the Grayhaven lighthouse and have *The Book of Lore*, you know which tune to play. The correct piece of music causes a secret door to appear. Behind it is a wooden box. Take the box but don't try to open or use it. The right time for that will come much later.

Observatory: Climb the ladder to the roof of the penthouse. There's a telescope there. Look through it at night only, or otherwise you'll get a zap from the sun. There are eight stars or planets to be seen, and three comets. The stars or planets represent the eight towns of Britannia, and the comets are the three Shadowlords. If a comet is next to a star, it means a Shadowlord is in that town, and you don't want to visit it while he's there.

That's pretty much it for Lord British's castle. There are not all that many interesting people to talk with, but you will want to come back to the storerooms in the basement occasionally. Oh, if every member of your party is killed, you will all be resurrected and find yourselves back on the top level of this castle, regardless of where you were killed.

Figure 12.3 A music lesson is critical to your success.

Major Keeps

There are three major keeps, all of which were encountered in your previous mission, but they are now much remodeled and enlarged.

Empath Abbey

Empath Abbey is the keep of Love, and is located to the northeast of Lord British's castle. If you can find Yew, you can use the road from Yew to Empath Abbey, which is a good road. It features a moon gate in the clearing near Yew, which you'll see at night.

There are two levels in Empath Abbey. A healer has set up shop on the first level, and the eternal Flame of Love burns brightly on the second level. Tim is Empath Abbey's bard. Ask him about Sir Kenneth, who was the court composer, and where he might be today. Lady Barbara is the keeper of the Flame and speaks to you of her vision. Lord Michael is the guy to discuss mountain climbing with, and he also knows the name of the Shadowlord of Hatred. You'll need that name later.

The Lycaeum

Sail due east from Brittany Bay, across the wide blue ocean, and you will come to Verity Isle, on which the Lycaeum and the town of Moonglow are located. The Lycaeum stands for Truth, and is Brittania's center of learning. The Flame of Truth burns bright within its walls.

There are three levels in the Lyceaum. In addition to the Flame, there is a pub (with lots of students in it, of course), a library, a healing shop, and a stable where you can buy horses. Some of the more important people to talk with are Lady Janell, who knows about the twins in Cove (who in turn know about the shard of Falsehood). Rollo, the scribe, can help you find the Amulet; and Shalineth, the Lord of the Keep, tells you the name of the Shadowlord of Falsehood.

Serpent's Hold

On a very small wooded island on the bottom left of your map is Serpent's Hold, the Keep of Courage. The keep itself is in the middle of the woods.

There are three levels, two above ground and one below. The Flame of Courage burns in the basement. An armoury and a prison are on the main level. Toede, a prisoner, helped construct the traps in Lord Blackthorn's castle. Kristi, the keep's cook, has skull keys for sale. Buy all she'll sell you. At a hundred gold pieces, they are an absolute steal.

In the basement talk to Gardner, who keeps the Flame of Courage burning. He knows how to find the Shard of Cowardice in the Underworld that you need to destroy the Shadowlord of Cowardice. He tells you its coordinates and what to look for.

The second level has a training room and a throne room where Lord Malone, the lord of the keep, holds sway. Monsieur Loubet, the fencing master, knows about magic carpets, and Lord Malone can be induced to reveal the name of the Shadowlord of Cowardice.

Minor Keeps

You will find, if you look long enough, four very well hidden minor keeps in out-of-the-way places. These are Bordermarch, Farthing, Windemere, and Stonegate. The latter is the home of the Shadowlords.

Bordermarch

You can only reach this keep by climbing mountains because it is located on a small, mountainous island to the west of the main continent. It has an armoury that sells Rings of Regeneration, which will restore your party's hit points as they travel. Dupre, a friend from the previous mission, is there, and he will join you if you have an open slot in your party. Lady Tessa knows about Lord British's Amulet. Sir Simon tells you about the Crown and the Sceptre.

Farthing

This is on a small island off the southwestern tip of the main continent. Again, you have to climb mountains to find it. Inside, Quinton the cook tells you about the biggest gossip in the realm. Dufus, a clumsy boy, tells you that the master of the keep, Lord Segallion, has a spyglass. When you find Lord Segallion, ask him about the spyglass. If you can tell him what the eight planets represent (Virtues), he gives you the spyglass. You can use it to keep track of the Shadowlords any time that it is dark. A mage tells you of her new spell for invisibility, but cannot remember the exact reagents. You have to carefully experiment to find them out.

Windemere

You meet Elistaria on this island in the far northeast of Britannia. If you know the password of the Oppression (Blackthorn's organization), she gives you the Black Badge of the Oppression. You need this badge to enter Lord Blackthorn's castle and retrieve the Crown.

Stonegate

Last and worst is Stonegate, the home of the Shadowlords. This abode of evil is in the mountains north of Cove. You have to climb mountains to reach it, and there is only one passable route (from the west side of the mountain range). Using gems is the only method of pinpointing this route. Don't try going there until you have killed all three Shadowlords. After that, you need to go there to retrieve Lord British's Sceptre. You'll be briefed on the steps to follow later.

Towns

You will find the same eight towns as in your previous mission—Britain, Jhelom, Minoc, Moonglow, New Magincia, Skara Brae, Trinsic, and Yew. They are still associated with the Eight Virtues, but much changed from those glorious days of yore during the Age of the Avatar. Britain, the capital, is supposed to promote Compassion, New Magincia's specialty is Humility, Minoc champions Sacrifice, Moonglow advocates Honesty, Jhelom bravely stands up for Valor, Skara Brae is the home of Spirituality, Trinsic feels duty bound to protect Honor, and Yew seeks Justice above all.

Of course, the usurper Blackthorn has twisted these fine ideals and during the times that a Shadowlord is in residence, things get even worse. Still, you need to visit all eight towns in order to garner the information needed to complete your quest.

Britain

Britain is located near Lord British's castle on Brittany Bay, as are the villages of West, North, and South Brittany. You can't miss it—this is the largest built-up area in Britannia.

There is an extensive two-story inn, offering both food and lodging. Explore the inn completely, and stock up on rations. The armoury in town sells the normal weapons and armor, plus magical bows. The latter are very expensive but a terrific offensive weapon. Gwenno, a bard, is in Britain. Seek her out. She'll join your party if you ask, and makes a strong addition to it. Lots of information here, too! Talk to everyone. Ask about the Mantra of Compassion; someone here knows it.

Converse intently with Annon, a wizard. He is a former Council member (Lord British's Council was disbanded by Blackthorn), and he knows the Word of Power that unseals the dungeon Deceit. He may not give this to you the first time you meet, but after you've completed two or three of the quests to the eight shrines, he thaws out considerably. He also gives you a hint about how to find another Council member. As you might expect, you need to find a total of eight Council members in all for the eight Words of Power. All eight dungeons were sealed after the previous era of troubles but, unfortunately, you have to open up all eight again to cure the current troubles by killing the Shadowlords and restoring Lord British to his throne.

Eb, the busboy in the tavern, knows the name of someone in Moonglow who can help you find the Glass Sword. Greyson can explain about the guardians of the Codex of Ultimate Wisdom. Telila is a gossipy cleaning lady. Ask her about gossip and she relates an important clue concerning the Mystical Arms and Armor. Terrance is dirty, but it's honest dirt. He knows someone in Yew in the Resistance movement.

Jhelom

Jhelom lies on an island southwest of the main continent. It has a moon gate nearby, which is indicated on your map. The two ways of reaching this town are either by moon gates, which work only at night, or by frigate. The latter mode of transportation gives you much more freedom of action.

As with any town, if you enter only to find an air of falsehood, hatred, or cowardice surrounding you, leave immediately. A Shadowlord is in residence, and now is not the time to irk one of *them*. Come back later when he's gone. If you can find a spyglass, check the heavens at night to see which of the eight planets or stars the three comets are near. This information tells you the Shadowlords' locations.

Jhelom is relatively small. There is an armoury, inn, and shipwright. Each of these establishments has a second floor. Four towers guard the four corners of Jhelom. To enter them, find the way to the top of the walls. You can search all the towers, climbing down into each.

Only the tower on the northwest corner matters. Goeth, a former Council member, lives here. He has a bit of a speech problem, and speaks backwards. Talk to him in the same way. He knows the Word of Power for the dungeon Destard. He also tells you how to find a moonstone (wait until a moon gate has just closed for the night and search for a strange stone). If you have one of these moonstones, you can plant it and generate a moon gate. During your retrieval of the three shards of Mondain's jewel from the Underworld, which are needed to kill the three Shadowlords, sometimes this might be the only, or at least the best, way to return to Britannia.

Bullwier tells you about Ambrose in the village of Cove, which lies far to the northeast on the other side of the continent. Ambrose was injured while on a quest for the Mystical Weapons and Armour. He only makes sense for an hour or so around midnight. Make a note, when you are in Cove, to talk with Ambrose at that time. The villages will be detailed later in this briefing.

Thorne is a fighter somewhat the worse for wear. He knows the Mantra of Valor, and quite a bit of useful lore concerning the dungeon Destard.

Minoc

In the far north and east of the main continent is the town of Minoc. This town has a good harbor, and the lighthouse Stormcrow will probably be a welcome sight to you if you're searching for this haven at night, as you can see its light from a good distance. A moon gate is located just over the mountains to the east.

The town is about the same size as Jhelom. There is an armoury, a healer, a mission for the poor, and a shipwright. Talk to everyone; someone here knows the Mantra of Sacrifice.

Fenelon is a sailmaker for Captain Blythe and is Fiona's daughter. She can tell you how to avoid the guard. Fiona manages the poor house and was a former member of the Council. She knows the Word of Power that unseals the dungeon Shame. Tactus is a fervent follower of Blackthorn, but ask him about the Oppression. He directs you to Judge Dryden in Yew (you need to learn the Oppression's password for your visit to Blackthorn's Castle).

Charity pays. In this case be charitable to the old beggar you find. He tells you to watch Shenstone, the merchant who runs the armoury and who sneaks around town at noon. Follow Shenstone and search the tree he goes to after he leaves. You find some of the ever-so-valuable skull keys, which open magically locked doors. (These are doors with a blue line around them.)

Moonglow

Moonglow is located on the same island as the Lycaeum, and a good road connects the two. You get to Verity Isle by sailing due east out of Brittany Bay. The lighthouse, Waveguide, is on a tiny island just to the west of the large island.

The town doesn't have a lot of interest, although it is the best place to buy food. There is a tavern and an apothecary shop where you can buy such necessary reagents for magic spells as sulfurous ash, garlic, ginseng, mandrake root, and nightshade. The prices are moderately good.

Find Lord Stuart in the tavern and ask him about the spell to make food. This spell could come in very handy. A gypsy knows the Mantra of Honesty.

There is an observatory on top of the central tower in town. Zaccariah, who tends it, is a former Council member. He knows the

Word of Power to open the dungeon Covetous. Astronomy, naturally, is a pet subject of his.

New Magincia

To the southwest of Verity Isle is a smaller island. It has a moon gate, which is indicated on your map, and the town of New Magincia. There is a tavern where food is available, but the real importance of the town is to be found in the conversations of the inhabitants.

Talk to a recluse to find out the Mantra of Humility. Kaiko can tell you about Hassad, a Council member now in the dungeon of Lord Blackthorn's castle. You learn about the daemon in the desert, and there could be a new member for your party here if you ask the right person to join.

Skara Brae

Skara Brae is located on an island just off the western coast of the main continent. A moon gate appears on your map on the same island. There is an apothecary shop (stocking ash, black pearl, blood moss, and ginseng), a healer (the most inexpensive in all of Britannia), an inn, and a mysterious tower in the center of town.

Getting into the tower requires a fifth-circle IN EX POR spell, or the expenditure of a scarce skull key. You have to fight a lot of bats, but do finally reach the top level. There is a very impolite wizard there, but mention the Oppression and he opens up. His only information of value is that you should talk to Tactus in Minoc about the Oppression, but I've already briefed you on that.

Three others have more worthwhile information. Saul tells you about Kindor, who is recovering from a battle with the Shadowlords. Talk to Kindor at 6 P.M. at the healers and he should tell you the Mantra of Spirituality, and who knows the location of that shrine. Froed is in a grove of trees. He asks you to carry a message to his father, who is imprisoned in Yew, which you should do.

Trinsic

Trinsic is the easiest town to find from Lord British's castle. Just follow the road south to its end. You pass the village of Paws on the way. The town is small. It has an armoury, a healer, and a stable. A bit farther to the south of the town is a moon gate.

Someone in Trinsic can tell you the Mantra of Honor. Sindar, an old wizard who walks in his sleep, knows the Word of Power that unseals the dungeon Hythloth. A certain Gruman could be induced to join your party if you approach him at the right time.

Yew

You need to learn both the password for the Resistance (the organization of those devoted to Lord British) and the one for the Oppression during your mission in Britannica. Situated in the large forest northwest of Britain, Yew is also connected by road to Empath Abbey. There is a moon gate on that road, not far outside of Yew.

The town is a little larger than most. There is an armoury that sells magic axes, an apothecary, a cemetery (there's a secret exit from the town here), a tavern, and a hall of administration and justice, housing the court and penal system for all of Britannia. Get arrested by a guard anywhere in the realm, and you'll wind up in jail here. Speaking of guards, the ones here are a pain, wanting you to donate money to "charity."

The Hall of Justice has administrative offices and the jail. There is also a trap door to the lower level. If you fall through the trap door, you wind up in a room on the lower level with a vicious rat. If you can defeat the rat, search for the secret door to escape the room. There are stairs leading back up. The Resistance quarters are down here, but you aren't ready yet to enter.

If you simply hang around town a little while, the guards arrest you, and you wind up in the middle cell in the jail. After you escape, the trap door is directly in front of the cell you were in.

Jerone is your cellmate. He tells you about the time he saw an apparition of Lord British while on a quest.

In the town is Chamfort, a cheerful blacksmith who runs the Arms of Justice, the armoury that sells those fantastic magic axes. Talk to Chamfort about the Resistance. He asks you who referred you to him. If you tell him that name, he tells you about Landon, the local leader of the Resistance, and what the password is. You reach Landon through the fireplace in Chamfort's shop, which gives entrance to a secret passage leading to the lower level.

Once you find the quarters of the Resistance movement on the lower level, you encounter Jaana. She's an excellent and actually critical addition to your party. She has magical powers that be very handy later on. Searching the lower level shows you a stairway that leads up to the jail. A secret door up there opens onto the middle cell where Jerone is imprisoned.

In the secret passage you should find Landon, who tells you that Lord British's Crown is located in Blackthorn's castle. He also suggests that you look for Sir Simon "on a mountain isle, west of the Spiritwood." This is where the minor keep, Bordermarch, is located.

Graymarch is a prisoner in the cells. He's concerned about his son, Froed, in Skara Brae. Tell him that his son is OK. Felespar, an old wizard, is a prisoner there, also. If you can give him the password for the Resistance, he tells you the Word of Power that unseals the dungeon Despise.

Others in the town of Yew that you need to converse with include Mario and Aleyn. They are father and son locked into the town stocks for passersby to ridicule. Talk with them, and then jimmy the locks to release them. The act of kindness will be good for you. Judge Dryden runs the town and can help you get into the Oppression, which you have to in order to visit Blackthorn's castle. Ask the Judge about the Chain of Oppression. He will want to know who sent you to him. He tells you then to visit Elistaria "on the northernmost isle of Britannia," and what password to tell her. (She gives you the Black Badge for the right password.)

Again, watch those guards!

Villages

Brittania has six villages. Three of them—East Brittany, North Brittany, and West Brittany—are just outside Lord British's castle. Paws is on the road south to Trinsic. Cove is in a, yes, cove far to the northeast of Brittany Bay, and Buccaneer's Den is on a small island in the ocean not too far southeast of Paws.

The Brittanys

In *East Brittany* a certain master shipwright named Hawkins here builds and sells skiffs and frigates. Search his building with great care, for the plans for the legendary *HMS Cape*. Using these plans when you have a ship makes it go considerably faster, although not without risk. Still, these plans can come in handy.

North Brittany is a small farming community with lots of food crops. However, don't take any food from the fields or off the tables, since this detracts from your virtue. One of the farmers might be willing to join your party if you know the Resistance password. You can get a horse at the stable. Kurt, the stable boy, should explain about horses in general, and tell you to see Treanna in the stable in Lord British's castle.

The tavern in North Britanny is an excellent place to park party members if you have recruited more than five and want to rotate them because of their varied skills.

West Brittany also is a hardworking farming community. There is little information of value to the quest at hand here, but you can learn some interesting background on the current troubles in Britannia.

Buccaneer's Den

Only a ship can take you to the small, isolated island that Buccaneer's Den is on, but the trip is worth it. There is a Thieves Guild with a hidden entrance. Search for it on the *outside* of the walls—you need either skull keys or an IN EX POR spell. The guild offers very useful items such as gems, torches, and regular keys. The village armoury is easier to find, and sells the Ring of Invisibility, which you need to have. There is a shipwright and an inn.

Buy the lady Tierra a drink, and she speaks to you of Bidney, the town drunk. Bidney tells you how to climb mountains and where to get the grapple you need to do so. Scalley is a bard, and he knows about David, a seaman who now tends a lighthouse in Grayhaven. David can help you with sextants when you visit him in the lighthouse.

Cove

Cove is pretty well hidden, just like it was in the previous mission. It's on a large inland lake northeast of Brittany Bay. It has an apothecary selling blood moss, black pearl, nightshade, mandrake root, and spider silk for your magic spells. There is also a Temple of Virtue and a healer.

In the temple are two beautiful young women who are twins. They can tell you how to find the Shard of Falsehood. Their directions are long, complicated, and a trifle vague. Note them down carefully.

Ambrose, who has been badly wounded, lives with the healer. He awakes at midnight only, and if you are there at that time he tells you about the mystical weapons and armor, and how to find them in the Underworld by entering it from the dungeon Hythloth.

Paws

Paws is easy to find. Just take the road south from Lord British's castle. Paws is located about halfway to Trinsic. It has an inn and a stable named the Wishing Well. The name is significant because sometimes you can get a horse by just wishing for one at many wishing wells in the realm. There is also a Thieves Guild in Paws where you can purchase gems, torches, and keys.

You will meet the mage Bandaii in Paws. Ask him about Smith, the fabulous talking horse. Smith can tell you the Word needed to restore the shrines destroyed by Blackthorn (although I know of nobody who has ever found a destroyed shrine). If you ask Bandaii the right question, he gives you a flying carpet.

The Isle of the Avatar

The large island in the far southeastern corner of your map is the Island of the Codex. The Shrine of the Codex is located on the southern portion of the island, and the path to it is pretty obvious.

You have to come here eight times, since you will be sent on a quest by each one of the Shrines. There are guardians at the Shrine of the Codex who let you pass only if you are on a legitimate quest. Everything is automatic here; after carrying out the quest, you can return to the Shrine issuing the quest and obtain your reward.

Figure 12.4 *You visit the Shrine of the Codex eight times.*

Lighthouses

The lighthouses of Britannia are indeed neat places. Be sure to visit them at night as well as in the daytime; they have pretty graphics then. There are four of them: Fogsbane, Grayhaven, Waveguide, and Stormcrow.

Fogsbane: Located on a small island near the entrance to Brittany Bay, this lighthouse is tended by Jothan and his granddaughter Jennifer. They are very friendly, but have no worthwhile information.

Grayhaven: Grayhaven is on the southern tip of the main continent, south of Trinsic. The most important person here is Lord Kenneth, the former court composer. He teaches you to play the harpsichord using the music found in *The Book of Lore*. You have to master this song to complete your mission.

David, the lighthouse tender, is an expert in navigation. He gives you a sextant if you talk to him about it, and Arbuthnot, the royal coinmaker, relates the story of the Coin of the Codex.

Stormcrow: This is on a spit of land to the west of Minoc. The only useful information you'll get here is a warning not to leave a ship in the port of Minoc.

Waveguide: This lighthouse is just off the west coast of Verity Isle, where Moonglow and the Lycaeum are situated. It is tended by Gregory, an exceptionally surly man. His wife, Jacqueline, is about as spaced out as one can get. There's nothing of benefit to you here, but it's a pretty lighthouse.

Huts

Four huts exist in widely scattered, isolated locations, and you have to find and visit all four.

Iolo's Hut: A warm and cozy little retreat in the deep woods, this is the easiest place in Britannia to find, because it is here that you are injected into this mission. Explore the area around the hut thoroughly. You'll find a wishing well (wish for a horse), and a hidden stable. Search the stable, and come back later in the mission. Smith, the talking horse, will be here then.

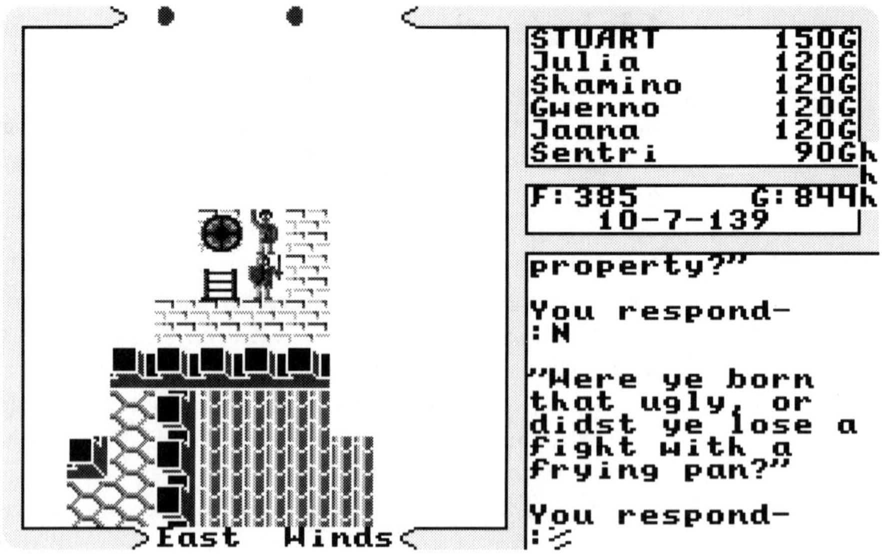

Figure 12.5 *Gregory does not mince words.*

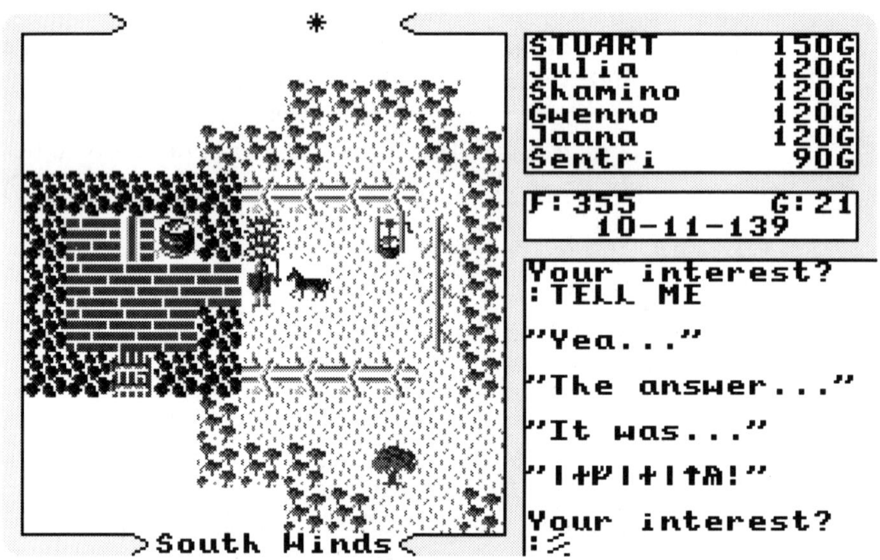

Figure 12.6 *Smith, the fabulous talking horse in the stable at Iolo's hut, finally gives you a valuable hint, if you can translate it. Smith won't let you ride him, but if you make a wish at the well here you might get a horse.*

Alchemist's Hut: The Alchemist's hut is in a swamp on the shore northeast of Brittany Bay. You need a flying carpet to get across the swamp without being poisoned. Talk to the large rat you find there, which is really the Alchemist who has come on hard times. He teaches you a spell that is exceptionally useful, especially against dragons.

Daemon's Hut: The Daemon who lives in this desert hut in the far northeast desert can tell you where the Shard of Hatred is located in the Underworld, and which two dungeons (Covetous and Wrong) may be used to reach it. Use the magic carpet to cross the desert to avoid the sand traps.

Sutek's Hut: Far down in the southern ocean is a tiny island with Sutek's hut on it. It's very swampy, so use your magic carpet again. Sutek gladly discusses how to use the shards to destroy the Shadowlords.

Shops

Thieves Guild shops are scattered around at various places also, such as in the village of Paws. You need large quantities of the items they sell.

Since you are probably already an Avatar, it should not be necessary to warn you about stealing. An Avatar does not steal.

Food and Drink

Savory meals are available at restaurants, taverns, and markets, but they do not sustain you throughout the rigors of traveling. Such places also sell the more usual packs of rations for adventurers. Prices vary from place to place.

Pubs, as has always been traditional, are great sources of refreshing libations and useful gossip. It pays to cultivate bartenders and chefs, and they often repay your patronage with valuable information, especially if you tip well. Many pubs and restaurants offer live musical entertainment. Be sure to talk to all musicians.

Arms and Armor

Armories have combined the function of the separate weapons and armor shops seen in earlier ages. Most armories gladly purchase used or found equipment, providing you with a ready source of income. The prices realized are less than the retail price of new items, since the armourer must make a profit. The types of goods sold at armories vary widely. Visit all you can find and inquire of their stock.

From the first, try to arm your party with as many long-range weapons as possible. Slings are cheap and ammunition for them is plentiful. They're better than nothing in the early going. As you can afford it, purchase bows and crossbows. These require arrows and bolts (called quarrels), which have to be bought as well.

Magic bows are very effective but highly expensive weapons. Magic axes are even better! Anyone can use them and, when thrown at an enemy, they always return to the hand of their owner. They can also reach anywhere on the battle field, whereas most missile weapons have range limitations. Magic axes are for sale at the armory in Yew, or you can find them as treasure. Reapers are the monsters most likely to have magic axes. They exist only in dungeons, so you have to go down after them.

Other weapons available include daggers, long swords, short swords, two-handed swords, and flasks of flaming oil. Some weapons require great strength on the part of the wielder; among these are clubs, maces, morning stars, two-handed hammers, polearms, and halberds.

Magic

Visit apothecary shops regularly. They stock various reagents you need for those important magic spells. These establishments tend to stock local ingredients, with fewer stocks of things from outside the area. Prices are not consistent, so shop and compare.

The ingredients for all spells are given in a table included in your adventurer's kit, along with what the spell does. There is no guessing. All you have to do is build up to the level needed to utilize the spell and mix up the ingredients.

Scrolls should be highly prized. Anyone, even someone who is not a magic user, can employ the magic on scrolls. First-level adventurers may even thus cast eighth-level spells, should they be so incredibly lucky as to find such a scroll.

Lodging

Several villages and towns have inns. Staying overnight in an inn, if you *pay* for lodging, has a healing effect on all members of the party, It is also a safe way to spend the night. You may also leave party members there, paying for their stay by the month. Inns are where you can park a current member of your party when his or her services are not needed, to free up a slot for a more desirable person.

Transportation

Shipwrights are hard to find in their shops, since they are very busy people. They sell you skiffs at reasonable prices, or frigates for much more. Frigates usually come with skiffs on board. You can also steal frigates from pirates, if you can catch one close to shore. Other aspects of transportation closely resemble those of the previous mission.

Stables

Stables are rare, but there are a few around. Some even exist in castles and private residences, and often these sell to the public. All offer supplies for the well-equipped rider. If you purchase horses, be aware that they do not stay put as in prior ages, unless they are at a hitching post. Remember this or you'll find your steed gone upon your return.

Healing

Healers are widespread. They offer cures for poison, healing of wounds, and even resurrection of your dead comrades. Prices vary from reasonable to stiff. The healer at the town of Skara Brae is the most altruistic, sometimes even healing those with no money at all.

Written Language

General literacy has come to Britannia, but the writing is of a runic variety that is sometimes not immediately obvious to outland adventurers, such as yourselves. Often you need to translate signs, gravestones, and other items letter by letter. A complete translation table may be found in *The Book of Lore*, and I encourage you to make use of it.

Your Challenges

The increased resources in this mission do not come free. You will find some not-so-nice changes as well. One is the change in moral structure. During the previous mission—in the Age of the Avatar—you could count on a town being virtuous. Britain was known for its compassion, Trinsic for its honor, and so forth. With the disappearance of Lord British, and the ascension of the Shadowlords, all this has changed.

The Shadowlords, through their human minion Lord Blackthorn, have perverted the virtues. Read the final section in *The Book of Lore* to see how the virtues have been evilly twisted. This is very important in helping you to understand what you are up against.

One of the most significant changes is the day/night cycle. It gets dark, very dark at night now. Sometimes you will want to camp for the night, since proceeding in darkened terrain can be extremely dangerous, especially if you wander into a swamp.

Monsters are pretty much the same as they were in the previous mission.

Lord British's Crown

A huge challenge is getting to Lord British's Crown, which is in the Castle of Lord Blackthorn, the renegade usurper who has taken over the government of Britannia. This human minion of the Shadowlords is not a nice person, so you want to be very careful in visiting his home, which is indicated with the symbol of a castle on a small island on the lower southeast of your map. (The large island next to it, by the way, is where the Shrine of the Codex is situated.) Unfortunately, you *have* to visit Lord Blackthorn's perilous castle—to retrieve the Crown. Luckily there is a way, although it requires a lot of travel and preparation to have any chance at all of success.

The only way to reach this island, surrounded as it is by deep ocean, is by frigate. Frigates may be obtained by buying them from a shipwright, such as the one in the village of East Brittany, or by taking them from pirates. With a such a ship, you can visit Lord Blackthorn at any time, who will be delighted to see you so naively strolling into his clutches, since he knows who you are and plans on eliminating your threat to his power.

Two things are absolutely necessary, unless you would like to spend a lot of time being tortured in Blackthorn's dungeon. The Black Badge and the password of the Opposition allow you to wander about this castle freely. Judge Dryden in the town of Yew knows the password, but you have to talk to Tactus in Minoc before the judge gives it to you. Once you have the password, Elistaria in the minor keep of Windemere (on an island in the far north) can help you acquire the Black Badge. To get to Windemere, by the way, requires the ability to climb mountains. Lord Michael at Empath Abbey has a helpful grapple for you.

Now you can go to the castle. Exploring it while wearing the Black Badge, you'll find that it's very large, and full of magically locked rooms, and stairways that are not always completely logical. It's not necessary to look in every room, and if you tried, you would quickly run out of the hard-to-obtain skull keys anyway. Talk with Hassad, a former Council

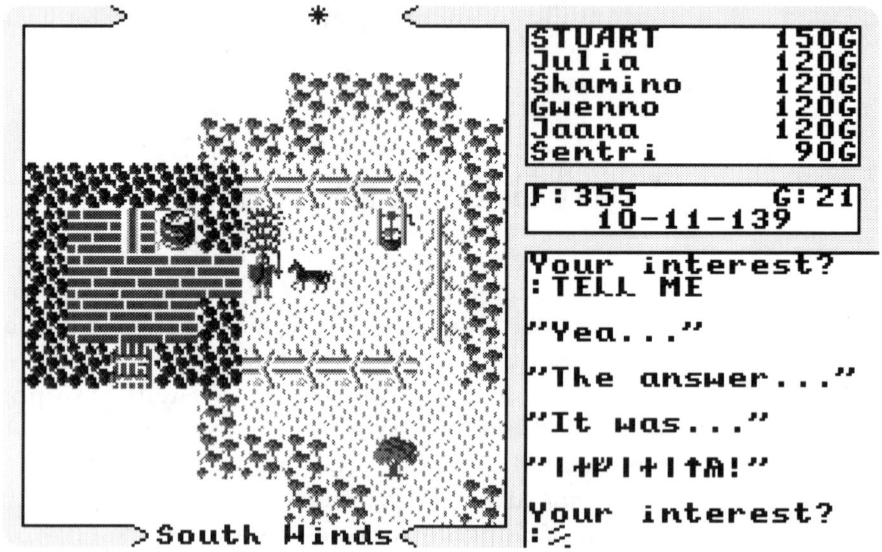

Figure 12.7 *If you can brave their cannon and get close enough, you can capture ships from pirates.*

Member, in the dungeon. He has a powerful word to relate. Gorn, who is also imprisoned, has more useful advice about the castle.

Following Gorn's suggestion, enter the castle from the rear. Be careful in the hallway just inside, because it has hidden trap doors. Stay next to the walls and take the stairs up to the second level. There's an old mage sitting in a chair who offers to help. Ignore him; he really won't. Four sets of steps lead up to the next level. Take any of them, it doesn't matter which, and enter the third level.

Search the level until you find Blackthorn's throne room (it won't be locked). He's there, but just stay to the side and, because you are wearing the Black Badge, he ignores you if you don't call attention to yourself. Edge around the walls and go to the door on the north side of the throne room.

On the other side of the door is Blackthorn's bedroom, currently empty. Search it well. There are several useful items here and you deserve them after all the trouble of getting here. Then take the stairs to the roof of the castle.

There are trap doors up here too, so use your magic carpet to avoid them. Flying along the southern wall you find a walkway leading to Lord

British's Crown. Unfortunately the stone gargoyles decorating the walls come alive and attack you. Two strategies work here. If you are strong enough, just kill them all. If your party is weak, but one member has a ring of invisibility, leave him on the battlefield alone and the gargoyles will think you are all gone and leave. You need a skull key or the IN EX POR spell to open the door and get the Crown.

Getting out of the castle is relatively simple if you keep the Black Badge on and give the password whenever a guard stops you. Once away, however, take off the badge. Otherwise, anyone who is on the side of good will not talk to you.

Your Strategy

You start at Iolo's hut, and you should search the surrounding area thoroughly. Next, the first part of this quest involves many complex preparations for your final dramatic deeds of journeying to the Underworld, destroying the Shadowlords, and rescuing the rest of Lord British's emblems of power and finally Lord British himself. Thus it might help to consider the first stage as a preparation stage and as encompassing both survival goals and building up goals. The final stage has several aspects, which I'll explain after these general remarks.

General Considerations

The lengthy preparation portion of your mission is devoted to exploring all the towns, castles, keeps, villages, and huts. You should also be keeping close notes about all the people you talk to, and what they say. You will accumulate experience, rise in level, obtain various weapons, armor, and artifacts, go on quests from all eight Shrines to the Isle of the Avatar, and so on and so on.

There's a lot to do, but if you are painstaking in talking to everyone, and finding all the locations mentioned above, plus those of the shrines and dungeons, completing the last stage is relatively straightforward.

Conversations

Most of the clues needed to complete your mission are obtained through talking to people. If you are a veteran of the mission immediately previous you'll probably note that even though towns are larger now, there are smaller populations. This means that one individual may have information on several subjects. Question everyone closely, and write down all key words that might trigger additional information.

Asking "JOB?" is a good icebreaker when meeting someone for the first time. Often he responds to your questions with one of his own. Always answer truthfully; it is greatly to your benefit to do so. Lying only gets you into trouble. Avatars do not lie.

I'll reemphasize—should you enter a town and at once sense an air of cowardice, falsehood, or hatred, *get out immediately*. It means that one of the three Shadowlords is in that town (they move from town to town). You are simply not ready to fight a Shadowlord yet. None of your weapons can hurt it. The only spell that affects it is the seventh-level Xen Corp, and that only makes it go away.

If you come back after the Shadowlord has left, the townspeople will be cooperative, and you can continue amassing your clues.

Figure 12.8 *Here's a warning that a Shadowlord is in town. Leave now!*

Combat

Actual combat takes place over larger areas than it did in the previous mission, although combat in general is not quite as important. Disperse your troops to take advantage of battlefield terrain, protecting your flanks while mobilizing firepower toward the enemy.

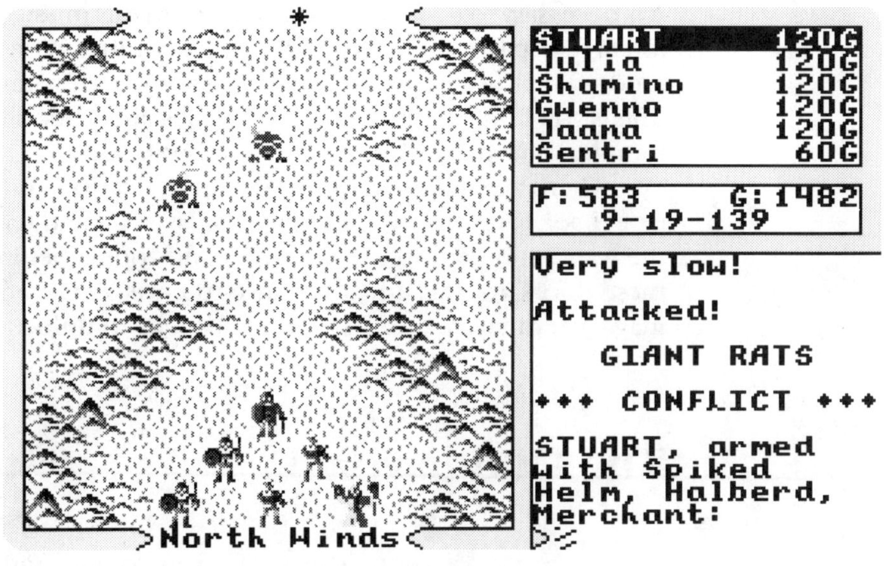

Figure 12.9 *Your party in combat with huge rats.*

It is important that those with missile weapons have an unrestricted field of fire, although they can stay behind party members who have to get within closer striking distance. It is safe to fire over the heads of your own people. Safe for you, not the enemy.

Exercise caution by keeping those who use bows or slings out of hand-to-hand combat. If the enemy gets close to them, their weapons can be interfered with, and you lose considerable firepower, sometimes with drastic results.

Magic users can shorten combat dramatically with the right spells. Keep a mage well back and let him or her loose the thunders and lightnings of, so to speak, your heavy artillery. A high-level mage can either annihilate the enemy in one fell swoop, or soften them up and make victory easy for your frontline fighters.

Searching

It is necessary to do a lot more searching in this mission. Have your most intelligent party member examine everything, With the exception of food—which you must not steal under any circumstances—most of the things you find are yours to keep. Scrolls and potions, for example, are found in odd places like barrels and bookcases.

There are many hidden doors in the various buildings to investigate. Look carefully for them (use the 'L' spell and try to spot a nick on the wall), and explore the passages and rooms behind them. Some of these doors are locked, so be sure to have plenty of keys. A fifth-level magic user may also cast IN EX POR spells to unlock doors.

The Underworld

The real battle does not come until you are built up and ready for it. The real battle does not start until you enter the Underworld. From then on things get hairy in a major-league way. Beneath the dungeons, but reachable through them, is the incredibly vast Underworld. *Do not*, *do not* go down there unless you know exactly where you are going and why. Its creatures are virtually indestructible, and it is filled with hardships and troubles beyond imagining. Alas, you have to go there to get the three Shards, Lord British's Amulet, and mystical weapons and armor, as well as to enter the dungeon of Doom.

You have a choice of how to get to the Underworld. The first way is the worst, sailing into a whirlpool. You wind up lost with no way back to the surface, unless you have some moonstones (remember how to get those by searching just after gates have closed?). So this is not the recommended way.

Or you can get there through entrances in the dungeons, or through the one direct entrance near the Spiritwoods.

There are several preparations to make before attempting to go into the Underworld. As far as weapons go, you can never have too many of your party armed with magic axes. All members of the party should be at least fifth or sixth level. Be sure you have a magic carpet, the grapple to climb mountains, loads of gems for viewing, and all the reagents for spells that you can afford. You'll use the AN NOX cure poison spell a lot. Take along several moonstones, too.

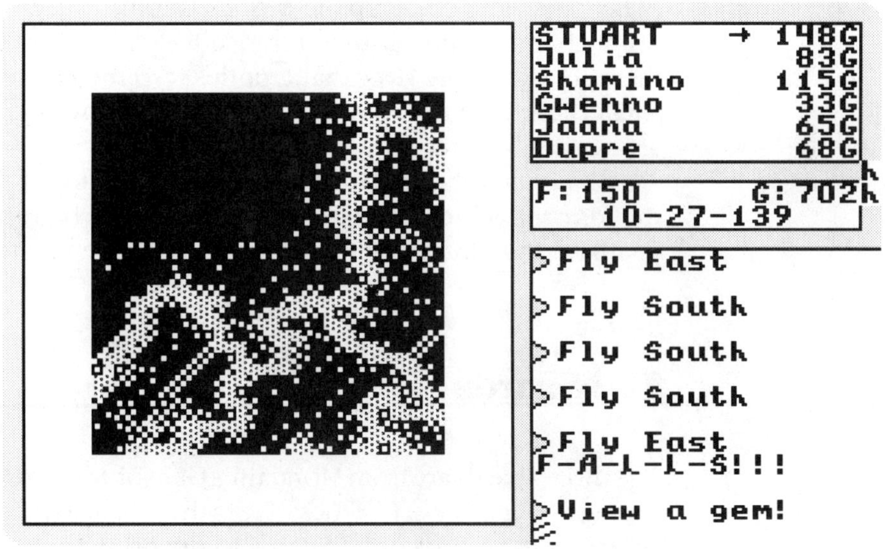

Figure 12.10 *Use gems often to map the Underworld or you'll never find where you have to go.*

Finally, the Ring of Invisibility helps you survive the trip down through the dungeon to the Underworld. To use it, have one member of your party wear it during combat, then remove everyone else from the battlefield. The monsters will think you have left and leave, too, thus letting you win the battle.

Lord British's Amulet

Once you are ready to face the Underworld, it is best to retrieve Lord British's Amulet first. This is moderately easy since you have an exact record of his travels included in your adventurer's kit—Remoh's *Journal*.

Use the entrance to the Underworld located in a small lake to the southwest of Lord British's castle. It requires that you be in a skiff. The best way to arrange this is to sail your frigate around to the western side of Britannia and come up the west coast until you encounter a group of uninhabited islands at the entrance to a large bay. Use the skiff from there to sail up the river that empties into the bay until you come to a small lake that empties over a waterfall. Sail into the waterfall and you are suddenly in the Underworld.

To find and retrieve the Amulet, simple follow the instructions in the *Journal*, which are extensive and will not be repeated here. Once you have the Amulet, plant a moonstone to return to the surface.

The Shards

The three Shards are from Mondain's Gem of Immortality, which existed during the First Age of Darkness. From these Shards the three Shadowlords sprang, and you need the Shards to unspring them into eternity.

All three Shards, naturally, are in hard-to-reach places in the Underworld, and you need to approach from various dungeons to find them. The Shard of Falsehood is closest to the dungeon Deceit. You can reach the Shard of Hatred either from Covetous or Wrong. The Shard of Cowardice is near Hythloth.

The twin ladies in the Temple of Virtue in Cove gave you very detailed instructions on how to reach the Shard of Falsehood. Follow those instructions to the letter. After you have the shard, return to the world above by planting a moonstone.

The Shard of Hatred is not too difficult to find. Entering the Underworld from the bottom level of either Covetous or Wrong, use a gem to find an area surround by paths. It is surrounded by mountains, and you have to search for the way through them, but it's not hard to find. You wind up using several gems and fighting monsters a lot. Once you find the Shard, you have to retreat back toward the dungeon entrance to plant your moonstone. For some reason, moonstones don't seem to work in the area enclosed by the mountains.

Entering the Underworld from the dungeon Hythloth can kill two stones with one bird, so to speak. The mystical armor and the mystical weapons are in the center of a huge lava cross north of the dungeon entrance. Getting to it requires mountain climbing, which is rough on hit points. Have some healing spells or potions handy. At the lava field, walk out into it and position yourself just south of its center. Have each member of the party search twice.

To get the Shard of Cowardice, you have to enter a nearby area that is like a lot of rooms without any doors. You need lots of IN POR (blink) spells to explore this area, which is a large rectangle. The Shard is not concealed, so you will see it immediately when you're in the right place. Just use IN POR to search the area until you find it.

Once you find the Shard, return to the dungeon. Hythloth appears to be the only one that lets you return to the surface, so save a moonstone here unless you are in a real hurry.

It's now time to waste some Shadowlords!

Destroying the Shadowlords

Now that you have the Shards, killing the Shadowlords is finally possible. To kill the Shadowlord of Cowardice, travel to the keep of the opposite principle, the Keep of Courage (Serpent's Hold). Stand next to the Flame of Courage and summon the Shadowlord by yelling its name. Once the Shadowlord arrives and steps on the flame, throw the Shard into the flame (invoke the 'U' spell).

Repeat this procedure to kill the Shadowlord of Hatred at Empath Abbey (using the Flame of Love) and the Shadowlord of Falsehood at the Lycaeum (using the Flame of Truth).

Once the three Shadowlords are dead, you can go to their former home, Stonegate, and retrieve Lord British's Sceptre.

Lord British's Sceptre

A daemon guards the door to Stonegate and poses a riddle. If you answer it correctly, he promises, you can pass unmolested. The answer to the riddle is 'a well,' but don't bother playing the daemon's game, because he'll not keep his promise even if you win. Just go ahead and attack him.

The Sceptre is in the center of the keep. The only way to get it, however, is by using your flying carpet. Get the Sceptre and leave. There is nothing else to keep you in this dangerous place.

The Final Stage

You've killed the Shadowlords and retrieved those three very important artifacts, the Crown, Amulet, and Sceptre of Lord British. Now you can turn your attention to rescuing Lord British.

This last part is the hardest part. You might be able to complete all the quests leading up to this end section with party members at only fifth or sixth level, but to save Lord British *you*, the Avatar, need to be eighth level. So at this point you might have to spend some time getting experience points and building up to that level so you can use eighth-circle spells.

When your party is finally ready (that is, when you all have the maximum in points), it's time to journey to the dungeon Doom. There's no turning back once you enter Doom, so be sure you have everything you need. Again, you must have those three artifacts which constitute the crown jewels of Lord British. Also make sure you have that mysterious sandalwood box that was hidden in Lord British's penthouse atop his castle. Take lots of food and all the reagents and mixed spells you can.

Enter the Underworld through the dungeon Shame and board your magic carpet to cross the deadly swamp. Keep moving due east for as far as you can go. When you can travel no farther east, use a gem. You see an area of grassland to the west which is bordered on the east by water. Use IN POR to blink yourself to the east, and then fly the magic carpet to the island you see. The island has several lava flows and high mountains.

Now you need to use the Amulet (invoke the 'U' spell), and enter one of the lava flows (yes, it burns). Walk toward the center of the islands until you find an area of darkness. Enter this area and use a gem. Because of the Amulet, you will be able to "see" the entrance to Doom. Enter it, even knowing that there is no return.

Doom!

Doom has eight levels. After you enter you're in a strange room with even stranger walls. There appear to be no exits, but use Lord British's Sceptre and you can walk right through the walls. Find a ladder down and descend to level two.

Level two is easy. Use a gem to find the down ladder and descend to level three. Head east until you find the secret door and enter the room behind it. You see daemons immediately! By now you should have developed the tactics that allow you to defeat them. Afterwards, if you find your way impeded by a ghostly wall, use the Sceptre again.

Now things get complicated. Find the down ladder and descend two levels to level *five* (remember to invoke the 'Q' spell all along through here). On level five, there are two ways up to level four, the level you just bypassed. Take either one and you should be in a room shaped like a cross. Go to the center of the cross and you can descend to level five again (although at a different place). Pay close attention now, because the directions get almost weird.

On Level five again, go east to where the ways cross, turn right and go forward twice. Take the ladder you find here back up to level four. Yeah, level four again. Go a couple of squares east, then find the portal and descend to level five. There is a ladder there to take you (finally) to level six.

There's some fighting to do on level six. Once you are victorious over the monsters, use a gem to find the ladder down to level seven.

You could take the ladder on down from here to level eight, but it would only cause you to wind up on level six again (yes, Doom is very, very confusing). Instead, there is a small room to the south. It's full of lots of nasty beings, and this is the time to use your eighth-level spells such as IN FLAM HUR and IN VAS GRAV CORP, which should wreak havoc nicely. There is a ladder down in the center of the room. Use it.

Prepare for more ups and downs. On level eight you are in a room full of beings who are looking forward to having your entire party for breakfast, and that's right *now*! There is a secret door in the northwest corner, which you can trigger by throwing magic axes at it. When the secret door opens, a horde of mongbats surges out. Use eighth-circle spells to crisp them, then enter the secret passage and take the ladder there back up to level seven (sigh).

More monsters to fight! Once these are defeated, find the three triggers on the east wall that open another secret passage. Go north and you find another way to return to level eight.

Go west on level eight and take the ladder back up to level seven.

Dizzy yet? See why you need a briefing?

On level seven, view a gem. In the middle of the C-shaped area is a way back down to level eight. Use it.

This time, on level eight, you're on a tiny island in the middle of an equally tiny lake, and besieged by monsters. Fight your way to the north and look around for a trigger, which should open a secret passage in the northeast corner. Go into this passage and push on the walls at various places. Another secret passage opens and . . . well . . . yeah . . . back to level seven.

Kill all the daemons you find here, then use the Sceptre and move to the east, leaving the room and searching to your front. You finally find a pit, which takes you down once more.

The room you wind up in is a surprise, and so is the final "puzzle" that completes your mission. I won't spoil your final triumph. Enjoy!

As helpful as specific strategic directions are, hearing the adventures of someone who has actually experienced the events and challenges awaiting you is even better. So now listen closely to what Kurt the stable boy learned about this mission.

13 Stuart, Master of the Silver Sword

Kurt was fourteen the day the Heroes rode into the tiny farming hamlet of North Brittany one hot and muggy summer's evening. To the day of his death some sixty years later, he never forgot that first moment when he looked up and saw them on the path to the stable. In startled awe he dropped the scoop. Oats spilled onto the floor.

"Take the noble knights' horses, Kurt," Theoan, the owner of the stable prompted from behind him. "Don't stand there like a dummy."

When the visitors got closer to the stable, Kurt shyly took the reigns of two horses and led them back to the paddock behind the stable. Theoan brought two more, and the tall, bronzed leader of the adventurers led the last two. His companions milled around in the coolness of the stable, brushing the dust of their travels from clothes and armor.

"And how long will you be staying, milord?" Theoan asked, knuckling his forehead in respect.

Kurt was surprised. He'd never seen his usually surly master quite that respectful before, not even to Lord Blackthorn's guards when they came to collect taxes. But then, the guards were a known quantity, and not as dangerous-looking as this tall adventurer and his five well-weaponed and armed companions.

"Just overnight," the leader said. "My name is Stuart."

He reached into a pouch on the leather belt around his chain mail and pulled out several coins. "Will this suffice to lodge the horses for the night and to feed and water them well?"

Theoan took the coins, now seeming close to awe himself. Kurt guessed he was thinking how seldom it was in these troubled days that good hard currency was put into his callused hands.

"Aye, milord. Just fine, just fine," he said, quickly pocketing what was three times his normal stabling fee.

Kurt was admiring the large silver sword that hung in an open-work scabbard from Sir Stuart's belt. On the other side of the knight hung a shimmering magic ax. A sudden buffet on his right ear jerked him back to his own world.

"Feed the horses, lout!" urged Theoan. "And quickly now. I'll be in the inn."

He stood with hands on his hips for a moment, watching Kurt until he walked over to the oat bucket. Satisfied, he tugged his forelock in greasy subservience to Sir Stuart, and departed the stable. Kurt knew that Theoan would make a beeline to the wine casks in the common room of the inn and drink the night away. None of that money would be given to his poor overworked apprentice.

Knowing Sir Stuart was watching him, Kurt hustled about busily, just as he always did anyway. He grabbed the bucket and poured oats into the horses' feeding trough, spreading it out thoroughly so that all the horses, including the ones already in the stable, would have a chance at the feed. Rushing, he went back to the barrel and filled the bucket again. And again.

Next, he got the large water bucket and went down to the stream to fill it. Barely able to carry the full bucket, water sloshing over its rim, he staggered over to the watering trough, and managed to tip the bucket into it, nervous that the knight was still standing there watching. He was sweating and out of breath from his effort, but he started back toward the stream for more water. It would take him five or six trips to fill the large trough.

"Hold it, boy," Sir Stuart said, his voice kind. He turned and called back into the stable. "Shamino! Dupre! Come out here. Your strong backs are needed."

Then, to Kurt's surprise, the knight walked over and took the bucket from his hand. Two of the adventurers, seeing their leader's actions, had found buckets in the stable and came outside also. The three of them soon had the trough filled while Kurt gave extra oats to the horses. He didn't care if Theoan beat him now for the extravagance, these people were nice and deserved something nice in return.

"Very good," Sir Stuart said, seemingly pleased at seeing the animals eating and drinking their fill. He clapped Kurt on the shoulder."You are a hardworking but scrawny lad. Come up to the inn and we will stand you to a good meal."

"I w—would like to, honored sir," Kurt said with a stammer," but there's the evening chores to do and—"

Another man and two women had come out to where they stood now.

"No problem, we'll help you with the chores," one of the ladies said good-naturedly, "after all we've been through, shoveling out a stable is nothing."

"True, Julia," Shamino said, and they laid into Kurt's chores with a will as dusk turned to darkness.

In the torchlit inn, the six adventurers ignored Theoan's fumbling attempt to ingratiate himself with them in the hope of cadging free wine. Theoan had to seat himself across the room. They called for a table for seven, and ordered up heaping helpings of roast mutton, removing and laying aside the more uncomfortable parts of their armor. Kurt gazed in awe at the wonderful magic axes and other weapons. These were very experienced adventurers indeed.

"Eat up, son, eat up," Sir Stuart said, smiling as the innkeeper's daughter brought the first course of their dinner.

Kurt was amazed at the amount of food the adventurers put away. They cleaned their plates and asked Lothar, the innkeeper, for more, which was speedily brought.

"Never know where the next meal is coming from in our business, Kurt," the grizzled fighter the others called Shamino said to him with a wink.

Kurt grunted understanding, his own mouth being full. He was putting away quite a bit of food himself. Stable work used up a lot of energy, and he seldom got to eat here at the inn. He reached for another chunk of bread to sop in his plate of gravy, determined to take full advantage of this wondrous meal.

After a time, however, they were pleasantly full and in a mood to while away the rest of the evening. They talked and the woman called Julia occasionally sung in her sweet, haunting voice. It was a magical time for Kurt.

They had introduced themselves when they first sat down at the table. Sir Stuart, the famous Avatar, he had been hearing tales of for years. Julia was a beautiful, dark woman who carried her weapon and armor with a feminine yet very competent air that completely captivated Kurt. Shamino and Dupre were fighters, gruff and friendly veterans who accepted him as an equal. Jaana had an elfin beauty; she told him she was a mage and made blue flames flicker along her fingertips for just a moment, playfully winking at him. Gwenno, like Julia, was a bard, and the quietest of the group, but the times she did speak, all listened respectfully to her wit and wisdom.

Kurt, in the unaccustomed glow of acceptance by these mighty warriors and of the celebrity status it was giving him in this inn, blurted out, "It's always been a dream of mine, milord, I think I'd be an excellent Avatar."

To his relief, they did not laugh but took it quite seriously. "You do, eh?" Sir Stuart said. He paused and looked meaningfully at Dupre, who silently nodded and left the table.

"Yes sir," Kurt said, leaning back and feeling his stomach full for a change. "The world out there is all messed up now and I want to help right it." He paused to blink away a sudden tear. "The troubles killed my parents, you know."

Julia looked at him with sympathy. "Do you want to talk about it, Kurt?"

So Kurt told them how a band of evil bears had caught his parents outside the village and killed them three years before, orphaning him. The minion of Blackthorn who ran the village was not very caring about it, and got rid of the problem of the orphan by apprenticing little Kurt into the anything but gentle clutches of Theoan the stable owner.

Dupre returned and whispered into Sir Stuart's ear. The knight nodded and smiled. "Good work, as usual, Dupre." He now turned his smile onto Kurt. "We've just paid off your apprenticeship, Kurt. Lothar confirmed to Dupre the hardship and virtual slavery to which we suspected Theoan has subjected you. Old Theoan is a bit in his cups now, but he was sober enough to see reason when Dupre offered him one hundred gold pieces for your apprenticeship."

Kurt's leaping joy knew no bounds. "Then . . . then I belong to you, Honored Sir? I'll do my best, I swear I will! Polish your armor, anything!"

Sir Stuart's smiled broadened. "You misunderstand, Kurt. The Way of the Avatar would not condone us enslaving another. You are now free to do as you please." He paused and winked at his companions as Kurt, a little crestfallen, tried to assimilate the idea of no master and no task to do next.

"But . . ." he said, "but what will I do?"

"Well," Sir Stuart said, seeming to think and then suddenly brighten with a solution (as Julia, Dupre, Gwenno, and Jaana chuckled), "you could come with us, of course. I mean, if you wanted to. Being a free man now, you have the choice."

Shamino, a little slower than the others, had caught on now also. He slapped Kurt on the shoulder. "You could even learn to be a fighter like me, eh, Kurt?"

The boy was thrilled at being called a man and agog at the prospect of traveling out into the world with these great adventurers and warriors.

"Let's go!" he said.

They laughed. "We thought we might wait until in the morning," Jaana said. "Maybe even get a little sleep tonight."

Kurt reluctantly agreed, but knew that he would slumber little, as excited as he was.

After a couple of hours in the hot sun and dust on the road to Trinsic, Kurt's excitement was beginning to subside a little, but he had a feeling it would quickly return. He was riding the horse that they had purchased for him from Theoan. The grouchy stable owner, head obviously pounding from a hangover, had not dared play games with the warriors, and Kurt's horse was one of the better ones. He had fed and cared for this old friend often.

He tugged at the unaccustomed weight of his leather armor, then let his hand drop to proudly brush the shiny, lethal-looking dagger hanging at his side. They had outfitted him with rather limited arms and armor—only what he had the strength to carry and use, but Kurt felt like a real man now, and ready for any battle.

It was a grand new life he had entered on. About an hour ago he had inwardly rejoiced as he saw the village of North Brittany and the turrets of Lord British's castle disappearing from view.

"If we are attacked," Sir Stuart had told him, "you stay in the back and let us handle the combat. Until we can give you some training and build up your strength, fighting is too dangerous for you."

Kurt had nodded his understanding, but now, with the weight of the armor on his body and the weapon at his side, he was feeling a lot more dangerous. "Let them come," he muttered under his breath, "I'm ready."

Shamino, who was riding by his side, overheard. "No, lad, you're not. But stick with us and we'll help you learn enough to fight and survive."

The road was now winding by a small copse of woods in a narrow defile, an ideal place from which monsters could ambush unwary travelers. Such was the rapport between the adventurers that Sir Stuart had only to make a small hand gesture to put the others on maximum alert.

"Could be trouble here, lad," Shamino said. "If there is an attack in this kind of terrain, we'll dismount to fight. You stay back with the horses and we'll protect you."

Kurt grunted noncommittally, still feeling like he could take care of himself. His confidence was overlaid a bit with fear, however, as his eyes took in the dark clump of forest ahead. Were those flashes of light in there reflected from the feral, gleaming eyes of long-fanged predators, or merely from moisture on leaves?

"I hear something to the southwest," Shamino said calmly.

"Orcs," Julia said just as calmly. A pack of the great slobbering, ape-like creatures bounded out of the woods, screaming in rage and waving huge clubs.

All of a sudden things started moving very fast. Kurt was not sure how it happened, but now they were off the horses and standing in a combat formation with himself at the back. The charging orcs were much closer now.

Sir Stuart had his silver sword in one hand and his magic ax in the other. There was a sudden *whirr* sound as the magic ax leaped from the knight's hand to stagger an orc by a blow to its head, then the ax returned gently to the hand that had thrown it.

There were equally sudden silver blurs as first Dupre, then Shamino released their silver axes at the same orc. After the latter hit, the orc was nothing but a splatter of blood on the ground.

"Yea!" Kurt said, waving his dagger. "Hooray!"

Julia smiled reassuringly at him, and stepped over to guard Jaana, who was concentrating deeply. She made mysterious sounds and movements of her hands and, abruptly, a wall of fire appeared that consumed two orcs.

"Wow!" was all Kurt could say. "Wow!"

A sense of duty overcame him then, and he looked behind to make sure the horses were okay. They were. Battle hardened, they contentedly munched grass and ignored the screams of the monsters. Kurt smiled and turned back to watch the fight, only to see a mouthful of wicked fangs leaping for his throat!

"Look out, Kurt!" Shamino yelled, throwing his magic ax. Unfortunately it blurred past the orc in a clean miss before arcing back around in a return path to its owner.

Kurt, in complete terror as the fetid breath of the beast washed over him, still managed to get his dagger up so that the momentum of the orc plunged its chest onto the blade as they went down together. Figuring he was one dead boy, Kurt still retained the presence of mind to keep twisting the knife in the wound as the orc tore at his armor. Four times he heard the tough leather shredding and felt the claws dig into his flesh.

He was about to black out from the horrible pain when he felt a soothing balm coursing throughout his body, bringing relief. He heard a thud and simultaneously felt a pounding shock from above; then heard and felt both again. (He later realized that these were two blows from magic axes being transmitted through the orc's body to him as he lay below.) The orc screamed in pain, and leaped to its feet to deal with its attackers.

Groaning, Kurt struggled to his own feet, just in time to see another ax resound off the orc. The monster roared—weakly this time, and staggered, obviously on its last legs. It turned yet again on the boy. Kurt raised his dagger and thrust it home into the beast's neck. To his surprise, it collapsed, kicked a couple of times, and was dead.

He looked around in surprise to see that all the other orcs had been dispatched, and that the adventurers, also showing various gashes and other signs of combat wear and tear, were grinning at him.

"I'll be a swamp toad," Shamino said proudly, "the kid just made his first kill."

Sir Stuart nodded in pleasure. "I told you he had potential, Shamino. Congratulations, Kurt."

"Stand aside," Jaana told them briskly. "This young hero needs another healing spell to stop all his bleeding."

Kurt, in surprise, looked down to see that his chest was a mangled mess. And now, it *hurt*.

Once more the party was on horseback. Kurt, restored to health, had on new leather armor. They rode through the now peaceful countryside, almost knee to knee.

"I'm ready now," Kurt said, the glow of victory still in him. "Let's go to the Underworld and get on with our quest!"

Sir Stuart smiled tolerantly. "It will be a long time before you are ready for the Underworld, Kurt. We're taking you down to Trinsic now. We're going to put you in training. You'll study fighting techniques and learn about Honor there. Later we'll see that you go to other towns and keeps to further your education. In a few years, *then* you will be ready to tackle the Underworld."

"You don't want to go to the Underworld anyway, Kurt," Shamino said with a wry smile, twisting around to a comfortable sideways position in his saddle. "It's pretty much a boring place. Just swamps and mountains and various waterways."

"Goes on forever, though." Julia added. "It's huge. Twice I got lost for a few hours."

"Right, I wouldn't ever go there unless I knew exactly where I was going," Stuart added. "Pop in, complete my mission, and get out. I certainly don't stay around to admire the scenery."

"I didn't find it all that dangerous," Gwenno asserted in one of her infrequent comments. "Except when the mongbats attacked us. We all were strong enough to be down there in the first place, so they were the only monsters we had to worry about."

"Oh, yeah, I'll never forget those horrible beasties flapping their wings behind my ears," Jaana shuddered.

"*Behind* your ears?" Kurt asked hesitantly. "Were you—running?"

Jaana nodded matter-of-factly.

"Is—is it okay for an Avatar to retreat from battle?" Kurt asked doubtfully.

"Sure it is," Dupre said. "Mongbats come in large packs and are hard as blazes to kill. Our best bet was to exit since our mission was not to mess around with mongbats but to retrieve the Shards, or whatever it was that time."

Kurt was soaking all this up, gazing wide-eyed at these wonderful, wonderful people as the sun beat down on his head and through his armor.

Stuart smiled. "An occasional retreat hasn't seemed to have affected my virtue. And a live Avatar is far more effective than a dead one. Believe me, I have tried both states and much prefer alive."

"Speaking of alive," said Shamino, "I'm starving. Let's stop for some lunch."

As they munched on their rations, nobody said much of anything. Kurt was glad. He had absorbed so much since yesterday! He was still tired from his first combat, and beginning to feel sleepy. But he perked up as they rode along after lunch, because the others were eager to share their experiences with him and he was learning a raft of useful tips.

The afternoon started to cool off, and the horses picked up the pace a bit. Julia was saying, "The monsters you have to watch out for, Kurt, are daemons, wisps, and gazers. They have the ability to actually possess members of your party, even the Avatar himself. This can get a party wiped out in a hurry."

"Yes," Stuart said, "to ward that danger off, throw up a nullify magic spell, then use hand-to-hand combat to kill off the monsters. If there are too many of them for that, retreat while the nullify is still in effect."

"If just one or two of the party become possessed," Jaana added, "don't worry—the cure is simple. Finish the battle and move all the unpossessed party members off the battlefield. The possessed persons will fall asleep and wake up as themselves again."

"Dragons are what you really want to watch out for, Kurt," Shamino commented. "They are hard to kill, and can shoot really vicious fireballs a considerable distance. Worse, if you don't hit them with a nullify spell, they can gate in more dragons or call for daemons to help them. Then you will have *really* serious trouble on your hands."

Sir Stuart had stood in his stirrups to look ahead. "Ah, there's the village of Paws," he said. "We'll spend the night there."

After the tasteless and dry field rations during the day, Kurt was glad to get another big meal into him. This adventuring stuff sure did raise an appetite.

"Bring me one of those berry pies over there," Shamino instructed the serving lass. "My friend Kurt here will help me eat it I'm sure."

Julia and Gwenno looked at each other and pulled musical instruments from their packs. Soon the room was filled with a rousing marching song, and their voices blended in perfect harmony. Good spirits continued to reign.

"Tomorrow morning," Sir Stuart told Kurt, "we'll have to take our leave of you."

Kurt felt sad at the thought of parting with his friends.

"We shall miss you," the knight said. "Now, as a parting gift to you, we'll give you some knowledge about things besides monsters to help you when the time comes for your own quest."

Jaana began.

"In my opinion, scrolls are the most overlooked key to success. Anyone can use them," she said, "and there are many places where you can find them. Search bookcases especially. There are purple, black, white, yellow, green, orange, blue, and red scrolls. Purple scrolls will turn your enemies into rats, which are very easy to defeat."

"Excellent way to deal with dragons," Stuart said.

"Yes, Stuart, and black scrolls will turn you invisible for combat."

"Just like a Ring of Invisibility?" interrupted Kurt excitedly, proud that he knew something about the magical tools an adventurer uses.

"Exactly,"answered Jaana. "And white scrolls invoke the sixth-circle WIS AN YLEM view spell, which will reveal hidden things around you and is very useful in the Underworld or in dungeons. Even if you're still only first level, you can cast this high-level spell using a scroll.

"Don't forget to tell him that scrolls lose their pretty colors after you first find them," interjected Gwenno. "But all you have to do to remedy that is just look at the runes on your equipment list."

"Right, Gwenno" confirmed Jaana. "Yellow scrolls are usually MANI or healing spells, but occasionally they're VAS MANI, the fifth-circle 'great heal' spell. There's no way to tell which it will be. Yellow and green I always steer clear of, because one is poison and the other puts you to sleep. Blue casts an awaken spell, and red is very useful, especially in swampy terrain, because it cures poison.

"And potions work exactly the same way as scrolls. The same color potion performs the same spell as that color scroll." She yawned and stretched. Kurt mentally reviewed what she had said, thanked for her advice, and ate some more berry pie. It was very juicy and sweet.

Dupre had been talking to somebody at another table, and now retook his seat. "I was thinking you need to know about keys, Kurt. Did you know there are two kinds? . . . You didn't? Well, most people know about the regular keys. Those are the ones available at Thieves Guild shops, along with gems and torches. If you have enough dexterity, they will open many doors. But some doors are not just locked, they are also sealed with magic."

Kurt started to ask how you could tell the difference, but Dupre went on. "Watch out for a blue outline around a door—that's the clue. It takes a special key to unlock these doors."

Dupre took an oddly shaped key from his pouch and held it out for Kurt to see. Yes, the twisted metal did look like a skull, and it shimmered with an innate magic. Kurt looked at it in awe until Dupre returned it to his pouch.

He took a sip of wine and smiled. "Now anyone who knows about Skull keys will tell you how rare they are. Usually, you can't buy them for love or money."

"Except for that cook at Farthing who sold us five at a hundred gold pieces each," Jaana said.

"She didn't know what she had." Dupre corrected. "They were worth a lot more than that. Anyway, Kurt, here's my—the famous courageous Dupre's—secret for a never-ending supply of Skull keys. Go up to the town of Minoc and search in the northwest corner of town after noon, and *every* day you will find five more keys. Now you never have to run out."

"Thanks, Dupre," Kurt said. "Thanks, *every*body. All these secrets will make my mission easy! And I swear I'll make you proud of me. But, why should I stay in Trinsic studying when I could be out doing useful things?"

"Well, I'll answer that for you," Julia said very emphatically, "by telling you we are almost ready for our final battle. Would you like to know what we are taking with us for the great rescue?" She barely paused. "Ninety nine gems, ninety nine torches, ninety nine regular keys, twenty Skull keys, our magic carpet, the Crown, Sceptre, Amulet, and the sandalwood box that we found in Lord British's apartment. Also, all the spells and reagents we can carry, plus about two thousand rations of food. And you know what? It took more than a couple of secrets to get that equipment assembled. Be prepared, boy. You have a long road ahead."

Soberly Kurt nodded. He understand much better the enormity of the task immediately ahead of them and, further in the future, ahead of him.

It was getting very late now. The torches were spluttering, about to go out. The sleepy innkeeper was impatiently waiting for them to seek their rooms and leave him to the lonely job of cleaning up.

Kurt yawned, in spite of himself.

Stuart smiled. "We won't have any time to talk or say goodbye, Kurt, once we reach Trinsic. So Farewell. You have been a faithful follower and stalwart companion. I hope you remember all we've taught you."

Kurt nodded gratefully. "Yes, milord, I will always try to live up to it!"

"Learn and abide by the Eight Virtues," Stuart said, "and you will be victorious."

Many years later, by then a successful and highly respected Avatar, Kurt again chanced upon Stuart.

"How can I ever repay you?" Kurt asked. "You and the others gave me a wonderful education, and I credit all of my success to the friendship and help you gave a poor stableboy."

"You already have repaid us, Kurt," the older Hero said. "Many times over, when you helped others as we helped you."

PART

7

Ultima VI — The False Prophet

14 The Gargoyles Are Grinning

O Brave veteran, once again Lord British needs adventurers. This time, only individuals already qualified as Avatars need apply. The threat of those denizens of the Underworld, the gargoyles, requires a Hero or Heroine who can assemble and lead a party through much hardship, danger, and turmoil to rescue Britannia from an invasion most foul.

Put aside all thoughts of the comfortable modern world, O Brave One. Turn off the entertainment box with its mindless series of colored pictures. Step forward through the red moon gate into stirring adventure. Step forward bravely, for all of our lives depend on the success you must achieve.

Background

In the last campaign, the fifth of the great missions, Lord British was rescued from the dungeon Doom and returned to his throne. As has happened often before, a triumph caused a karmic imbalance in the Underworld, which in turn resulted in vast and tumultuous geological upheavals.

Deep under Britannia the continent-sized tectonic plates ground one against the other, butting and riding up on their neighbors like gigantic blind leviathans fighting to the death. High above, the ground fell and rose rapidly. Volcanoes spewed forth rivers of glowing and sizzling lava. The waters of the world boiled in a maelstrom of towering tidal waves and hurricane force winds.

In the midst of the turmoil, the world actually *stretched*. Yes, it expanded. While the map of the world remains much the same as before in outline, distances between points are now greater, as you will find out when you set forth to follow the King's Road.

It was a terrible time, but mercifully short. The planet endured occasional aftershocks for a short period thereafter, but soon all returned to normal. Or so we *thought*.

Then, an expedition of royal seismologists, intent on checking underground conditions, were the first to encounter the gargoyles. The scientists had traversed a cavern deep in the world when they came across this subterranean civilization, once believed to be only mythical.

The gargoyles viciously set upon the party, and only a few survived to reach the surface again. The gargoyles, now aware of our existence, sent their armies forth. Scores of homes and villages throughout Britannia were destroyed by sword and torch. Yet again the good people of the land are forced to forsake the countryside and huddle in towns for protection.

Brave soldiers of the realm have gone up against these daemons of the night only to be utterly defeated. The monsters seem tireless in battle, and wreak horrible fates on any who oppose them. Even worse, the enemy has begun seizing our places of enlightenment and our holy shrines.

They *must* be stopped, and soon.

There is also a most disconcerting rumor that the gargoyles are seeking out any Avatar who would destroy them, in the hope of conducting a preemptive strike before the Avatar finds them. As you sit here in this briefing, they may be stalking *you*, or laying an ambush in order to take your very life. Walk with care, Avatars, this is your most dangerous mission yet.

Yes, this will be your greatest challenge yet, Lord British himself advises in the Adventurer's *Compendium*,

> Gird yourself with the infinite wisdom of Truth, Love and Courage, for at the end of your quest lies a destiny foretold in ancient times: "One shall arise who possesses the strength of an army, the vision of a prophet and the heart of a saint. This Great One will bring an end to the struggle between the Darkness and the Light."
>
> May you be that One.

Figure 14.1 *On a world far from Britannia, you watch television in boredom. Soon you will get a call, O Avatar, and return to adventure.*

Your Characters

As a veteran of the previous *two* campaigns, you may transfer to this one as a full-fledged Avatar. A special 'Transfer a Character' spell has been provided for your convenience. Invoke it before being injected into Britannia and your mission. Of course, character determines profession.

Your Profession

For newcomers, or those who would like to test their character anew, there is the option of visiting the same gypsy lady met during both the Age of the Avatars and the time of the Warriors of Destiny. Answer her questions honestly and to the best of your ability. The potion she mixes as you answer will define your attributes and profession at the start of the present mission. The professions available are the same as those for the previous quest.

The highest level you can hope to achieve, as in the previous mission, is eight. You attain the first level at 50 experience points, and each following level requires double the previous level. Thus level eight requires 6400 points.

At this time, the use of higher-circle magic by adventurers is restricted to Avatars only. Your party members have little or no magical ability compared to you. The burden of spellcasting is on you. A rare second-circle spell is about all the others are able to manage.

As you reach each new level, that circle of spells becomes available. Consult the *Compendium* in your adventurer's kit for a listing of the spells according to the circles of proficiency that they require.

Scrolls and potions are a different matter, and you should highly prize them. Anyone, even someone who is not a magic user, can employ the magic on scrolls. Thus, if you are a first-level adventurer you may even cast eighth-level spells, should you be so incredibly lucky as to find such a scroll.

Figure 14.2 *Suddenly your boredom is interrupted by a blinding flash of light!*

Your Party

This mission requires a totally different mindset from the previous one. Remember that there the realm had been subverted by the Shadowlords and you could trust no one. Now Britannia is restored and the threat is an external one. This means that you should structure your party toward completing the quest, rather than fighting ability. You can safely do this because Rings of Invisibility help you avoid a lot of combat. Then you can get on with more important things, such as finding the pirate treasures and lens, and restoring Shrines.

Another different recruitment criteria is the reduced need to consider magic-using ability. In the previous adventure you wanted to have as many magic users as possible to maximize mystical firepower. Now, with magic restricted mostly to yourself, you no longer need to consider that.

Also, building yourself up to level eight, as was necessary in the last mission, is not a requirement for this mission. Believe it or not, you can finish triumphantly as low as level five!

One reason for this is that monsters in general are fairly easy to kill, except for dragons, so you don't need a lot of high-level spells to put them out. This, unfortunately, makes most of the upper-level spells pretty worthless overall.

You may recruit up to seven companions. You'll start out with your three old friends and companions-in-arms; Shamino, Dupre, and Iolo. Actually, you could restrict your group to just these three, at least in the initial stages. One reason you might want to do this is that having some empty slots lets events transpire faster.

Two small exceptions to taking just anyone who will join you are Sherry, a nice mouse, and Beh Lem, the young gargoyle. You'll need to speak his language to befriend the latter. To get to Sherry, you'll need to search Lord British's castle and talk to the mice. Ask Lord British's permission to do so, however. Have some cheese with you and give it to her. She can do one very important thing for you later on.

On the other hand, it would be wise to ask others to join the party just for their utilitarian value. For example, Seggallion is strong and useful for carrying around extra items. He comes into the party as a level five fighter, so he is effective in combat. You'll run across him during your visit to Serpent's Hold (Sentri is also there). Ask Seggallion to tell you his story. Don't waste time asking people like Mariah to join the group.

Another possible party member is Jaana, your old friend the Druidess from Yew. Alas, she no longer has the strong magical powers she enjoyed in the previous mission, but she's still a decent fighter. Find her a magic bow and instruct her to go berserk during combat.

You can find Leodon and Leonna at the inn in Buccaneer's Den. Neither of them are of sterling quality, but Leodon does have an edge in strength and dexterity, and is a weak magic user. Julia and Gwenno are in Minoc. Although veterans of the previous mission, they aren't as important here, but Julia can help you with a quest.

The peasant girl Katrina, in New Magincia, is already a level five fighter and is well equipped with weapons and armor besides.

Talk to all your party members; they are surprisingly well informed.

Leave at least one slot open in your party when you enter gargoyle land, for you'll pick up a new member there.

Figure 14.3 *On a world far from Britannia, you found a black moonstone and came back to a new quest.*

The Lay of the Land

It's just as important in this mission as it was in the others to be familiar with the geographical makeup of the planet and the terrain you encounter.

Figure 14.4 *Were you a bit hasty in stepping through that red moon gate?*

Geography

Britannia, despite all the world-shaking upheaval it went through, is still much the same as when the Warriors of Destiny strode so bravely forth. It still consists of a large continent—broken up by natural features such as mountains, rivers, swamps, and forests—and several islands. There is much more detail now, of course, and distances between localities are greater because of the stretching of the world (although the towns remain in the same relative places).

Terrain

The largest portions of land areas are grasslands. Grass offers no impediment to travel, but also no concealment from enemies. Areas of brush and trees usually exist next to grasslands, consisting of taller grass and dense shrubbery. These slow down travel dramatically, since you must walk around the larger shrubs and the trees.

Swamps are still poisonous. You have to cross them from time to time, so be sure to learn how to cure poison early on. Doing it yourself requires an An Jux Ort spell, but there are healers in many towns, and Lord British will gladly restore your party to full health any time you request him to.

There are several rivers and many streams. Some of the streams are narrow and you can wade across them easily. You can ford the wider ones at the places where you see a couple of stepping areas that look like small islands in the stream bed. You can negotiate the wider rivers in a skiff or raft; because the latter is a slave of the current, it works only going downstream.

The oceans are larger and take longer to traverse than previously. On the plus side, however, they are not as rough and you can cross them just as well with a skiff as a frigate. The skiff has two major advantages: it's cheap, and, although it's heavy, a strong party member can carry one around wherever you go!

Travel on land is somewhat easier due to the road system. It's primitive but more extensive than the one in the last mission. The roads are brown dirt; you can easily discern them from the surrounding terrain.

Your Resources

You have many, many more resources at your disposal than ever before. Once more, as happened in the previous adventure, the world has gotten a lot larger. You can see everything in much greater detail, and objects remain at a constant scale. Many, many more items—in some cases, hundreds more—are available for use.

The richness of detail requires closer examination of the scene around you. Learn good searching habits. Investigate every nook and cranny. Look at every object, no matter how insignificant it may at first appear.

You receive the same number of initial points as you did on the previous mission.

Castles, Towns, and Villages

The Isle of the Avatar plus all the towns, castles, villages, shrines, major keeps, and most of the dungeons that existed during the time when the Warriors of Destiny fought the Shadowlords are in the same locations, but greatly enlarged and extensively remodeled. Some of the minor keeps, together with their islands, have disappeared, as have those wonderful lighthouses so useful to the Warriors of Destiny. Stonegate still exists, though.

In some towns there are government offices where day-to-day administration is conducted.

I suggest you check prior briefings for a description of the individual towns, castles, and villages. I will refer to them throughout this one only insofar as they affect your mission.

Locations Below Ground

Several important underground areas exist: they include the crypts of Moonglow, which are under Xiao's place (you'll need a Magic Unlock spell to get in) and the catacombs of Sutek, located under the late Blackthorn's former castle (be sure to have Magic Unlock, Dispel Field, and Telekinesis spells). The cellar of the Cyclops at Stonegate also is crucial; it requires Magic Unlock and Dispel Field spells, as well as a key obtained from the Cyclops. Of course you have to go to Dungeon Hythloth to see Captain John; you should enter it from the gargoyle side. You need a skiff to reach it easily.

You don't need to enter any of the other dungeons unless you are looking for pieces to the pirate's map, which are in Shame, Covetous/Wrong (same dungeon), Destard, the Ant Hill, and Pirate's Cove (not to be confused with Pirate's Den). The Pirate's Treasure is also underground. More about whether you should even bother with this part of the mission later.

Examine the map included in your adventurer's kit carefully, using a magnifying glass under bright light; you'll see several caves. None of them are critical to your mission, but they are interesting and fun, and the Spider Cave southwest of Empath Abbey is a good source of the reagent spider silk.

Important Shops

Shops are much the same as during the time that the Warriors of Destiny quested across Britannia, but there are two new types of shops.

The new shops include glassworkers, basketweavers, astronomers, ropemakers, and clockmakers, plus tailors, where you may purchase fine clothes, and fletchers and bowyers. This latter type specializes in arrows, bolts, bows, and crossbows. Iolo Fitzowen, owner of Iolo's Bows in Britain, is reputed to make the best of these weapons and their ammunition in all of Britannia. Visit him and his apprentice Gwenneth.

Since you are probably already an Avatar, it should not be necessary to warn you about stealing. An Avatar does not steal. You'll see many things left lying around in these shops, even when the shopkeeper is out. Wait until he or she returns and pay for what you want. It's the way of the Avatar.

Food and Drink

You can enjoy tasty meals at restaurants, taverns, and markets, but they won't sustain you during the rigors of traveling. Such places also sell the more usual packs of rations for adventurers. Prices vary.

Pubs, as usual, are great sources of refreshing libations and useful gossip. Cultivate the bartender or chef; they often repay your patronage with valuable information, especially if you tip well.

Arms and Armor

Most armouries still gladly purchase used or found equipment (if they sell that type), providing you with a ready source of income. You'll receive a price lower than the retail price of new items, since the armourer must make a profit. The types of goods sold at armouries vary widely. Visit all you can find and inquire of their stocks in trade.

Thieves Guild Shops

Thieves Guild shops are at various places also, such as in the village of Paws. You will need large quantities of the items they sell. Britain has no Thieves Guild shops, but a member of the Guild in Buccaneer's Den sells the same sort of supplies as any general store—at a better price to members, too.

Magic

Four mages of great wisdom and power will sell you spells, plus reagents for mixing up others: Xiao, whom you will find north of the Lycaeum; Horance, in Skara Brae; Rudyom, in the village of Cove; and Nicodemus, who is north of Britain between the two rivers. Additionally, Zotan, the wandering gypsy, has reagents for sale, although no spells. You'll run into him from time to time.

Several of these spells are necessary to the success of your mission. You'll need Dispel Field, Telekinesis, and Unlock Magic for sure. The Explosion spell, which is an excellent but noisy way to deal with locked doors as well as various monsters, is nice to have. Be sure to stand clear, though! Pickpocket is useful in the actions you'll need to accomplish to get the Pirate's Treasure, Invisibility comes in handy in several places, and Great Heal (a fourth-circle spell) will completely heal one person when you just don't have the time to travel back to Lord British's castle.

Here's where you can obtain the various spells:

From Xiao

Level of Spell	**Spell**
First	Detect Magic, Dispel Magic, Light
Second	Infravision, Reappear, Telekinesis, Vanish
Third	Dispel Field, Great Light, Peer
Fourth	Animate, Fire Fields, Poison Fields, Sleep Fields, Mass Dispel, Locate, Wind Change
Fifth	Energy Field, Invisibility, Reveal, X-Ray
Sixth	Clone, Negate Magic, Replicate
Seventh	Fear, Gate Travel, Wizard Eye
Eighth	Unknown

From Horance

Level of Spell	**Spell**
First	Harm
Second	Magic Arrow, Poison, , Magic Unlock
Third	Curse, Fireball
Fourth	Disable
Fifth	Explosion, Lightning, Paralyze
Sixth	Flame Wind, Hail Storm, Poison Wind
Seventh	Chain Bolt, Energy Wind, Kill, Mass Curse, Wing Strike
Eighth	none

From Rudyam

Level of Spell	**Spell**
First	Create Food, Douse, Heal, Ignite
Second	none
Third	Mass Awaken
Fourth	Great Heal
Fifth	Pickpocket, Seance
Sixth	none
Seventh	none
Eighth	Resurrect

From Nicodemus

Level of Spell	**Spell**
First	Detect Trap
Second	Sleep, Magic Unlock, Untrap
Third	Magic Lock, Mass Sleep, Protection, Repel Undead
Fourth	Conjure
Fifth	Insect Swarm
Sixth	Charm, Confuse, Mass Protect, Web
Seventh	Enchant, Mass Invisibility
Eighth	none

Apothecary shops are places you should visit regularly. They stock various reagents you need for spells.

Lodging

Several villages and towns have inns. Staying overnight in an inn, if you *pay* for lodging, has a healing effect on all members of the party. It is also a safe way to spend the night. If you have food for everybody, they will heal when camping, but this is not as safe as lodging in town.

Healers

Healers are widespread. They offer cures for poison and healing of wounds, and even resurrection of your dead comrades.

If things start getting too hot for your party and death from any source seems certain, casting the Kal Lor or Help spell will immediately resurrect you and your party before the throne of Lord British.

Transportation

An expanded world, as Britannia now is, offers many more areas for you to explore as you search out things you need. Alas, the downside is that it now takes much longer to go from place to place. There are two kinds of travel these days—very, very slow, and practically instantaneous. The fast way is to use the red moon gates, but these go to only a few places. Otherwise, you must walk or sail—either of which can take a very long time. You can also use the old familiar blue moon gates, but they operate only at night and according to the phases of the two moons as in prior missions.

First, the faster way to travel. To use the red moon gates you must first talk to Lord British about the Orb of the Moons. You get an explanation of the black stone you brought with you to Britannia and find that it is very handy to have, indeed!

The table below shows how to control the moon gates. There are twenty-four positions. Two are nulls, but twenty-two will instantly transport you and your party to various locations. Placement of the stone determines where you go.

Red Moon Gate Guide

Moonglow	Honesty	Britain	Compassion	Jhelom
Humility	Control	Lord British	Passion	Valor
New Magincia	—	*Avatar*	—	Yew
Spirituality	Temple	Diligence	Codex	Justice
Skara Brae	Honor	Trinsic	Sacrifice	Minoc

The 'Avatar' in the center is you. Visualize this grid around you and place the stone with the Using spell in the appropriate imaginary square. A moon gate then appears, which your party can step through to be instantly transported to the selected location. The direction you are facing is immaterial, because the grid is always oriented as shown.

The sixteen boxes located around the outside take you to the towns and shrines, each town being located next to its shrine. Thus Moonglow, in the upper left corner, is next to the shrine of Honesty; Britain, in the center, is next to the shrine of Compassion; Jhelom is next to the shrine of Valor; and so forth.

The six inner boxes take you to Lord British's castle, the Isle of the Avatar, and four places located within Gargoyle Land: the Shrine of Control, the Shrine of Passion, the Shrine of Diligence, and the Temple of Singularity. By the way, it takes more than an Orb of Moons to enter the Shrine.

Even though you can now jaunt down to Gargoyle Land, there is no reason to do so just yet. They won't like you and you will be unable to communicate with them because you won't know their language (see a fellow named Captain John for language lessons). Besides, you have more than enough to do in Britannia first.

Unfortunately, if you want to reach a place that's not listed in the moon gate table, such as Empath Abbey, you have to gate to the nearest location and walk the rest of the way. If your destination is on an island, you have to sail there.

Regarding the slower methods of travel, sometimes horses are speedier than walking. They are inexpensive and widely available.

Stables are rare, but there are a few around. Some even exist in castles and private residences, and often these will sell to the public.

When walking through swamps, you need special swamp boots to avoid getting poisoned. A handy source for them is Utomo in Yew. Make sure every member of the party has a pair.

Travel over oceans in frigates or skiffs. Your party can carry skiffs. The only advantage of having a ship is that it has armament (cannons) that can take care of the occasional sea serpents and other aquatic nasties that might try to impede your journey. Ships are not the easiest things in the world to maneuver, however.

Sailing the seas of Britannia requires navigation skills. Before taking that first ocean voyage, visit Ephemerides, who lives east of the Lycaeum, and buy a sextant. It will be cheap and it will be useful in many places. The Lycaeum is located on an island and has no moon gate, but Moonglow on the same island does. To get to Ephemerides, gate to Moonglow and walk to him via the Lycaeum. He sleeps until 3:00 PM, by the way, and spends the evenings in his observatory. The only time you can talk to him is between 3:00 PM and 9:00 PM, unless you awaken him (with Mass Awaken) when he's in his bedroom. On this island you'll be glad for your antipoison boots.

Shipwrights are hard to find in their shops, since they are very busy people. They will sell you skiffs at reasonable prices, or frigates for much more. You can also take frigates from pirates, if you can catch one close to shore.

Actually, there is an even faster way to travel that you should know about, although this does not befit an Avatar, and this one method can take you *everywhere*. To use it, you must be able to invoke the IBMish 'Alt 214' spell. There are three coordinates you must use in the spell—X, Y, and Z, where Z is the number of levels below ground.

Once you find an interesting place, invoke the 'Alt 213' spell and note the last seven digits of the numbers that materialize before your eyes. They are the X and Y coordinates and the level. Once you have the coordinates, you can return to this spot at anytime. Just remember to get the Alt 213 coordinates.

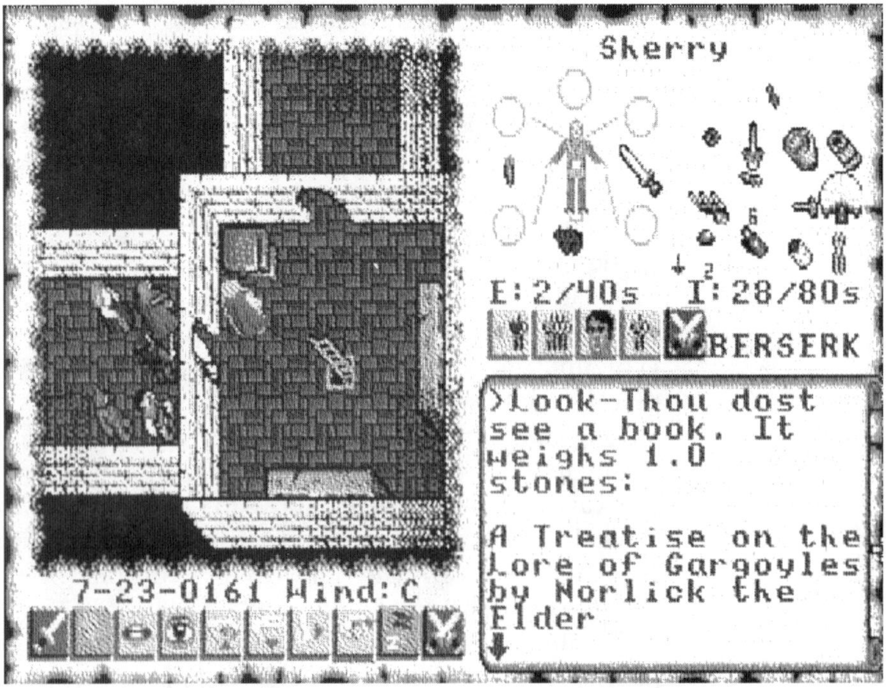

Figure 14.5 *The Lyceaum is the center of all learning for Britannia. Its huge library has several underground levels housing much arcane and useful knowledge.*

I cannot give you such critical data as the coordinates for the Pirate's Treasure, or the Temple of Singularity, but here are some interesting ones that will take some of the tedious and time-consuming travel out of your mission:

Blackthorn's Castle	X-313	Y-3C5
Britain Armoury	X-160	Y-17C
Cove	X-223	Y-162
Empath Abbey	X-091	Y-0DB
Ephemeries	X-3B2	Y-19A
Jhelom	X-097	Y-37B
Lord British	X-133	Y-15D

Lycaeum	X-37A	Y-1AB
Minoc	X-27B	Y-063
Moonglow	X-388	Y-1F3
New Magincia	X-2E0	Y-2A3
Paws	X-174	Y-244
Sawmill	X-2A3	Y-063
Serpent's Hold	X-223	Y-3B2
Skara Brae	X-051	Y-1F3
Trinsic	X-19B	Y-2E4
Yew	X-0FB	Y-0A8

Figure 14.6 *Boarding a frigate at New Magincia. You will need to have a deed showing you paid for the ship to use it. Also, see the magic shield lying in the left of this picture? Leave it alone. Avatars do not steal, so you have to be careful not to take anything you find unless you are sure you have the right to do so.*

Your Strategy

Now, it is time to get on with the actual mission itself: rescuing the eight shrines from the domination of the gargoyles and then ridding the land of these creatures. There are many things in the vast land of Britannia that divert time away from your mission. You will probably want to explore them when your major quest is successfully concluded. They can give you many hours and days of pleasant exploration. But for now, Brave Avatar, listen to the steps needed to save Britannia. First, some general considerations.

Conversations

You obtain most of the clues needed to complete your mission through talking to people. Those veterans of the mission immediately previous will note that keywords are now emphasized, making it easier to pick them out and further question the individual. Examine other words too, because sometimes they contain extra helpful information.

Asking "JOB?" is a good icebreaker when meeting someone for the first time. Often the character will respond to your questions with one of his or her own. Always answer truthfully; it is greatly to your benefit to do so. Lying only gets you into trouble. Avatars do not lie.

Combat

Combat not only is less important, it is very different in this mission. For one thing, you don't undergo random and therefore unpredictable attacks by monsters. Also, the other members of your party have much less freedom of action, and fight automatically as per your instructions. *You* are responsible for instructing them what to do in case of hostilities. You may order them to go berserk in wild attacks on whatever monster is near them, or you may dictate a more thoughtful assault. If a character is weak, your standing orders to that person should be to stay in the rear of the party for maximum protection, or even to retreat in case of combat. Order stronger characters always to station themselves in the front or on the flanks of a party. Your group will then perform these actions automatically until you change those standing orders.

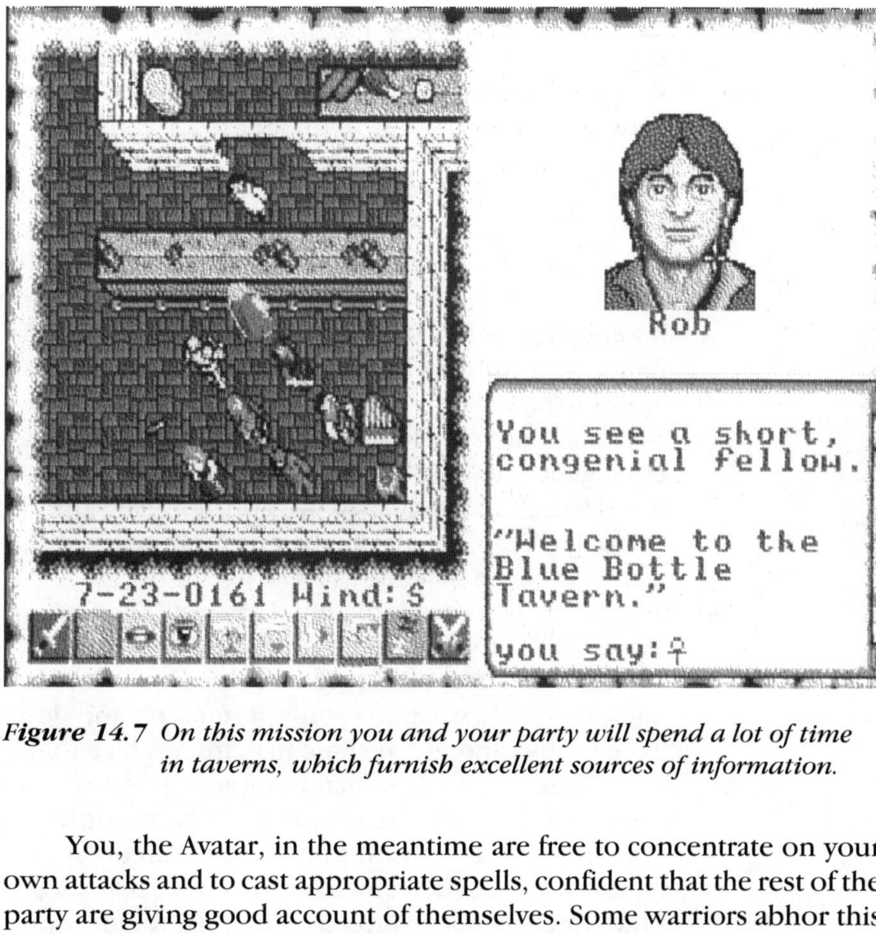

Figure 14.7 *On this mission you and your party will spend a lot of time in taverns, which furnish excellent sources of information.*

You, the Avatar, in the meantime are free to concentrate on your own attacks and to cast appropriate spells, confident that the rest of the party are giving good account of themselves. Some warriors abhor this new, automated method of fighting because it is less flexible, but it is somewhat faster and the leader has less to keep track of during the heat of combat.

I stated earlier that combat is not a major consideration in this mission, but let me temper that by adding that it is important if you are *in* combat, and you do need to fight to some degree. Although it's not necessary to attain a very high level, you must become at least level five. Accumulating enough experience points to achieve this level does, alas, require some combat.

Combat also lets you enhance your finances, either by finding gold after defeating monsters or by selling the weapons and equipment you capture. Also, sometimes combat will be forced upon you by monsters with larger fangs than brains. Nighttime is a good time to fight monsters because they come out then, and in case anybody is wounded, Lord British can heal you in the morning. Don't worry about missing sleep—you don't need much (you don't need much food, either).

The Warriors of Destiny found magic axes to be the supreme weapon during their quest. Unfortunately the secret of their manufacture has been lost in the present time. The closest equivalent is boomerangs which, when thrown at an enemy, strike a solid blow and return to your hand. Boomerangs are among the best ranged weapons available and even a mouse can carry one or two.

The only source for boomerangs is gargoyles. According to our intelligence reports, during the initial stages of your mission, you will most likely be ambushed in Lord British's throne room by three gargoyles. Search their bodies well for boomerangs, and those of other gargoyles you defeat.

Slings work well initially. They never run out of ammunition and are excellent for knocking out those annoying small attackers such as bats and rats. They also work surprisingly well on larger foes, and when you use missile weapons you can stand off and destroy monsters such as acid slugs and green slime that are not nice to be close to.

There is a wide selection of armor and weapons available, both through armouries and by capture. Most armouries will gladly buy used equipment, thus providing a constant source of funds. Weapons, armor, and other helpful items include arrows, black shields, bolts, boomerangs, bows, brass helms, chain coifs, chain mail, cloth armor, clubs, crossbows, curved heater/shields, daggers, door shields, force fields, gargoyle belts, gargoyle helms, glass swords (one hit only), guild belts, halberds, iron helms, kite shields, leather armor, leather boots, leather helms, maces, magic armor, magic bows, magic helms, magic shields, main gauches, morning stars, plate mail, ring mail, scale mail, slings, spears, spiked collars, spiked helms, spiked shields, swamp boots, swords, throwing axes, two-handed axes, two-handed hammers, two-handed swords, webs, winged helms, winged shields, wizard eyes, and wooden shields.

Take everything you find out in the field. While there are weight limitations on how much you can carry, Britannia is now an honest place, so you can park stuff almost anywhere and be assured that it will remain there until your return. Shrines are handy places to cache equipment, as well as easy to remember and find again.

I do recommend against leaving things in Lord British's castle. It is a quirk of reality, perhaps because so *many* items are there, but they tend to disappear in seemingly random patterns. Establish your caches elsewhere.

Getting Started

When you are injected into your mission, you arrive in Lord British's throne room with only your ankh and the black moonstone picked up in your home world. Luckily Shamino and Iolo are with you, having rescued you from those other gargoyles who wanted to sacrifice you.

After defeating the gargoyles, you have the opportunity to start accumulating equipment, taking what they had. Now, talk to Lord British and his mage Nystul. You'll find out that anything inside his castle is yours to use in your mission, and it won't be considered stealing if you take it. Be sure to ask him about moonstones so that you will be able to generate and use the red moon gates. Lord British also informs you that he has ordered a room set aside for your use while in the castle, which you will visit often to restore your party to health.

Your Room

Exit the throne room and take the oaken door to the west. This is the west wing of the castle. Your room is the first on the left.

Search the room well. There are swords, rations, lockpicks, a spell book, and several other items. Get everything.

There is food on the table. Take it all. Look in the pantry off the kitchen for cheese, which you'll need later for Sherry (actually you can buy cheese in some shops and pubs too). Look in the bag in the corner for more provisions.

Lord British's Room

Lord British's suite is directly across the hall from your room. Search it well—he won't mind. Use your lockpicks to open the locked chest in his closet. Within the chest is a sword, a dagger, a chain coif, and chain mail. Help yourself.

Nystul's Room

The royal mage's room is around the corner of the corridor and on the same side as your room. You'll find a chest containing a wand and other things. Get these things for your own use.

Potions

Beyond Nystul's room is a room with a ladder leading down into the sewers and a large crystal ball (which will show you various locations if you know their coordinates). Ignore this for a moment and check out the potion factory to the east. The potions do the following:

Yellow	Works similar to a healing spell.
Red	Like the Dispel Magic spell, also cures poison.
Purple	Protects, temporarily stops effects of poison.

Blue	Awakens party member from sleep caused by magic or orange potion. Will not awaken from normal sleep.
Green	Supposedly protects you from death, but more often poisons. Use cautiously.
White	Same as the X-Ray spell. Lets you look through walls.
Black	Same as Invisibility spell. Most enemies will be unable to detect you.
Orange	Puts you to sleep!

Sewers

After you have the above items from the rooms of the west wing of Lord British's castle, it's time to head for the sewers. No, I'm not kidding, you explore the sewers next. Enter them by climbing down the ladder in the room next to the potion factory.

People live down here, and you'll find several rooms with items in them. Below the sewers is a dungeon. There are some *very* nasty beasties down in this dungeon, such as the corpsers that will drag party members under if you're not careful. However, you can pick up lots of goodies too, such as Rings of Invisibility, Rings of Regeneration, and Rings of Protection.

The only reason to go into this dungeon is to gain experience and equipment in building up for your main mission. If you run across a woman named Phoenix, who lives north of the lake on level two, chat with her about belts.

If you go back up a ladder and then return, monsters *usually* regenerate. Take advantage of this fact by putting a party member in the dungeon alone and letting him or her wear an invisibility ring for protection. Then have your solo fighter go down and up the ladder repeatedly, killing the monsters at the bottom each time. This is an excellent way to build up that character's experience points.

The Shrines

The most immediate and pressing reason that Lord British called for you, O Most Courageous Avatar, is to free the Eight Shrines, all now so basely captured by the gargoyles. The Shrines of Compassion, Honesty, Honor, Humility, Justice, Sacrifice, Spirituality, and Valor are an integral part of both Britannia and the Way of the Avatar. For them to be in the hands of the gargoyles is blasphemous at best.

Saving the shrines not only is the first major portion of your mission, but also it will rapidly build up you and your party members. You'll need all the eight moonstones that you pick up at the shrines. The Orb of the Moon, that black moonstone you brought along with you, will make it easy to reach the cities and their associated shrines. Remember that each town stands for a virtue. Britain, the capital, promotes Compassion; New Magincia's specialty is Humility; Minoc champions Sacrifice; Moonglow advocates Honesty; Jhelom bravely stands up for Valor; Skara Brae is the home of Spirituality; Trinsic feels duty bound to protect Honor; and Yew seeks Justice above all.

The information that follows is just the bare bones of a how-to on freeing the eight shrines. Don't do just these steps. Spend considerable time in each town, talk to *everyone*, and note their replies. If you don't you'll have to do a lot of backtracking. This mission consists of much more than Shrine liberation, which is the easy part. I say this again, *take extensive notes*. Now, on to the Shrines.

Compassion

Since you are already so close to Britain, being in Lord British's castle, logically the first Shrine to liberate is the Shrine of Compassion. To do so, you need two things, the rune for the Shrine and its mantra. Those veterans of both the Age of the Avatar and the Warriors of Destiny campaigns already should know the mantras for all eight shines, since they are the same for all three missions. The Mantra of Compassion, which is no big secret by now, is "MU."

Figure 14.8 *Ignore the gargoyles and free the eight Shrines of Virtue. You'll need a mantra and a rune for each. Be sure to take the moonstone afterwards.*

Explore the town of Britain, which is just outside the castle. The museum (take the first path to the left after leaving the castle) has a number of interesting exhibits, and there should be a concert in progress. Ask Ariana the child about the rune.

Once the rune is in your possession, it's a short stroll to the Shrine. Take the eastern road out of Britain. Stay on the road until you've forded the second stream, then walk due east. You'll soon see the pillars that surround the Shrine.

The Shrine of Compassion has several gargoyles nearby. You can take the old hack-and-slash route and eliminate them as part of the liberation process. However, they are tough fighters and it's not really necessary to engage them at all. Once the Shrine is freed, they will eventually just go away.

To free the Shrine, approach it, use the rune and, when asked, supply the mantra. The Shrine will then be free and you'll see a moonstone lying on its altar. Take the stone.

Honor

This one should be the next-easiest shrine to free. Use the Orb of the Moon and travel to Trinsic. No need to search for the rune here, because it's lying out in plain sight on an altar in the center of town. Since you are an Avatar, it's not stealing for you to take the rune.

To go to the Shrine of Honor, you can either gate to it via the Orb of the Moon, or else just follow the road south out of town. The road leads you right to the Shrine. Follow the same procedure used above, use the rune, and say the mantra ("SUMM").

Justice

Gate to Yew next. Enter the tavern. The rune is hidden under a potted plant, which you'll have to move. Take the road east out of town, and it will curve around to the north. At the Shrine of Justice, use the rune, say the mantra ("BEH"), and take the moonstone.

Since you are in Yew already, you can take care of another little chore by finding the woodcutter in the forest west of town. Buy a log from him and take it with you.

Sacrifice

Minoc and the Shrine of Sacrifice are next. In Minoc, take the road east from town until you find the sawmill. Or go south of the red moon gate to get to the sawmill. Have the man there turn your log into a board. Go back to Minoc and find Julia in her shop (it's in the northern part of town). Talk to her about panpipes. She'll make you a set out of your board and, later, join your party if asked.

In the meantime, find Selganor, ask him about the rune, and show the pipes when he asks. He'll want you to do a little number for him, a familiar tune. If you haven't learned it yet on this mission just harken back to the previous mission and the song that Lord British's court composer taught you on the harpsichord, or find a townsperson to teach you. Same piece, a real golden oldie. After you finish, he'll give you the rune (the rune for the tune).

The Shrine of Sacrifice is a considerable distance east of Minoc, in the large desert shown on your map. The Shrine is exactly in the center. Rather than walking or riding, it's better by far to use the red moon gate to go there directly and free it. The Mantra of Sacrifice, as in the two previous missions, is "CAH."

Spirituality

Gate to Skara Brae and find the woman named Marney. She lives next to the boat dock north of town. Search her house, and especially look in the chest. Gate to the Shrine and free it, using the mantra "OM." Of course, before leaving Skara Brae talk to several other people and take note of their answers to your questions.

Humility

New Magincia has always advocated humility since its predecessor town, Magincia, was destroyed because of excessive pride. Antonio is the government representative there, and can be found in those offices (look for the blue sign). He'll give the rune to you for the name of the most humble man in New Magincia. I won't say who it is, but you might want to speak with Conor.

The Shrine of Humility is on the Isle of the Avatar, also the location of the Shrine of the Codex of Ultimate Wisdom. Use the red moon gate and free the shrine, using the mantra "LUM." Ignore any gargoyles there, get the moonstone, and leave.

Valor

Go to Jhelom and enter the tavern. You'll find a small mouse hole at its back. The rune of Valor is down that mouse hole. Too bad you don't have a mouse to retrieve it for you . . . but *wait*! Don't forget about little Sherry! That investment in cheese now pays off. Let Sherry go solo into the mouse hole and bring back the rune.

A raft is waiting at the southern dock in Jhelom. Use it to float south to the Shrine of Valor, or do the easy and logical thing—use the red moon gate to get there instantly.

Honesty

The rune to free the eighth and last shrine, the Shrine of Honesty, is the hardest one to get. Journey to the town of Moonglow. Find Bevlyn's cousin in the tavern there. Ask him about Bevlyn and tell him you have visited the tomb. Ask for the key. He will give you a key and some flowers.

Take the key and flowers to the sawmill on the northern end of the island, which is where Xiao lives (buy spells from her!). At the back of the sawmill is her room, which has a magically locked door. Unlock it with a Magic Unlock spell and go down the ladder. You are now in the catacombs, where there are lots of bones. (Another way to this dungeon is from the secret room off the kitchen in the Blue Boar Tavern.) Pick up the glass sword hidden near the ladder for use later in your mission. Search around for another ladder down. Watch out for those acid slugs!

The lower level of the catacombs has several rows of stone tombs. Look for the one with Bevlyn's name on it. Put the flowers next to the door and unlock it with the key. Search Bevlyn's bones and you'll find the rune of Honesty and a few other goodies. Take them, leaving the bones. Gate out from there to the Shrine (no need to climb all the way back up).

Be sure you have freed all eight shrines now and have all eight moonstones in your possession. Safeguard them, because they are critical to the success of your mission. If all the Shrines are now free, you are ready for the next major phase of your mission.

The Pirate's Treasure

The middle part of your mission, finding the Pirate's Treasure, is very long and tedious. It also, alas, is not necessary to the success of your mission. The only important piece of information to come out of this treasure hunt is the other half of the tablet that Mariah (she's at the Lycaeum) needs to translate the *Book of Prophecy* and tell you who the False Prophet is. Since you eventually learn the language and can read the book for yourself, the tablet is not really needed.

One other minor thing to get out of the Pirate's treasure is a magic fan that is useful when you finally have a balloon to fly in, but a few Wind Change spells do the same job.

That leaves you two options, O Avatar. You can forget the treasure and get on with more important things, or you can take the considerable time to track down and get all the pieces of the pirate's map and find out where to dig.

If you want to do it just for fun, that's fine. There are many, many red herrings and interesting but useless quests on this mission. Complete the main portion first. Then you can enjoy yourself with all the others. You can even visit our old friend Smith, the talking horse from the previous mission, who is still at Iolo's hut in the Spiritwood.

Should you decide to take the long detour to find the pirate's treasure, seek out Zotan the gypsy at or around the Blue Boar tavern in Britain. He will tell you that some time ago pirates stole the missing part of the tablet Mariah wants and that you should go to Buccaneer's Den for more information.

Sometime during all this process, find yourself a shovel to dig the Treasure up with, should you find it. If you want to take the time to find the Pirate's Treasure, here's how to do it.

Phoenix

Nobody in this pirate's village will tell you much unless you are a member of the Thieves Guild. This necessitates a trip down into the sewers under Lord British's castle before you leave for the small island that the Guild is on.

Enter the sewers by the ladder in the west wing of the castle. Several ladders lead down into the dungeon below the sewers, but you want to use the one at coordinates 8S-11E. (Use a Locate spell to determine coordinates.)

You are now on the first level of this dungeon, but the person you need to see is on the second level. Find the ladder down at 0N-7E, then travel north to 12N-19E. Phoenix is here. What you want is her belt. There are two ways of getting it—kill her or use the Pickpocket spell.

Once you have the belt, you can now join the Thieves Guild. So, travel to Buccanneer's Den. It's a long sea voyage unless you remember the 'Alt 214' spell described earlier in this briefing.

Join the Thieves Guild

In the back room of the tavern at Buccaneer's Den is the kitchen. Move the large cauldron to find a secret door. Through that door is another one; you have to pick its lock or blast it open with a powder keg. See the man inside about joining the Thieves Guild. If you have the belt, he'll let you into that fine but shifty organization (remember, Avatar, you are but pretending and do not subscribe to their warped moral values).

Return to the common room of the tavern and look for a man named Homer. Now that you are a member of the Guild, Homer will tell you where to find the different sections of the map in return for a certain deal he outlines to you.

Your First Stop

The dungeon Destard will be your first stop (it's still in the same place as in your previous mission). You need a dragon's egg, and there are *lots* of dragons in this dungeon. Having everybody invisible is the best approach here. Why fight when you don't have to? Especially since dragons are so incredibly tough to kill.

Go down four levels and then north as far as you can. There is a large group of dragons there, and where that many dragons gather you are sure to find eggs. Take one, but don't let the dragons detect your presence.

Now that you have the egg, you'll need a cook. I recommend Sandy, the cook at the tavern in Trinsic.

Trinsic, Pieces of the Map, and Gypsies

After you give the dragon's egg to Sandy in Trinsic, he will explain about pirates, tell you several places to go, and reveal that the mayor of this town is actually a pirate! Ask the mayor about Alastor Gordon, which is his real name. Keep at him and he'll break down and give you his piece of the map in return for your promise not to tell anyone.

Take the road out of Trinsic (it's the King's Way). You should come across a band of three gypsies. Talk to the one who calls himself Arturos. He owns a piece of the treasure map and will sell it to you for fifty gold pieces, if you bargain him down.

Next make sure you have three items: a gold nugget, a magic gem, and a curved heater (one of the shields with a snake emblem on it). Travel to Serpent's Hold by ship.

Between Serpent's Hold and Trinsic you'll need to stop at the shipwreck located at the small group of islands between Britannia and the larger island where Serpent's Hold is located. Search the wrecked ship and you will find another piece of the map.

The Magic Shield

At Serpent's Hold, seek out Korunada in the Government Building around noon. Converse with him, mentioning the Guild and the word 'shield.' Then go south of that building to the blacksmith's shop and talk with Gherick. If you have the items necessary (see the preceding paragraph), he'll make you a Magic Shield.

Now go north to the road, then east until it forks, and follow the northern fork. You are looking for Morchellas' house. Talk to her about the map and keep talking until she decides to trade you her part of the map for the Magic Shield (now that you know how they are made, you can always have more constructed).

Dagger Isle

Yes, I did warn you that the quest for the Pirate's Treasure was long and tedious. Prepare for yet another lengthy sea voyage. Journey to Dagger Isle. It's a small island north of the larger one on which Moonglow and the Lycaeum are situated.

Some mountains ring the north side of this little island. Inside lives an old hermit who has yet another piece of the map. You'll have to use gems or the 'Alt 213' spell to find his house.

Inside the house, move his piano and climb down the ladder. Search everything until you find the piece of map stuck in a bag.

From Ocean to Desert

More or less north of Dagger Isle is the large desert that has the Shrine of Sacrifice in its center. South of the Shrine (at coordinates 20N-67E) is a large anthill.

Enter the anthill (and be prepared to do a lot of fighting unless you are invisible). Find your way down three levels and look for a large open area in the northern part of that level. Among the horde of ants, the queen will be on a pedestal. South of the queen ant is the body of a human (coordinates 25N-85E). Search it for yet another piece of the map.

The Dungeon Wrong

Now go to Minoc (at least you can use the red moon gate to get there quickly). Your next stop will be the dungeon Wrong, which is across the bay in the mountains. Go down to level two, then look for a lever. Use a Telekinesis spell on it; then go back west and you'll find a a ladder at 40N-19E. Climb down it.

Walk south to the first room on the east. There's a hydra in the room, and also a secret door (37N-27E), behind which is a corridor. In the room at its end is another piece of the map.

The Dungeon Shame

On the end of the mountain range surrounding Britain is the dungeon Shame. You'll have to use a skiff to go down the river. The exact coordinates of its entrance are 23S-20W.

Go down a couple of levels and look for Ybarra. Ybarra is *very* hungry. He promises you his piece of the map for food, *but* if you give him food, he'll keep eating until you have none left. Also the smell of food will attract hungry gremlins. If you refuse him food, he'll collapse and you won't get the piece of the map. So just use the Pickpocket spell on him, get the map piece, and get out of there.

Back to Buccaneer's Den

Now, you have all the pieces of the map except one. Go back to Homer and tell him you have all but one of the pieces. Make the deal with him and he will give you the last piece of the map.

The Treasure

You now have a complete map. The Pirate's Treasure is buried on a small island southeast of Buccaneer's Den. There will be three stones on the northern part of the island. Move to the center of the stones. Go south three paces, west nine paces, then south twelve paces. Your location then should be 59S-50E.

Now is not the time to find out you forgot to bring a shovel. Digging down will get you into the Pirates' Cave. Almost immediately you see a sign reading "This Way."

Only a fool would believe pirates, so go in the opposite direction. It's a winding way around, but you are looking for a ladder at 69S-19E. When you find it, go down, then southwest to the Maze of Death. At the center of the maze is another ladder leading downward.

On the next level, you will see several ladders leading further down, but the one at 68S-25W is the one for you. It's in a larger open area than most of the rest. Go down and then along the corridor, past the first set of poison fields, and Dispel Field the next two poison fields. You will then come to a door. Pick the lock or blow it to smithereens with a powder keg.

Inside the building you can take everything you want—and there are quite a few items! Above all, however, be sure to get the Tablet and the Storm Cloak. Take the Storm Cloak back to Homer at Buccanneer's Den, thus honoring your part of the deal, and the Tablet to Mariah at the Lycaeum. She can now decipher the book and inform you who the False Prophet is.

Or, you can skip all of the above and forget about the Pirate's Treasure.

Stay On Track

Don't let all this very un-Avatar-like concern with treasure divert you from your mission, which is to end the gargoyle invasion and save Britannia.

By this point, you should be strong enough to descend into the gargoyle world and set things aright. But, there is one very important preparation to make first. You must find the plans for a hot-air balloon and have one constructed.

The level of technology has decreased considerably since the spaceships and time machines that existed in ancient Sosaria. Now even hot-air balloon technology has been lost and is not widely available. In fact, the only set of plans known to exist lies under Sutek's castle (77S, 60E), which was formerly owned by the usurper Lord Blackthorn, the late minion of the defeated Shadowlords.

Retrieving the Plans

When you go to Sutek's castle, take Magic Unlock, Telekinesis, and Dispel Field spells. Blow away the front door of the castle and cast Telekinesis on the crank to lower the drawbridge. Beyond you will find a decorative sword on a wall mount. Move the sword and wall mount to reveal a secret door. Go east after entering.

Look for another secret door on the western walls after you leave the corridor. Enter it and you will see three levers. Move the left and middle levers to the right, and the right one to the left. Exit and take the door to the right. Look for another secret door on the north wall, then walk west until you find a hydra. There is a secret door in that room on the south wall. Behind that door is a ladder. Climb down.

The next level is small. You'll find a room to the northwest that has several switches in it. Do not touch the ones on the floor. The ones on the walls open doors.

Go south from there and you will find a ladder at 80S-59E. After you climb down, search the room for a secret door. Go east, descend another level, follow the corridor, and climb down the ladder located at coordinates 65S-63E. You will find a human corpse on this level at coordinates 65S-51E. Search it and you will find the balloon plans.

Now, that was easy enough, wasn't it?

Building the Balloon

If you've been talking to everyone in towns and taking the extensive notes recommended earlier, putting all this together should be easy.

Michelle in Minoc will build the balloon's basket, and make it large enough for eight people. Arbeth in the village of Paws can supply silk, and Mortude in the same place has rope. Take that to Charlotte in New Magincia and she will turn the silk thread into cloth. Return to Paws and commission Marrissa to sew the cloth into a bag. Now go to the sewers below Lord British's castle and find yourself a good cauldron. With all these prerequisites completed, use the plans and your balloon will be finished.

Remember to leave at least one slot open in your party, because you will be picking up a new member in Gargoyle Land.

Gargoyle Land

You are ready now for the land of gargoyles!

This place is full of mountains, earthquakes, volcanoes, and lava flows. The balloon will be invaluable for getting around, as long as you can control the direction of the wind.

Your first stop will be the gargoyle side entrance to the Dungeon Hythloth. It's at 64S-72E. There should be a young gargoyle by the name of Beh Lem there. Don't hurt him, you want Beh Lem to join your party! There is the problem of communication, however. You need to learn the gargoyle language.

Enter the dungeon. Nearby you will find a scholarly human, Captain John. He'll teach you how to speak gargoyle. Now you'll be able to converse with Beh Lem and the other gargoyles down here in this doomed world.

Next you want to talk with Beh Lem's father, and he will give directions on how to get to Lord Draxinusom. After learning all you can from the father, talk with Lord Draxinusom.

Tell this gargoyle leader that you surrender. He'll not believe you at first, so use the word "Sacrifice." You'll be asked to wear an amulet, the Amulet of Submission. Now the gargoyles will talk to you without fear (before this, you would have just been wasting your time trying to talk to them).

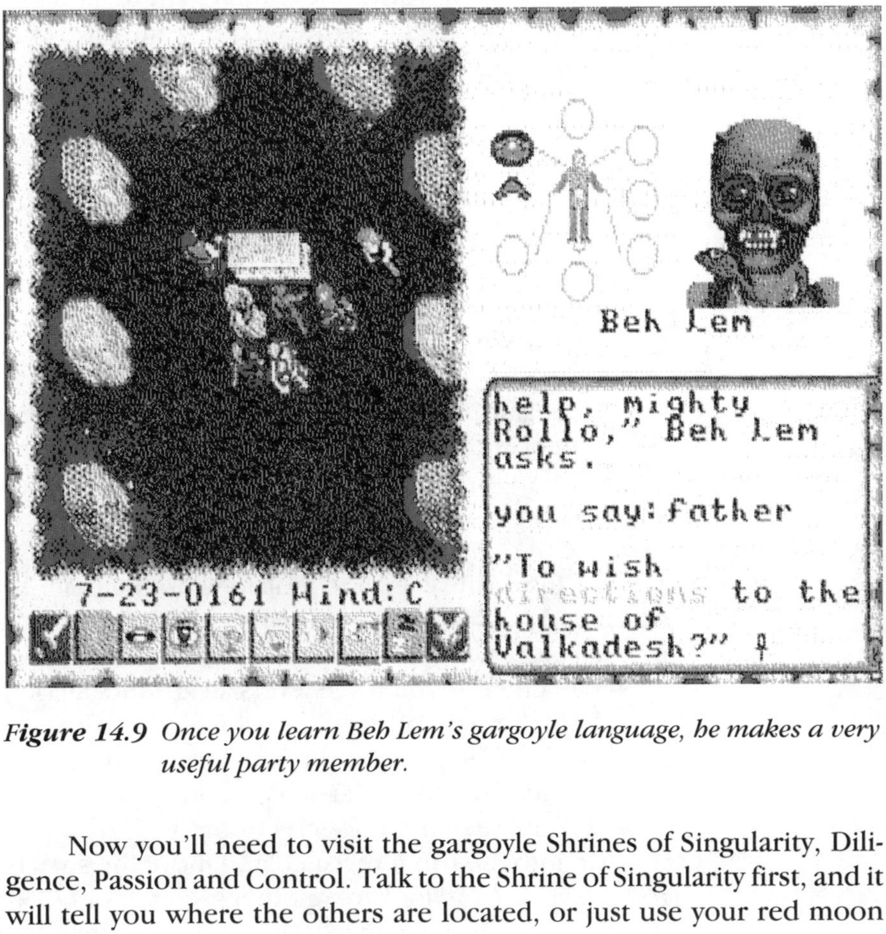

Figure 14.9 *Once you learn Beh Lem's gargoyle language, he makes a very useful party member.*

Now you'll need to visit the gargoyle Shrines of Singularity, Diligence, Passion and Control. Talk to the Shrine of Singularity first, and it will tell you where the others are located, or just use your red moon gates.

When you've talked to the altars in the Shrines of Diligence, Passion, and Control, return to the Shrine of Singularity. Use the mantra "UNORUS" and you will be sent on a sacred quest to the Codex of Ultimate Wisdom. Use the red moon gate again to get there.

If you've tried visiting the Codex before this, the guardians will have refused you passage. Now that you're on a sacred quest, you'll be allowed in. Talk to the Codex and you will learn how to save Britannia!

The Avatar Triumphant!

Saving the known world does require a little more effort on your part. You now must get the Vortex Lens from the Hall of Knowledge in Gargoyle Land (look in the town south of the entrance to the Shrine of Singularity). Be sure to read all the books there; then pay a visit to the gargoyle seer. He'll inform you that the lens needs to be repaired, and that you have to have a second lens.

Luckily there is a gargoyle lens maker northeast of the seer's house. Go there and he will repair your Lens. Return to the seer for additional instructions.

Now it's back up to the surface of Britannia. Visit Minoc first and have the glassworker there make you a glass sword, then journey to Stonegate.

Stonegate is the former home of the late, unlamented Shadowlords. It's south of Minoc in the mountains, and the best way to get there is to take a skiff south along the shore. You'll need to use gems or the 'Alt 213' spell to find its exact location, which is not too far from the village of Cove.

Go inside the keep and look for a fishing pole. Take the pole to the ocean and catch a fish. Give the fish to the papa Cyclops. You get a key in exchange. Go back into the keep and look for a secret door at 10N-37E. Enter it. You'll see levers all around, all of which you need to move. This reveals ladders, any of which you may take down. Downstairs, walk to the room in the southeast corner. Descend the ladder at 4N-43E, then find the one at 8N-39E and go down one more level. Locate 10N-39E and search for a secret door.

Go into the room revealed and move the switch. Go into the new room revealed and look for another secret door (13N-35E). Behind that door is a small room with a door in it. Unlock that door with the key the Cyclops gave you, and you'll be able to retrieve the Vortex Cube.

Easy enough, huh?

Now, gate on down to Moonglow. There's a Lens Maker east of the Lycaeum. Use the word 'lens' and he will examine your Vortex Cube and offer to shape it into a concave lens for a glass sword. Give him the glass sword you got in Minoc. This is the 'gargoyle lens,' and the repaired lens is the 'Britannia lens.'

Now, with both lenses, you're ready to complete the mission. Gate back to the Codex of Ultimate Wisdom. Enter the Shrine and drop the Britannia lens halfway between the left flame and the Codex. Rays of light will spring out when you have it placed correctly. Next drop the Vortex Cube or gargoyle lens halfway between the right flame and the Codex. Again, rays of light confirm correct placement. Drop all eight of the moonstones into the Vortex Cube and 'use' the cube.

The rest is an automatic sequence that you will find awesome to behold.

Now, O Avatar, harken to the saga of Rollo, the Savior of the known universe. He walked bravely amid danger and pain, and did not flinch. When all seemed lost, he only tried harder. When Death came to take him, he spit in its eye and went on to achieve glorious victory. Emulate him and you might, just might, survive to become legend yourself.

15 Rollo, Savior of the Known Universe

The private quarters of the king were spacious and homey. Multicolored tapestries depicting scenes from various areas of Britannia gave tasteful splashes of color to the gray stone walls. A bright fire burned cheerily in the large fireplace, and a huge oaken table groaned under its weight of choice cuts of meat, large hoop cheeses, fresh crisp loaves of bread, and a selection of fine wines. Tonight, the ruler was expecting an old friend.

There was a discreet knock on the door. The monarch rose from his comfortable lounging chair near the fire. He was tall, bearded, and of indeterminate age. From his physical features he looked to be in his fifties or sixties, but his dignity suggested that he had been around for a lot longer than that. Tonight he was wearing his favorite robe—old, decrepit, snug—which he donned only when he was at ease and far from the tiresome and intricate formalities of the royal court.

The door opened and the palace majordomo ushered in a man equally as tall as the king. Blond and burly, the newcomer moved with the agility of a cat. Intelligent eyes missed nothing, taking in the room at a glance. He was wearing no weapons, no armor, but was obviously ready for any and everything.

The monarch waved the majordomo out. "Thou mayest leave now, Alfred. We two old friends can perform thy services, as we have in the past."

The door closed softly and the two men stood looking at each other for a moment. Then they closed to exchange bear hugs and hearty slaps on the shoulders.

"You're looking good, Rollo. I trust you are well?"

Rollo nodded. "Yes, your majesty." He eyed the laden table. "But this feast threatens to make quick work of my waistline!"

The emperor grinned, poured himself a glass of wine, and sat back down in his chair. "A good quest will take off any excess pounds."

Rollo also helped himself to some wine and cut a few pieces of cheese to nibble on. He passed a couple to the king, saving one in case his old friend Sherry should happen by.

They talked of many things long into the night, these two friends and kindred spirits. The titles 'Avatar' and 'majesty' had been taken off and set aside like hats in a house.

"The historians and tacticians," the monarch observed, "have made much of your mission. Many learned scrolls have already been written about your varied travels across Britannia—how you and your party backtracked here and there, went from Minoc to Trinsic and back to Minoc again. Much has been read into your wanderings. They say the mission was the most complicated ever, and that it would take scrolls of great magnitude to list all the steps that were taken."

Rollo laughed, making a deep booming sound that filled the room pleasantly. "To tell you the truth, we *were* wandering aimlessly at times. Britannia has grown so huge and complicated, that we found many, many leads that had to be chased down and disposed of only to turn out to be red herrings—dead ends that led nowhere but back to our starting point. Actually, there are really just a few steps needed to complete the mission."

The king nodded and stretched his legs out so that his feet were closer to the fire. "You cut through all the extraneous stuff, eh?"

"Right, but it did take awhile. Just getting my party equipped was a challenge...."

A boomerang hit Rollo in the side with a resounding *whack*. He grunted in pain and whirled, swinging his sword at the barely glimpsed red flash of an attacking gargoyle.

"There's three of them!" Shamino yelled, raising his own sword to fend off an attack. "They followed us through the red moon gate!"

The royal throne room echoed to the snarl of the attacking monsters. Rollo was busy, very busy, trying to survive, but he could see the emperor out of the side of his eye just sitting there on the throne. An old man who looked like a wizard stood by his side.

"Must be some sort of test," Rollo thought, managing to barely wound his gargoyle assailant. "He has to be testing our worthiness, otherwise he or that mage would use their magic to shrivel these red monstrosities into so much dried-up leather."

"OW!" Dupre screamed as an ax bit into his left arm, but his strong right arm scythed his sword through the air with an audible *whirr*, sinking into the side of a gargoyle and evoking a much louder scream from the heavily wounded beast.

Iolo, always tall and elegant even in a battle for his very life, was hitting hard and fast, ignoring the blood trickling down the right side of his face from under his helmet.

The fight raged hot and heavy around the throne room, but Rollo, Shamino, Dupre, and Iolo were obviously going to be the victors. They had the three gargoyles outclassed in speed, agility, intelligence, and armor. Only the one gargoyle with a boomerang was doing any serious damage to them. Rollo suddenly ended that threat, lunging forward with a mighty lightning thrust that put his sword through the gargoyle's breastbone and all the way out of the now-dead creature's back.

Rollo twisted his weapon free and spun in search of another enemy, but the other two gargoyles were now also lifeless hulks on the stone floor. He took a deep breath to calm himself, then searched the gargoyle's body. He looked at the various items he found and took the boomerang for himself; it looked like a very handy weapon to have.

"Search those bodies well," he ordered the others, and walked forward to talk with the emperor.

The emperor recognized Rollo, from past adventures, but still posed three questions to him to be sure that it was indeed he and not some impostor. Rollo answered correctly and was given a full explanation of the problem facing the planet as well as several bits of helpful information, which the Avatar noted down carefully. The royal mage also spoke with Rollo.

In spite of what they had learned from the emperor, as Rollo and his party left the throne room that first time, they were not sure of exactly how to get started on their mission. There were just four of them—Shamino, Dupre, Iolo, and, of course, Rollo the Avatar and leader. They had been told everything in the palace was theirs to use, and the guards were very respectful, but still, it requires a little courage to help yourself to a king's possessions.

"This must be the room he said was for us," Iolo said, as they entered a spacious chamber directly across the hall from the King's Suite.

"I could eat a dragon," Shamino said, looking around the room. Spying a bag in the corner, he peered inside. "Ah ha! Provisions. Here's mead, bread, grapes and one, two, three, four . . . twenty-two portions of meat. This should last us awhile on the trail."

Dupre was feeling the cloth on a pair of trousers neatly hung on a valet stand. "Good material, but too fancy for out where we're going."

Iolo had picked up a shield from the floor and hefted it experimentally.

"Use it, Iolo," Rollo urged. "It's yours. Search the room well, men; all you find here that can be of use is OK to take."

"What about down in the town?" Shamino asked, examining a sword hanging on the wall.

"No, that would be stealing. We have permission only to use what's in the palace," Rollo explained. "Meanwhile, I'll take the spellbook here since I'm the power magic user. Dupre, get those lockpicks over there—they may come in handy."

They loaded up and, feeling brave, decided to check out the King's Suite next. After all, the emperor had said they had the run of the castle.

Dupre whistled in awe when the party entered the King's Suite. No expense had been spared in decorating this large apartment. Priceless tapestries hung on the walls. Scented candles burned in solid gold candelabra, and a fire burned brightly in a fireplace as big as the hut of many a peasant.

"Very nice," Iolo said, looking over the emperor's satin-covered bed. "I could sleep well there, even with the cares of the State on my head."

Meanwhile, Rollo was looking through the suite. Although the rooms were large, there were only three—the bedroom/sitting room that they had first come into from the hallway, a book-lined study, and a huge walk-in closet. There was a key on a table and he picked it up.

"In here," he ordered, and they went into the closet. It seemed logical that useful equipment would be stored there, since very few people, not even rulers of worlds, would want weapons and armor cluttering up their bedrooms.

"Here's a mouse hole," Dupre observed from the back of the closet.

Rollo considered for a moment. "Hmmmm. I doubt the emperor would allow a mouse hole to remain in his closet unless it was there for a reason. I'll ask him about it when we return to the throne room. Meanwhile, Dupre, see if you can use your lockpick to open this chest."

Dupre knelt and begin fumbling at the chest's lock. While he was doing that, Shamino picked up a kite shield that was lying on the floor.

"Can I use this, Rollo?"

"Sure," Rollo said distractedly as he watched Dupre finally get the chest open.

"Nice!" Dupre said. "Here's a sword, a dagger, chain mail, a chain coif, and some leather boots." He took the items out of the chest and Rollo and Shamino helped him don the armor.

They then continued to search the apartment and take items that might prove useful.

They moved into the bedroom of Nystul the royal mage, which, while small, was interesting. "You think it's safe to mess around in a wizard's bedroom?" Shamino asked, shuddering a little.

"Of course it's all right," Rollo assured him. "Anything in the palace is ours to take. Dupre, here's another chest for you to open. Might be a clue in it."

A few seconds later the chest was open. "There's a wand," Dupre said, pointing to where it lay in the chest.

Rollo lifted it out carefully. He intended to exercise caution until he found out how it worked. Inside was not the place for that. "I think it's a lightning wand," he said, examining it.

"Here's a scroll, too," Dupre added.

Rollo nodded and looked at it, reading aloud. "If you're looking for the clue, there's something for you under a plant in Serpent's Hold."

"Long trip from here," Shamino commented.

Dupre shrugged, grinning. "I imagine we'll be going there and a lot of other places again before we're through."

"That's for sure," Rollo said, and led them down the hall to where they found a potion factory.

The emperor halted Rollo's story.

"Yes, old friend, I know. You explored the castle well, talked to the people who would talk to you, found little Sherry, explored the sewers a little bit, and so forth. I know all that. I asked you about your activities there because I wanted to see whether my sources had missed anything; evidently they didn't. I even know about your buying reagents from that gypsy fellow—Zotan's his name, I believe. But what happened after that?"

Rollo said. "Well, after leaving the castle, we explored the town and talked to a lot of people. It soon became apparent that we needed to start freeing shrines.

"The plan was to obtain the eight mantras and runes and liberate the Shrines of Compassion, Honesty, Honor, Humility, Justice, Sacrifice, Spirituality, and Valor. The town of Britain being to hand, we decided naturally to start with the shrine of Compassion."

"This is it," Shamino said, "the eastern road out of town."

They began walking. The late afternoon shadows were lengthening, but they had torches in case darkness caught them.

"Traveling with you guys is fun," Sherry the mouse said. "Could I have a little more of that cheese now, you think?"

Rollo smiled down at the rodent. "Later, Sherry. Right now we have to liberate the Shrine of Compassion."

"I hope finding the rune and mantra for each of the other seven shrines turns out to be this easy," Dupre said.

"I have a feeling it will get harder, a lot harder," Iolo said. "Otherwise, why would we need someone special like Sherry?"

"True," Rollo agreed. "Keep a sharp lookout now. There will be gargoyles near the Shrine."

"I'll mow them down like summer hay!" Shamino vowed.

"Negative, Shamino," Rollo said. "From what we saw in the throne room, I think we can pretty much ignore them. Avatars do not kill just to be killing."

"You're the only Avatar here," Shamino protested, but his smile betrayed that he was teasing.

Shamino suddenly paused to listen. "Something to the east," he said.

They came to the shrine of Compassion then—a circle of stones with a stone altar in the center. A pulsating violet light glowed on the altar's top. Several gargoyles were lounging about, but made no immediate move to attack.

"Follow me," Rollo said, stepping quickly and confidently up to the altar. Suddenly the gargoyles *did* attack.

"I could have been wrong," Rollo said with a sigh. He freed the shrine, using the rune and mantra. The violet light disappeared, leaving a stone lying on the altar's surface, which Rollo picked up and put in his pack.

"Let's go," he said, turning and walking away.

The gargoyles followed, pressing their as-yet-unanswered attack.

"I imagine, now that the shrine's free, they eventually wander away," Rollo added.

Iolo laughed in relief. "This is *easy*." Then "OW! That hurt!"

Rollo smiled grimly. "Don't count on it staying this simple, Iolo. We'll endure a lot of hardships and shed much blood, some of it ours, before this quest is over."

The gargoyles increased the fury of their attack.

"Oh, all right," Rollo said. "Let's wipe out these idiots and gain a few points."

The ensuing combat was fierce but relatively short-lived. At least the attacking gargoyles turned out to have short lives.

Rollo paused to refill his glass. "As I suspected, freeing the other seven shrines was more difficult. We traveled to all eight towns of Britain, and many other places, too. We talked to all kinds of people and found many clues to other things besides the runes and mantras we needed.

I faithfully recorded everything.

"Two new members joined our party along the way—Jaana and Katrina. Jaana I knew from a previous mission. She's a little weird, being a Druid, but a staunch companion and good fighter. Katrina was a young peasant woman, proficient at arms and a pleasant addition to the group. Sherry was having so much fun that I let her tag along."

"Weren't you running out of time?" the emperor asked.

"We'd only used about half our allotted days by then. Time only became really pressing after the shrines were freed, since our levels had built up and we knew we had to move fast."

"What then? The balloon?"

Rollo grinned. "You make it sound so easy. But getting the plans was no easy task. We had to sail to Blackthorn's old castle for that."

The emperor grunted. "I hear the wizard Sutek is squatting there now. He ought to be evicted. Anyway, glad you didn't get sidetracked hunting the pirate's treasure."

"No, we were smarter than that. We found the balloon plans, got all the materials we needed, and made the balloon. It was tedious but easy enough since we picked up all the clues needed through various conversations.

"After that, following other clues, we went on a quest to find the Vortex Cube. As you know, it was in the former home of the Shadowlords. And then it was time to pay a visit to the land of the gargoyles."

"Far beneath the surface," the king grimaced, "and you definitely needed the balloon down there."

They stepped from the red moon gate into the Land of the Gargoyles. The ground shook to a not-so-minor earth tremor. On all sides the glare of active volcanoes blazed against the black clouds they had created. The smell of sulfur was heavy in the air.

"This place is coming apart at the seams," Dupre observed.

"No kidding," Jaana said, barely managing to keep on her feet as the ground rumbled and swayed violently yet again. "This, of course, is why the gargoyles are attacking the human world up above."

"If their world is destroyed," Rollo said, pointing out the obvious, "then so is ours, since it's all the same. Let's get moving. No time to waste. Our first task is to find the entrance to dungeon Hythloth and talk with Captain John. He can teach us the gargoyle language, and then maybe we can accomplish something."

The others nodded in agreement and they set off in search of the dungeon, using a sextant to check their position. Both the balloon and the skiff that Shamino carried came in handy several times for skirting volcanic areas and for crossing streams and arms of the sea.

Captain John was one level up in the dungeon. All knew that the dungeon went on up, past many monsters, clear to the surface of Britannia and that they could have tried to enter it from the top. They were glad they had the Moon of Orbs and did not have to fight their way down through those levels of death to get to Captain John.

The captain provided them with a quick language course, and Rollo mastered the gargoyle language in short order. Which was good, because when they came back out of the dungeon, they spied a young gargoyle standing nearby.

Rollo approached him and struck up a conversation. His name was Beh Lem and he agreed to join their party.

"You must talk with my father," the young gargoyle insisted. "He can help you save us all."

Glancing at the rest of the party to confirm their acquiescence, Rollo agreed. Beh Lem told them where his father was, and they went there as quickly as possible through the hellish Land of Gargoyles.

In the gargoyle town, Rollo had tried to talk to other gargoyles, but they all screamed something about 'the False Prophet,' and refused to have anything to do with him. Beh Lem's father explained why.

"You have to surrender to us first," he said, "and wear the Amulet of Submission. Only then will you be accepted."

Rollo sighed. "And where do I get this amulet?"

Beh Lem's father then gave them instructions on how to reach the gargoyle lord who would accept his submission.

"Hard for a Hero to surrender, eh?" The emperor commented.

Rollo smiled. "True. Not something you would normally think of doing, but it's necessary. While we were there in the gargoyle city, acting on clues already noted, we got the purple lens from the museum. It was broken, but a gargoyle lens maker repaired it for us.

"Also in the Land of Gargoyles, we visited the Temple of Singularity and the shrines of Passion, Control, and Diligence, talked to their altars, and noted the responses they gave us.

"That caused us to activate the red moon gate and return to the surface of Britannia. Our task now was to get a blue lens made. Having talked to a lot of people and noted their clues, we already had a pretty good idea of how to accomplish this.

"With all that done, we were now ready to visit the Shrine of the Codex of Ultimate Wisdom on the Isle of the Avatar. I read the Codex and followed its instructions. Then it was just a matter of sitting back and watching the universe right itself."

The emperor scratched thoughtfully under his beard. "It all sounds moderately easy, but I know you spent days of pain and much time in combat. Only the most virtuous Avatar could have kept his party together in the face of such tremendous adversity."

"Oh, I lost my temper now and then," Rollo admitted. "Especially on the days we sat waiting for shops to open. That's the worst thing about Britannia today—the merchants keep lousy hours, and they are all *different*!

"But you live and learn. It became obvious that most merchants closed up shop in the evening and didn't open up very early in the morning. So we used those times and night also to do whatever we had to do in the dungeons and other underground areas.

"Afternoons were the best time to catch merchants, although a few took off for lunch at odd times in the afternoon. One exception was the four mages who sell spells. They tended to be night owls. The throne room clock was invaluable for checking on the time of day or night."

"We also learned to camp out during the dark hours, but got up early when we had a long walk ahead so that we'd get to our next destination while everyone was still up and available. Otherwise, a full night would be wasted waiting for people to wake up again."

Rollo had stopped and fixed himself a gigantic ham and cheese sandwich. The emperor, seeing it, became hungry himself and made one just as large.

"You know," Rollo said with a minor spray of crumbs, "Adventurers should be warned about a couple of other things that waste time, just like the Pirate's Treasure does."

"Umpf?" asked the emperor, in the middle of a huge bite.

"The ghost in Skara Brae is one. Quentin is his name. You can't communicate with him very well or even do much about finding out who killed him, except make a guess. No way to bring the killer to justice even if you do find him, either.

"And all the steps leading to Smith the talking horse at Iolo's hut! We went through considerable motions, all for him to tell us to take the sandalwood box along. That was useful for the Warriors of Destiny but completely inappropriate for this mission."

"What about the book?" the emperor asked.

Rollo smiled. "Yes, I know, the standing offer of twenty gems for *The Wizard of Oz*. It's somewhere in those vast underground stacks at the Lycaeum's library. Finding and returning it is a nice gesture, but contributes nothing really to the mission."

The emperor sighed. "This sure isn't Kansas, Toto."

It was getting very late now. The grandfather's clock by the fireplace had just chimed two A.M. Rollo gave a great yawn and hastily covered his mouth.

"Your room is right across the hall," the king smiled. "Let me know if you need anything. Stay as long as you like."

"Thank you," Rollo said, and got to his feet. "I could use a good rest."

"Just one more question." The emperor rose also. "What do you really think of Britannia? You've got the viewpoint of a man from another world. Are we doing a good job?"

Rollo paused and gave the question serious consideration.

"There are flaws, but that's life. Britannia, with its warts and all, is a grand place. Following in the Way of the Avatar brings immeasurable rewards. There are adventures galore to be had. I love it!"

The ruler smiled and opened the door for Rollo.

"Then you would come again should we call for a Hero to follow a new and dangerous quest?"

"In a flash!"

The emperor clapped him on the shoulder. "Would that it were not so, but I suspect your services will be required sooner than later. Gird yourself for the coming battle."

Rollo stepped out into the hall and the door closed behind him. A guard was stationed there to protect the royal slumbers.

"Greetings, Lord Rollo! It's good to see you again."

"Hello, Dan," the Avatar smiled in recognition.

"You know," Dan lowered his voice to a whisper, "I love the king. I'd give my life for him in a second. But how do you stand it in there with all those 'thee's and 'thou's? It's so archaic!"

"Tell me, Dan, if you had that kind of power, how would you talk?"

Dan thought for a moment. "Any darn way I pleased?"

Rollo grinned and headed for his room. "Say good night, Dan."

In the royal bed chamber, the king sat staring into the flames. He sensed new evil growing somewhere and felt that it would soon strike once more in his beloved land. The test would be severe and the need for a Hero overwhelming.

Casting off the loneliness of his high position, there in the quiet of the wee, small hours, he smiled. Let evil come. There were plenty of Avatars like Rollo who would spit in its eye and take on any challenge. That was the strength of Britannia, its salvation and its glory.

The monarch then climbed into his bed and slept well, secure in the knowledge that his real wealth was not gold and precious jewels, but the friendship and support of the legions of Heroes and Heroines such as Rolf, Nimsman, Flavian, Lavonda, Stuart, and Rollo. Thousands upon thousands of them out there, wonderful people.

PART

8

Glossary

Glossary

Avatar A human who, after a long period of study and mastering of the Eight Virtues of Compassion, Honesty, Honor, Humility, Justice, Sacrifice, Spirituality, and Valor, has become a paragon of integrity and a symbol of all that is worthy in Britannia. The Avatars are always in the forefront of Britannia's battles against evil.

Beh Lem A young gargoyle who joined the Avatar's party and helped discover who the False Prophet was.

black pearl A rare pearl that serves as a reagent in many of the spells available to spellcasters. Only one oyster in ten thousand yields a black pearl.

Blackthorn's Castle A mighty castle built by the usurper Blackthorn on an island in the far southeast ocean. After Blackthorn's defeat by the Warriors of Destiny, the wizard Sutek took over the castle for his own use.

blood moss A type of fungus that is a reagent used in spells.

Bloody Plains The site of a vicious war, located northeast of Cove, across the mountains. The bloodstained, barren soil remains as a memorial to the thousands of soldiers who died there. Mandrake root and nightshade are found in this area.

bobbits A race of small beings friendly to humankind who existed for a time in ancient Sosaria. The bobbits resembled hobbits down to their hairy toes. Unfortunately, after the fall of Exodus, the bobbits, hobbits, elves, and dwarves all were seen no more and humans became the only race of the new empire of Britannia.

Britain The capital city of Britannia, located on the shore of Brittany Bay. The center of Compassion, it also has a first-class inn and a good selection of shops. Lord British's castle overlooks the town. As were the seven other major towns of Britannia, Britain was founded shortly after the fall of Exodus.

Britannia A large empire on the world of Sosaria, far away in time and space. The society is mostly medieval, although various implements of a highly technological society occasionally are to be found. Magic works in Britannia, and powerful mages cast amazing and wondrous spells. Unfortunately, pockets of evil exist that often fester and erupt, necessitating major quests to eradicate them. The demand for Heroes and Heroines is so great that the longtime ruler of Britannia, Lord British, maintains a recruitment program to attract adventurers from other worlds.

Buccaneer's Den A pirate settlement on a small island in the ocean east of the village of Paws. Buccaneer's Den is also the headquarters of the outlawed Thieves Guild.

Cove A village on the shores of mountain-bound Lost Lake in the northeast of Britannia. The isolated out-of-the-way hamlet is home to a surprising number of healers, magicians, and alchemists. There is also a temple to Virtue.

dungeons Abodes of evil, multilayered pits of peril, breeding grounds for monsters, holes of horror, tunnels of terror, floors of fear—abandon hope all ye who enter them. These vast underground labyrinths hide legions of frightful monsters who live out their lives preying on those who dare to enter to obtain gold and other important items.

Dupre A brave and vibrant fighter.

eight A number of mystical significance. In Britannia there are the Eight Virtues, eight towns, eight mantras, eight runes, and eight shrines of virtue—all of which have played and continue to play important roles in the history of Britannia.

Empath Abbey A retreat for those who wish to contemplate and reflect on life and the universe. Calm and tranquil within its walls, it is located between the western edge of the Deep Woods and the sea.

Exodus The "child" of Mondain and Minax. Exodus wreaked havoc on Sosaria during the Third Age of Darkness. A brave party of adventurers finally destroyed this last member of the Triad of Evil.

Gargoyles A race of red-skinned beings whose vast underworld habitat was almost completely destroyed in the cataclysms following the death of the Shadowlords and the rescue of Lord British by the Warriors of Destiny. In desperation, the gargoyles invaded Britannia, taking over the Eight Shrines.

garlic A powerful reagent for spells when carefully and properly mixed with other reagents.

Garriott, Richard C. A pseudonym sometimes used by Lord British.

ginseng A savory root and powerful reagent.

helm An archaic term for helmet. Several styles of leather and metal helms are available. No adventurer should go into combat with an unprotected head.

Iolo A bard and adventurer whose hut in the Spiritwood played a significant part in the mission of the Warriors of Destiny to rescue Lord British.

Isle of the Avatar An island to the far east of Britannia where the shrine housing the Codex of Ultimate Wisdom is located. During the Age of the Avatar, the retrieval of the Codex of Ultimate Wisdom from the Stygian Abyss caused a mighty upheaval that formed this island.

Jhelom A town in the far southwest of Britannia, on the largest of the Valorian Isles. This town espouses the cause of Valor. A shipwright, inn, and fine armoury are among the business establishments catering to adventurers.

kine The plural of *cow*—a type of livestock much favored by the peasants of Britannia in their agrarian society. Unfortunately, during times of troubles, livestock and peasants alike were considered tasty snacks by various kinds of monsters, which tended to disrupt farming.

Lord British Britannia's founder and only monarch down through the centuries. A benign ruler, he often relies on adventurers from other worlds to perform his many quests. From his early days as a minor king in Sosaria through the present as ruler of Britannia, the mightiest empire on that world, the regal and mysterious Lord British has always worked for the common good of his people and has led them victoriously through six major times of trouble.

Lycaeum The seat of learning for all of Britannia, on Verity Isle. It houses a large library, an observatory, various laboratories, and other facilities for the collection and study of knowledge.

mage A wizard. Well versed in the arcane knowledge of magic, a mage can cast a variety of useful and awesome spells. Having a mage along has saved many a party of adventurers.

mandrake root An herb growing in or near swamps, and an effective and much sought-after reagent for magic spells.

Minax Mondain's female apprentice. Her seizure of power caused the Second Age of Darkness. One of the Triad of Evil, this evil enchantress caused many deaths before a brave adventurer ended her days.

Minoc A town far to the north of Britannia on Lost Hope Bay. Sacrifice is the Virtue revered here. Many skilled artisans in the fields of metalworking, armouring, glassworking, and clock making live in Minoc.

Mondain The first wizard of the so-called Triad of Evil. Mondain's takeover of Sosaria spawned the troubles now known as the First Age of Darkness.

moon gates The most efficient way to travel in Britannia. Moon gates have existed since the time of Exodus. Stepping through one takes you to a far away destination in the blink of an eye, the location of which usually is dependent on the phases of Sosaria's two moons. Normal moon gates are blue; special moon gates, which are made by gargoyles and lead to their land, are red.

Moonglow A town located on the southern tip of Verity Isle. It is dedicated to the virtue of Honesty. Many mages and scholars frequent this town because the Lycaeum, Britannia's seat of learning, is nearby.

moonstones Mysterious gemstones that can produce moon gates. If you have a moonstone you can plant it and generate your own moon gate. Sometimes this might be your only method of returning to less hostile climes. Moonstones became available in the era after the destruction of the Shadowlords.

New Magincia An island town built on the site of an older city, Magincia, which was destroyed because of its pride. Thus, it is not surprising that New Magincia supports the virtue of Humility. The people are mostly simple farmers, humbly living the rural life.

nightshade A hallucinogenic mushroom and a rare but necessary ingredient in several powerful spells.

Paws A village on the royal road between Britain and Trinsic. Being halfway between the two, it is a good stopover, and it boasts a stable and inn.

princesses Princesses were routinely captured and kept prisoner in the castles of kings during the First Age of Darkness, before the Princesses' Equality Movement. Many an adventurer during that period rescued princesses to his or her great advantage.

reagents Substances which, when combined properly, make the casting of various magic spells possible.

Serpent's Hold A castle in the Southwest ocean on the Isle of Deeds. Serpent's Hold is the headquarters for the Order of the Silver Serpent, which only the flower of Lord British's chivalry is invited to join, and the training headquarters for Britannia's militia.

Shadowlords Three evil beings who sprang full-grown from three shards of Mondain's Gem of Immortality. They are the Shadowlords of Cowardice, Falsehood, and Hatred. They subverted a once-noble lord named Blackthorn to do their bidding, kidnapped Lord British, and took over the reigns of government with Blackthorn as their front man. The Warriors of Destiny foiled this plot, killed the Shadowlords, and rescued Lord British, who banished Blackthorn.

Shamino A strong and brave fighter who staunchly defends his Avatar. It is said that Lord British has honored Shamino's valiant deeds by assuming his likeness while traveling incognito on Earth.

Sherry A little mouse who went adventuring with the Avatar against the gargoyles and proved to be of great assistance, so great in fact that some call her a supermouse.

Shrines Places of mystical significance that serve as centers of virtue. During the Age of the Avatar the adventurer needed to visit these eight: the Shrines of Compassion, Honesty, Honor, Humility, Justice, Sacrifice, Spirituality, and Valor. Important during the time of the gargoyles are the Shrines of Love, Courage, Truth, and the Shrine of the Codex of Ultimate Wisdom, which are in Britannia, and the Shrines of Singularity, Passion, Diligence, and Control, which are in Gargoyle Land.

Skara Brae The town that espouses spirituality, just west of the Spiritwood on a small coastal island.

Smith A talking horse.

Sosaria An ancient world that endured many mighty battles against evil. After the first evil wizard was destroyed, the minor king Lord British began consolidating the planet's many warring fiefdoms. This took several hundred years and was interrupted by various major conflicts, but eventually he united the known world into the present empire of Britannia.

spider's silk Delicate parts of spider webs used as a reagent in magic spells, especially as a binder to make the spell stronger.

Stonegate A small, almost inaccessible mountain keep north of Cove. This was the home of the Shadowlords during the time that the Warriors of Destiny fought to rescue the kidnapped Lord British.

Stygian Abyss The most dangerous dungeon ever found. The Codex of Ultimate Wisdom was hidden on its bottommost level until retrieved during the Age of the Avatar.

sulfurous ash A reagent that adds energy to spells. It is the product of volcanic eruptions.

time doors During the Second Age of Darkness, doors that enabled adventurers to travel back and forth to five different eras in the past and the future. Actually, adventurers were forced to use the time doors because the deeds of the evil enchantress Minax had warped Time itself. Going through a time door leads you to a different place as well as a different time.

Trinsic A town on the far southern tip of the main continent of Britannia, just above the Cape of Heroes. Trinsic is the center of Honor. Some of the best horses in the realm are available from the stable here.

Yew Britannia's second largest city, located in the Deep Forest northwest of Britain. Justice is its specialty; the Supreme Court of Britannia is here.

Index

C

D

J

K

L

M

  - G'L", F'G", 214-215

N

O-P

Q-R

S

T

U

V

W

X-Z